Christianity and the Challenge of History

BC 6-19-06

Christianity and the Challenge of History

by

John J. Mulloy

Christendom Press
Front Royal, VA
1-800-877-5456

ISBN: 0-931888-61-1

Acknowledgments

Thanks are due to the Editor of *The Wanderer*, A.J. Matt, Jr. for many of the articles included in this volume, which first appeared in that paper in a column entitled *The Catholic Tradition*. Some of the other articles appeared in a quarterly historical journal devoted to the thought of Christopher Dawson, *The Dawson Newsletter*, edited by the present writer. A part of the article on Marxism appeared in *The New Oxford Review*.

In addition, the author deeply appreciates the financial assistance given by The Wanderer Forum Foundation, which made the publication of this volume possible.

Special thanks are due to Sister Mary Michael, M.I.C.M., of the Sisters of St. Benedict Center in the town of Harvard, Massachusetts, for her faithful transcription of the author's manuscript and her cheerful willingness to accept the many changes which the author introduced.

Contents

Preface

Part One of this volume deals with certain themes in the interpretation of history developed by the Hebrew Prophets of the ninth to the sixth centuries B.C., and how Christianity built upon and expanded these for its own interpretation of history and its own special mission. At the same time, the contrast is recognized between the Christian view of history and that which was adopted by post-Old Testament Judaism, which led to a divergence in the understanding of each of them concerning the role and purpose of the Messiah.

Part Two of this volume deals with the ideas of history held by different philosophers of history of our time and, in fact, back to the time of the Enlightenment. These are compared with the Christian interpretation of the same events and movements which have caught the attention of these philosophers. For the critique of their views from a Christian and Catholic standpoint, the author has relied greatly on the thought of Christopher Dawson.

The arrangement of these thirteen chapters in Part Two has been in chronological sequence, according to the period and movement dealt with, not in accord with the time of the philosopher of history whose views are being discussed. Thus, for example, Karl Jaspers, dealing with the axial period before the Christian era, appears before Voltaire, who preceded him by two centuries. The only exception to this is with some philosophers of history of the twentieth century.

The premise on which this volume is based is that views of the meaning of world history are at the basis of most secular ideologies of our day, and give direction and fervor to the efforts of their adherents. It thus seems valuable to provide a critique of these different secular views of history when judged from a Christian and Catholic standpoint.

CHRISTIANITY AND THE CHALLENGE OF HISTORY

PART I: The Origins of the Christian Conception of History

Introduction: The Old Testament and the Christian View of History

The Christian conception of history is based on Judaism and on the Jewish Scriptures, as we see from the inclusion of the Old Testament in the Christian Bible. The Old Testament has a twofold character to it; one of these aspects deals with the fate of all mankind, as in its account of the Creation and the Fall, and later of the Flood; the other aspect deals with the history of the Jewish people, from the time of Abraham and the Patriarchs onwards. As history develops in the Scriptures, it is the Hebrew people who are the center of attention, with their triumphs and defeats and their being tested by God to make them effective instruments of His purposes.

Nevertheless, the Gentile peoples are present also, often as enemies of the Chosen People. We see this, for example, in the case of the Egyptians, with whom Moses had to battle in order to be allowed to liberate his people from Egyptian servitude and lead them on their way to the Promised Land. Later, for the possession of that land, the Hebrews had to engage in long drawn-out wars with the Canaanite peoples who possessed it. Two centuries after their entry into Canaan, the Hebrews achieved some spectacular triumphs under the leadership of King David and gained control over all of Palestine and part of Syria. This military ascendancy was relatively brief, however, for, after the reign of Solomon, David's son, the kingdom split in two, each going its separate way and each weakened by the disunion.

During the period of the writing Prophets, from the eighth to the sixth centuries, the great Gentile empires are triumphant over the Hebrew people and carry them off into captivity. This happened to the northern kingdom of Samaria in 722 B.C. with Assyria serving as the rod of God's anger, as the Prophets expressed it. The same fate of conquest and captivity befell the southern Kingdom of Judah in 587, as the Babylonian king and his armies destroyed both Jerusalem and the Temple. Fifty years later, Cyrus, king of the Persians, conquered Babylon, and issued a decree allowing the Jewish people to return to their homeland. Only a minority of the Jews chose to do so, but these began the rebuilding of Jerusalem and the Temple, although on a less lavish scale than before. At a later date, about 330 B.C., Alexander the Great conquered the Persian Empire and included all of the Near East in his dominions. Thereafter, for about two centuries, the Jews were ruled by one or other of the Hellenistic kingdoms which succeeded Alexander, one centered in Egypt, the other in Mesopotamia. When the Seleucid king of Mesopotamia attempted to impose pagan religious rites in the Jewish Temple about 160 B.C., the people rose in revolt and, under Maccabean leadership, were victorious. They then set up an independent kingdom which lasted for about a century. This was brought to an end when the Roman general Pompey and his armies occupied Jerusalem in 63 B.C. and made Judea a part of the possessions of the Roman Republic. Some twenty years later, the half Jewish general, Herod, won a series of victories over his enemies, and, under the sovereignty of Rome, ruled as king from 41 to 4 B.C. It was in the last years of his reign that Jesus was born in Bethlehem.

These, then, are the major developments in the history of the Jews down to the time of Christ. Looking at the events in the Scriptures from a theological standpoint, for the events were means by which new advances were made in Divine Revelation, we have these stages:

(1) The Creation of man and the world, when God looked upon His work and saw that it was good. (2) The Fall of Man, in which Adam's disobedience to God's command lost Adam and the human race the special graces Adam had been given. This left humanity in a state of alienation from God, in which it "should seek God, and perhaps grope after Him and find Him," to use the words of St. Paul in his speech to the philosophers of Athens. (3) The Flood, as a punishment for the almost universal sinfulness of mankind, from which Noah and his family alone were rescued. Later, this element of divine retribution was to be a recurring feature in the history of the Jewish people. (4) The calling of Abraham by God to leave his native place in Mesopotamia and settle in the land of Palestine, which the Lord promised to give to him and to his descendants. Abraham thus became the father of the Hebrew people. However, there was also a provision here for the Gentiles, for in Abraham and his offspring all the peoples of the earth should be blessed. (5) After the Hebrew people had left Egypt, they assembled at the foot of Mount Sinai and Moses went to the top of the mountain to converse with God and to receive from Him a covenant which made the Hebrews the specially chosen instrument of God's purposes. The Covenant

established the rites of the Hebrew religion and also included the Ten Commandments and the Mosaic Law to govern the lives of the Jewish people. It was their failure to live up to this covenant in subsequent generations which led to divine punishments being visited upon them. (6) The conquest of the two kingdoms of Samaria and Judah by the Gentile world empires, which led to a new conception of God's action in history as proclaimed by the prophets Isaiah, Jeremiah, and Ezekiel. What this conception involved will be discussed in later chapters of this book. (7) The coming of the Messiah and His life, death and resurrection, which inaugurated the New Testament or Covenant and created a new Israel as a fulfillment of the Messianic promises made to the Old. (8) Finally, we have the growth of the new Israel as the Church, which preaches the message of salvation to all mankind. Christopher Dawson describes this stage as "the extension of the Incarnation in the life of the Church, through the Sacraments, the liturgy, and the lives of the saints, and the progressive incorporation of the human race and its cultures into the new unity of regenerated humanity."[1]

Or, as Dawson in another place discusses the role of the Church in the traditional Christian conception of history, it involves "the expansion of the Kingdom of God by the incorporation of the nations in the Kingdom and the enrichment of the Christian tradition by the various contributions of different national cultures and traditions;" and, in relation to this, "the idea of a providential preparation through which all the positive elements in the pre-Christian and non-Christian world find their fulfillment in the Kingdom of God."[2]

---

[1]From Memorandum of Christopher Dawson to John J. Mulloy, August 22, 1953.

[2]Christopher Dawson, *The Crisis of Western Education* (Sheed & Ward, 1961), p. 163.

1

Creation and the Christian Worldview

The Jewish and Christian conception of world history is based upon a close link between the universal and the particular. In this way there are communicated truths valid for all of humanity, through the agency of specific persons and events, with all the limitations and obstacles that this may involve. The cosmic perspectives into which Judaism and Christianity expand in the course of their historical development—one thinks of the prophecies of Isaiah and Daniel in the Old Testament and of the Letters of St. Paul and the Book of the Apocalypse in the New—are rooted in the historical experience of one particular people. This people was one of the smallest and least successful in worldly fortunes among the nations of the Near East, but which nevertheless carried within its destiny the universal reign of the Kingdom of God.

Thus, when the Christian Gospel is preached to all the nations of the world, it is the prophets and kings of this one small people of the Jews who are seen as embodying in their experience the meaning of mankind's relationship to God. And it is one particular historical Person, born in the reign of Augustus and crucified in the reign of Tiberius under Pontius Pilate, in whom the God of all the earth and the Creator of the starry heavens, reveals Himself to man and makes known His work of salvation.

As Christopher Dawson has remarked, this has always been a scandal to the rational mind, which wants to have things follow a certain preconceived order and have them fall into a proper and neatly disposed arrangement.

The individual character of the Christian Revelation, its avoidance of formless generalities, is especially to be seen in the Christian doctrine of creation. This is in contrast to the more generalized and indefinite outlines offered to us in the various evolutionary hypotheses. Even when evolution is linked up in its origins with some idea of creation, the emphasis, the guiding spirit, is to be found, not in God's creative act, "Let there be light," "Let us make man in our own image and likeness," but in the long drawn-out accounts of

7

the unrolling, the evolving, of the different forms of life from some primordial mass of matter. In evolutionary theory there is no sense of the complex and distinctive constitution of living beings. When one looks at the tremendous variety of the innumerable forms of life, each with its own specific character, one cannot but be struck by the fact of how a creating God, with His own particular purposes and a love of individual things, accounts for all that in a way that evolution does not. The testimony of living things as we actually see them is strongly in favor of the individual nature of creation, what we might term its arbitrary character, as though the God who made these infinitely varied forms had His own element of choice, His own enjoyment of this and that creature in His mind as He made them.

Nevertheless, science also needs to have its roots in a sense of the particularity and contingency of things, for otherwise it is apt to treat its subject from the viewpoint of *a priori* principles and generalizations. Under such circumstances, it is likely to decide in advance what the world should be like, rather than allowing the world to tell the scientist what it actually *is*, and what is the specific character of the different things which make it up. According to Fr. Stanley L. Jaki, only the seventh American to give the famed Gifford Lectures since their inception in 1885, this tendency toward *a priori* generalization has been the bane of scientific thought in many cultures and has led to the stifling of creative scientific advance. It is precisely because of the influence of the Christian worldview, founded on the idea of a creating God, that science in the West has been able to break loose from preconceived generalizations, and to come to a maturity in the West which it has attained in no other culture.[1]

C.S. Lewis also notes the singularity of things when one looks directly at reality: "It will be agreed that, however they came here, concrete, individual, determinate things do now exist: things like flamingoes, German generals, lovers, sandwiches, pineapples, comets and kangaroos. These are not mere principles or generalities or theorems, but things—facts—real, resistant existences."

And from this he concludes to the individual character of the God who made them, in contrast to the Pantheist ideas of generality and diffuseness in conceiving of God: "Let us dare to say that God is a

---

[1]Stanley L. Jaki, *The Road of Science and the Ways to God* (Univ. of Chicago Press, 1978).

particular Thing. Once He was the only Thing: but He is creative, He makes other things to be. He is not those other things. He is not 'universal being:' if He were there would be no creatures, for a generality can make nothing."[2]

The Christian conception of history, then, begins with the fact of Creation, and of God as the Creator. It is this idea of the relationship of all created things to the God who made them which is set forth with such profundity and freshness in the opening chapters of Genesis. And it is that which is decisive for all future events and developments in human history.

---

[2]C.S. Lewis, *Miracles* (Macmillan, 1947), pp. 105-106.

2
History and the Fall of Man

Before undertaking the examination of particular historical cultures, it would be well to consider the general character of the history of mankind as it shows the influence of certain basic principles. History reflects the apparently innate religiosity of human nature, and the need of man to communicate with the transcendent powers which rule man's life. And yet at the same time, it shows the effects of man's fallen nature upon his culture and achievements. It is therefore apparent that to understand history requires theological insight.

Of the nature of man, as he seeks after the Unknown God in various religious rites and symbols, Vatican Council II has said:

> From ancient times down to the present, there is found among various peoples a certain perception of that hidden power which hovers over the course of things and over the events of human history; at times some indeed have come to the recognition of a Supreme Being, or even of a Father. This perception and recognition penetrate their lives with a profound religious sense.[1]

Of the omnipresence of God in the achievements of human history, as seen in pre-Christian experience and cultures—a presence that is obscure rather than clearly perceived—John Henry Newman has written:

> Anticipations or reminiscences of His glory haunt the mind of the self-sufficient sage, and of the pagan devotee; His writing is upon the wall, whether of the Indian fane, or the porticoes of Greece . . . . He is with the heathen dramatist in his denunciations of injustice and tyranny, and his auguries of divine judgment are upon crime. Even on the unseemly legends of a popular mythology He casts His shadow, and is dimly discerned in the ode or the epic, as in troubled water or fantastic dreams. All that is good, all that is true, all that is beautiful, all that is beneficent, be it great or small, be it perfect or

---

[1]Vatican Council II: Declaration on the Relation of the Church to non-Christian Religions, Section 2.

fragmentary, natural as well as supernatural, moral as well as material, comes from Him.[2]

Yet in looking at the overall course of mankind's history, Newman is impressed rather by a sense of the absence of God and His Providence, and by the spectacle of mankind left to its own devices in a world which God has forsaken:

[O]ur first feeling is one of surprise and (I may say) of dismay, that His control of the world is so indirect, and His action so obscure . . . . What strikes the mind so forcibly and so painfully is, His absence (if I may so speak) from His own world. It is a silence that speaks. It is as if others had got possession of His work. Why does not He, our Maker and Ruler, give us some immediate knowledge of Himself? Why does He not write His moral nature in large letters upon the face of history, and bring the blind, tumultuous rush of its events into a celestial, hierarchical order? Why does He not grant us in the structure of society at least so much of a revelation of Himself as the religions of the heathen attempt to supply? Why from the beginning of time has no one uniform steady light guided all families of the earth, and all individual men, how to please Him? Why is it possible without absurdity to deny His will, His attributes, His existence? . . . I see only a choice of alternatives in explanation of so critical a fact: either there is no Creator, or He has disowned His creatures. Are then the dim shadows of His Presence in the affairs of men but a fancy of our own, or, on the other hand, has He hid His face and the light of His countenance, because we have in some special way dishonored Him?[3]

Blaise Pascal, the brilliant French religious thinker writing in the mid-seventeenth century, had a similar view of the tragic condition of mankind. Here the emphasis is not on man's history, but on the condition of the human race amidst the vastness of the universe:

When I consider the blindness and the wretchedness of man, when I regard the whole silent universe, and man without light, left to himself, and, as it were, lost in this corner of the universe, without knowing who has put him there, what he has come to do, what will become of him at death, and incapable of all knowledge, I become

---

[2]John Henry Newman, *The Idea of a University* (Longmans, Green & Co. 1912), pp. 65-66.

[3]John Henry Newman, *A Grammar of Assent* (Univ. of Notre Dame Press, 1979), p. 309.

terrified, like a man who should be carried away in his sleep to a dreadful desert island, and should awake without knowing where he is, and without means of escape. And thereupon I wonder how people in a condition so wretched do not fall into despair.[4]

The Christian understanding of the alienation of man from his Creator is based on the Fall of Man, and its consequences for the subsequent history of mankind. Of the influence upon history of the Devil who brought about mankind's fall from grace, the Tempter who promised our first parents that their disobedience would make them to become as gods, Pope Paul VI spoke in one of his allocutions:

> We know many things, however, about this diabolical world, which concern our life and the whole history of man. The Devil is at the origin of the first misfortune of mankind; he was the cunning and fatal tempter of the first sin, original sin. (*Gen.* 3; *Wis.* 1, 24.) From that fall of Adam the Devil acquired a certain dominion over man, from which only Christ's Redemption can save us. It is a story that is still going on: let us recall the exorcisms of baptism and the frequent references of Holy Scripture and the liturgy to the aggressive and oppressive "powers of darkness." (cf. *Lk.* 22, 53; *Col.* 1, 13.) He is the enemy number one, the tempter *par excellence*.
>
> So we know that this dark and disturbing spirit really exists, and that he still acts with treacherous cunning; he is the secret enemy that sows errors and misfortunes in human history.... He was "a murderer from the beginning... and the father of lies," as Christ defines him (*Jn.* 8, 44-45); he launches sophistic attacks on the moral equilibrium of man. He is the treacherous and cunning enchanter, the one who finds his way into us by way of the senses, the imagination, lust, utopian logic, or disorderly social contacts in the give and take of life ....
>
> This overhanging fateful presence is mentioned in many passages of the New Testament. St. Paul calls him "the god of this world." (II *Cor.* 4, 4). He warns us of the struggle in the dark that we Christians must wage not against one Devil only, but against many of them: ... For we are not contending against flesh and blood, but against the principalities and powers, against the world rulers of this present darkness, against the spiritual powers of wickedness in the heavenly places (*Eph.* 6, 11-12).[5]

Possibly the most concise summary of the fateful effects of the Fall

---

[4]Blaise Pascal, *Pensees*, no. 692.
[5]Pope Paul VI, Allocution of Nov. 15, 1972.

of Man on the rise and fall of nations in human history, and the undermining of man's social progress by the fault that lies within man's own soul, is in this passage of Christopher Dawson:

> It is, in fact, when we look at the history of mankind in the mass that the evils of human existence are most apparent. We see empires built on oppression and the blood of the poor, by degrees falling into ruin, and being replaced by some equally bloodthirsty but more barbarous power which goes at last to meet the same fate. Nor does civilization bring freedom; for the spectacle of a civilized society dominated, not by one unconscious natural instinct, but by a conscious lust for pleasure or power or wealth, is even more horrible than the other . . . .
>
> This is the fundamental problem which has pressed on the human race for thousands of years and which is as living now as it was in the days of Buddha . . . .
>
> Civilization after civilization in the past has stagnated and fallen into ruin, because they are tainted at the source, in the spiritual will which lies behind the outward show of things. The only final escape for humanity from this heart-breaking cycle of false starts and frustrated hopes is through the conquest of the world by charity—the coming of the Kingdom of God.[6]

It is true that the effects of the Fall are counteracted, even in pre-Christian times, by graces flowing from the Redemption. However, the influence on human society of the Redemption is an invasion by the Divine of territory formerly held by the Enemy, the prince of this world; and in this struggle fallen man should not expect any given society or social structure to become the realization of the Kingdom of God. The final victory will not be realized until the end of human history, when history has passed into another dimension from the present one; in other words, its fulfillment is eschatological, not utopian.

---

[6]Christopher Dawson, *Enquiries* (Sheed & Ward, 1933), pp. 323, 343.

3

Jewish Monotheism Versus the Worship of the Baals

When we consider Judaism, we encounter the religion culture which, in the Christian interpretation of history, was divinely guided in its historical development and in its religious teaching. And we are also in the presence of one of the world religions which, on the level of merely human understanding, requires to be compared with the developments taking place in the Orient. How is Judaism similar to the other religion cultures, and on what points does it differ from them? Does it give definite evidence that here we have the finger of God, the intervention of divine Providence in human history, and not simply man's striving after God which is characteristic of the other world religions?

We wish to consider this question in relation to the element of criticism and even denunciation of the ritual sacrifices, which finds expression in a number of the Hebrew prophets. This fact links the prophetic movement in Judaism with the reaction against the archaic culture which characterized the rise of the other world religions.

The Hebrew prophets, beginning with Elijah in the ninth, and Amos and Hosea in the eighth century B.C., were a parallel development to the Oriental higher religions, preceding these by one or two centuries, but engaged in the same conflict with the practices of nature worship. Only, the Hebrew prophets were not content to reject these idolatrous practices for themselves alone, but demanded the adherence of all the people of Israel to the worship of the One God. The conflict manifested in Elijah's challenge to the prophets of Baal, by means of their respective holocausts on Mount Carmel, portrays the goal of the Hebrew prophetic movement. That is, to force the issue of idolatry out into the open, and to have the people of Israel make a definite choice as to whether they would serve God or Baal. Unlike the Oriental development, the intolerance of the prophets was related to their intense awareness that the whole of Hebrew society had to be involved and converted, if the monotheistic goal of the prophets was to be achieved.

So Ahab [King of Israel, the northern kingdom] sent unto all the children of Israel, and gathered the prophets together unto Mount Carmel. And Elijah came unto all the people, and said, "How long halt ye between two opinions? If the Lord be God, follow Him; but if Baal, then follow him." And the people answered him not a word. Then said Elijah unto the people, "I, even I only, remain a prophet of the Lord; but Baal's prophets are 450 men. . . ."

And when it was now time to offer the holocaust, Elijah the prophet came near and said: "O Lord God of Abraham, and Isaac, and Israel, show this day that you are the God of Israel, and I your servant, and that according to your commandment I have done all these things. Hear me, O Lord, hear me: that this people may learn that you are the Lord God, and that you have turned their heart again." Then the fire of the Lord fell, and consumed the holocaust, and the wood, and the stones, and the dust, and licked up the water that was in the trench. And when all the people saw this, they fell on their faces. And they said: The Lord He is God; the Lord He is God . . .[1]

From the viewpoint of the religion culture of the Jews, Elijah's purpose was to gain a united commitment of the entire people to the worship of the One God. It would not allow for syncretism with the existing practices of Baal-worship to which the Hebrews were given; it would not allow them to call upon Baal to make up for the deficiencies they might find in the response of Yahweh to their petitions. The success of the prophetic movement in restoring to the Hebrew people what the prophets proclaimed to be the original Mosaic tradition led to the eventual triumph of monotheism as the characteristic religion of the Jews. This was in marked contrast to the polytheism of the peoples who surrounded them in the ancient world.

Thus, while the religion of the Hebrews involved a sacred ritual order, emphasizing the Temple and the Holy City of Jerusalem—and this corresponded to the features of the archaic ritual culture—its center was the worship of Yahweh and the carrying out of His Commandments. Unlike the archaic culture, where the performance of the ritual was not related to moral prescriptions for the individual, and where the ritual might indeed involve moral evils such as temple prostitution and infanticide, the continuing demand of the Hebrew prophets was for moral righteousness. Without this, the ritual would be looked upon as an abomination by Him to Whom it was being offered.

---

[1]II Kings 18:20-39.

And this brings out a predominant element in the message of the prophets. The worship of Yahweh was of no value if it did not correspond to an interior sacrifice, by which the people strove for conformity to the will of God, through the keeping of the Covenant and the Commandments. Otherwise, the sacrifices would be merely a means by which to purchase God's favor and indeed to control Him for their own ends. In this self-centeredness, we see the effects of original sin manifesting itself at the very center of Jewish religious life.

Fr. Louis Bouyer describes this basic challenge to the honor of Yahweh which the prophets had to confront:

> Nonetheless, He consents to come down to earth, to make Himself the companion of His people, as they wander here below seeking the city to come. But let man not, for all this, have the outrageous presumption to try to take possession of Him in order to shut Him up in His own political system, to make Him an obedient cog in a machine for dominating the world in which man himself is to remain the sole master. It was precisely this, indeed, which was implied for the Canaanite religions in the dwelling of a Baal in his temple. Kept from sight like a valued hostage and regularly fattened by sacrifices, the Baal was held there at the people's disposal, like an all-powerful but docile apparatus to make the earth fertile and to frighten away enemies.[2]

In this connection, we find an expression of Yahweh's dissatisfaction with His people in the *Book of Isaiah*: "Offer sacrifice no more in vain: Incense is an abomination to me. The new moons, and the sabbaths, and other festivals I will not abide. Your assemblies are wicked. And when you multiply prayer I will not hear, for your hands are full of blood.... Cease to do perversely. Learn to do well: Seek judgment. Relieve the oppressed. Judge for the fatherless. Defend the widow."[3]

After giving this passage, Fr. Bouyer adds: "The Psalter with its numerous sacerdotal prayers includes many passages like this."[4]

For the prophets, this view of God's judgment upon the people for their injustice and their immorality gave a quite different meaning to the

---

[2]Louis Bouyer, *The Meaning of Sacred Scripture* (Univ. of Notre Dame Press, 1956), p. 44.

[3]*Isaiah* 1:11-17.

[4]Louis Bouyer, *The Paschal Mystery* (Henry Regnery Co., 1950), p. 188.

Day of Yahweh than existed in the popular conception. To the Jews in general, the Day of Yahweh was a day of judgment by which the God of Israel would triumph over His enemies and exalt His own people. To Amos and to succeeding prophets, the Day of Yahweh involved a judgment upon the Jewish people also, even more searching than that visited upon the Gentiles; for "You only have I known among all the peoples of the earth. This is why I will punish you for all your iniquities." Consequently, we have this passage in which Amos proclaims the new meaning of the Day of Yahweh to the people of the northern kingdom:

> Woe to them that desire the Day of Yahweh. What will it be for you, the Day of Yahweh? It will be darkness and not light. It will be like a man who flees from a lion, and see, a bear comes to meet him; he goes into his house, and leans his hand on the wall, and the serpent bites him! . . . Is it not darkness, the Day of Yahweh, and not light, obscurity in the place of splendor?[5]

This was the principle by which the prophets explained to the Jews the meaning of the misfortunes that were to befall them, as in the conquest of the northern kingdom in 722 B.C., and of the southern kingdom in 587, with the people in each disaster being led away into captivity by the Gentiles. The Day of the Lord would eventually be visited upon the Gentiles also, but first it would mean punishment of the People of God for the evils they had committed.

In the lifetime of Jesus, more than seven centuries after the prophecies of Amos, the majority of the Jewish people still held the same expectation that the coming of the Messiah, who would be the instrument for the Day of the Lord, would mean the triumph of the Jews over their enemies—and especially over the Roman Empire which now held the Jewish people in subjection. This belief was in fact the reason for the desperate uprising of the Jewish people against the Roman power in the war of 66 to 70 A.D., which led to the destruction of Jerusalem.

The refusal of Jesus to meet this expectation, and His deliberate intention to give to the idea of the Messiah the content of the Suffering Servant of Isaiah (*Is.* 53), is what finally led to the rejection of Jesus by the Jewish people and to His crucifixion. Nevertheless, the teaching of

---

[5]*Amos*: 3:1-2; 5:18-20.

the Hebrew prophets, including that of the last and greatest of these, Jesus Himself, found fulfillment in those members of the Chosen People who accepted the new covenant with God, sealed in the blood of Jesus. These became the foundation for the New Israel, intended to embrace all of mankind, the Catholic Church of Jesus the Messiah.

4

History: Cyclic Repetition
or Divine Purpose?

In this chapter we wish to discuss what is of the greatest significance for the Jewish conception of history, what is indeed its keystone, and the foundation for the Christian interpretation of history as well. That is, its doctrine of divine Providence, and how that Providence expresses itself through the events of human history. This is a concept peculiar to the Jews, for all other cultures based on the world religions and the new philosophies, which were arising in the ancient world of East and West in the middle third of the first millennium B.C., tended to discount the significance of history. In fact, they saw history as something from which man had to escape in order to find salvation.

Here, for example, is the idea of history as conceived by Hinduism; this same view was inherited by Buddhism, and formed the framework for the Buddhist doctrine—release from pain through attaining Nirvana. Of this Hindu concept of history, R.C. Zaehner writes:

> For the Hindu, life in space and time is without beginning and, unless the way of liberation is found, without end too; and eternal life in *this* sense becomes a crushing burden in its endless, pointless, senseless repetitiveness; and as the twin doctrines of *karma* and *samsara* developed, the revulsion against never-ending life through never-ending death in a manifestly imperfect world became more and more extreme. For the Hindus, the world was not created once for all nor was there any end to it: from all eternity it had been re-creating itself and dissolving back into its unformed and "unmanifest" condition....
> ... Such is the Hindu concept of the cosmos beginningless and endless in time as well as in space and the soul of man must ever anew embark on this journey that has no end, passing from one life and from one body into another like a caterpillar moving on interminably from one blade of grass to the next.[1]

Nor was this conception of history as cyclic repetition confined

---

[1]R.C. Zaehner, *Hinduism* (Oxford Univ. Press, 1962), pp. 80-82.

only to India. It was present also in the Near East, under the idea of the Great Year, and it was an important element in the thought of the philosophers of Greece and Rome. Speaking of the influence of the thought of Plato upon Greek ideas of man and the cosmos, Christopher Dawson observes:

> It became impossible to attach any ultimate importance to the changes of the temporal process. For though the earth was not itself eternal, it was modeled on an eternal pattern, and time itself "imitates eternity, and moves in a circle measured by number." And since the perfect motion of the heavenly spheres is always circular, the process of temporal change must be circular also. It is not only plants and animals that go through a cycle of growth and decay. All created things have their appointed numbers and revolutions, and the cycle of the world and of time itself is fulfilled in the perfect year, when the heavens have performed a complete revolution and the planets find themselves in the same relation to one another that they were at the beginning. Then the cosmic process begins anew and all things recur in their former order.
>
> This theory of the Great Year . . . is not, however, peculiar to Plato, since it had already made its appearance in the Greek world as early as the days of Heraclitus.[2]

Moreover, its influence was so powerful on the world of Greek thought that even a thinker with the strong philosophical realism of Aristotle succumbed to this conception of history:

> To him, also, the highest knowledge was to be found in the contemplation of the universe as a manifestation of perfect and unchanging Being. All progress is but a part of the process of generation and corruption, which is confined to the sublunary world—"the hollow of the Moon"—and which depends on the local movements of the heavenly spheres.
>
> All such change must necessarily be cyclic. "For if," he says, "the movement of heaven appears periodic and eternal, then it is necessary that the details of this movement and all the effects produced by it will also be periodic and eternal" (*Meteora*, I, xiv). Nor is this to be understood solely of material changes, for Aristotle expressly states that even the opinions of the philosophers themselves will recur in an identical form, "not once nor twice nor a few times but to infinity."[3]

---

[2]Christopher Dawson, *Progress and Religion* (Sheed & Ward, 1929), p. 142.
[3]*Ibid.*, p. 143.

It is indeed curious that the Greeks, who were creative and experimental and open to new approaches in so many things, should have been so enchained and lacking in freshness in the picture they accepted of the universe as a whole, and of man's history within it. It is a testimony to the power of Oriental thought, over even the most open and creative of the peoples of the West, that this cyclic recurrence theory should have been incorporated into the Greek worldview.

Thus man and the universe are condemned to these endless cycles in which nothing new or creative can ever emerge. It was as though man's alienation from God, by means of the Fall, was implicitly recognized by these theories, which bound humanity up within the prison of a universe from which there was no escape.

In contrast to these ideas, there was the Hebrew conception of the relationship of Israel to Yahweh. Through the creative intervention of God, Abraham and his descendants were invited to cooperate with Yahweh in the realization of the true purpose of human history. The history of this one people, whom God had chosen, would serve to show forth God's power and glory to all humanity; and the Providential events in their history would become the means by which all the peoples of the earth would be blessed. Instead of history being meaningless, therefore, it would have for the Jews almost too much meaning, for they would not be left to their own devices and purposes, but would find the significance of the Covenant expanding in a way that they had not anticipated. As proclaimed by Moses and by the prophets of the ninth to the sixth centuries, the events of Jewish history were filled with a transcendent meaning, a part of which would be punishment for their transgressions and for having fallen away from the Covenant, by which they had become a people specially dedicated to God.

But beyond all punishment and immediate disaster there lay the promise of the Messianic hope, a hope which became ever more vivid and intense with the passage of the centuries, and which served to fortify Israel against every external defeat and misfortune.

> Behold my servant, whom I uphold; mine elect, in whom my soul delighteth; I have put my spirit upon Him; He shall bring forth judgment to the Gentiles.... I the Lord have called thee in righteousness, And will hold thine hand, and will keep thee, And give thee for a covenant of the people, For a light of the Gentiles;

To open the blind eyes, To bring out the prisoners from the prison,
And them that sit in darkness out of the prison house.[4]

Are not these cyclic conceptions of history indeed a kind of prison house, from which the Gentiles shall be delivered with the advent of the Messiah promised to Israel?

---

[4]*Isaiah,* 42: 1, 6-7.

5

The Apocalyptic Character
of Sacred History

In this chapter we shall examine certain key features in the Jewish interpretation of history, which have been taken over by Christianity as part of its heritage from the Old Testament. Here is how Christopher Dawson identifies these elements of historical continuity between Judaism and Christianity concerning the meaning of history:

> The Christian interpretation of history... was in fact the creation of the Hebrew prophets and was handed on without essential change to St. Paul, St. John, and St. Augustine.
>
> In the Old Testament, especially in the prophets, we find first the guiding idea of divine Providence and divine intervention in history—the conception that the great events of history are all integrated in a divine plan leading to a divine judgment.
>
> There is also a historical dualism—there are two principles at work in history. True history—sacred history—is not the same as apparent history or secular history. The spiritual meaning and value of history are hidden under the veil of outward political and economic change.[1]

The first of these principles, divine intervention in human history, we have referred to in a preceding chapter in connection with the Day of the Lord. As we saw there, the older Jewish idea of this Day was redefined by the prophets to include a judgment upon the Jews, as well as upon the Gentiles. But what made belief in divine intervention most difficult for the Jews to accept, was the fact that judgment was being visited first upon the Jews rather than upon their enemies. When this happened, the most natural interpretation was that the catastrophe which had struck the Chosen People was a sign that God's arm was indeed shortened, that His claims through the prophets to universal power and sovereignty were strikingly contradicted by what had happened to His people. When the Jews saw the northern kingdom of

---

[1]Christopher Dawson, *The Formation of Christendom* (Sheed & Ward, 1967), p. 81.

Samaria conquered by Assyria in 722 and its people led away to deportation and exile, never to return, and when the southern kingdom centered in Jerusalem was conquered in its turn by Babylon in 587 and its people sent into exile, they might well have given up hope in the special meaning they had ascribed to their own history. It appeared that Yahweh Himself was defeated and discredited in the conquest of His Chosen People.

That this was not the meaning which the Jewish people ultimately attributed to these events, that they continued to believe in God's Providence as shown in the events of their history, was due to the inspired teaching of the prophets before and during their time of exile. The meaning which was brought out by the prophets involved a certain fore-shadowing of the Crucifixion; and the Suffering Servant of Isaiah can be seen as applying both to the Messiah Himself and to the people whose fate was in some ways not dissimilar to His. Here is Christopher Dawson's summary of the prophetic interpretation of the history of Israel:

> Consequently when the Assyrian world power conquered the lesser peoples of the Near East, the religion of Yahweh did not share the political fortunes of the nation, as was the case with the other peoples. For the prophets saw in the material ruin of Israel, not a proof of the powerlessness of Yahweh to protect His people, but a manifestation of His universal power in a higher and more mysterious sense. Assyria itself was but an instrument in the hand of the God of Israel, which would be discarded and broken when His purpose was accomplished, and Israel was to look for salvation not to "the arm of the flesh," but to the mysterious workings of divine omnipotence.
>
> Thus the crisis which destroyed the existence of Israel as an independent nation, was also the time of travail in which Judaism was reborn as a world religion. The series of national calamities which culminated in the destruction of Jerusalem and the period of the captivity only strengthened and enlarged the prophetic belief in the sovereignty of the divine purpose in history. And this purpose was no longer limited to the fate of Israel—it had an even wider significance. "It is too light a thing that thou shouldest be my servant to raise up the tribes of Jacob and to restore the preserved of Israel; I will also give thee for a light to the Gentiles, that thou mayest be my salvation unto the end of the earth (Isaiah, 49:6)."[2]

---

[2] *Progress & Religion*, pp. 152-153.

The second feature of the Jewish view of history, the contrast between history's apparent meaning and its ultimate spiritual meaning which is working underneath the surface of historical events, is implied in what we have just described of the course of Jewish history; but it would be well to give a more specific illustration of it. It is what might be called the apocalyptic nature of sacred history; and it is what makes Revelation a stumbling block to Rationalists who expect history to follow certain ordered patterns, whose causes can be perceived and determined. Voltaire's protest against the interpretation of the history of the ancient world empires, seen from (the viewpoint of) the meaning given to it by the Jews of the Old Testament, is an illustration of why the Jewish and Christian interpretation of history is bound to cause hostile reaction from the Rationalist mind:

> Reason, indeed, cannot make us believe the Jews; but we submit to them by faith. . . .
> What I admire most in our modern compilers is the wisdom and good faith with which they prove to us that everything that happened in former days in the greatest empires in the world happened only in order to instruct the inhabitants of Palestine. If the kings of Babylon, in the course of their conquests, fall in passing on the Hebrew people, it is solely in order to punish this people for its sins. If the king known as Cyrus becomes master of Babylon, it is in order to allow some Jews to return home. If Alexander conquers Darius, it is to establish Jewish old-clothes dealers in Alexandria. When the Romans annex Syria to their vast domains and enclose the little country of Judea in their empire, it is once again in order to instruct the Jews. The Arabs and the Turks appear on the scene only in order to chastise this attractive people. It must be admitted that it has had an excellent education; no other nation has had so many teachers; and all this shows how useful history is![3]

This is of course, vastly amusing. But what Voltaire overlooks is that this interpretation of Jewish history by the prophets which he ridicules has been verified by history itself. The influence of the Jews on the future history of mankind has been far more important than that of the Assyrians, the Babylonians, the Hellenistic empires which followed Alexander, or even the Roman Empire itself.

Dawson portrays this same contrast and contradiction as Voltaire

---

[3]Voltaire, *Essay on the Custom and the Spirit of Nations.*

does, but sees it from the viewpoint of the Christian reflection upon history:

> The real meaning of history is something entirely different from that which the human actors in the historical drama themselves believe or intend. For example, to a contemporary "scientific" historian the rise of the world empires in the Near East from the 8th to the 6th centuries B.C. would have seemed the only historical reality. He could not even have imagined that 2,000 years later all this drama of world history would only be remembered insofar as it affected the spiritual fortunes of one of the smallest and least materially civilized of the subject peoples. And in the same way what contemporary observer could have imagined that the execution of an obscure Jewish religious leader in the first century of the Roman Empire would affect the lives and thoughts of millions who never heard the names of the great statesmen and generals of the age? . . .

Thus "the Catholic interpretation of history preserves the prophetic and apocalyptic sense of mystery and divine judgment. Behind the rational sequence of political and economic cause and effect, hidden spiritual forces are at work which confer on events a wholly new significance."[4]

---

[4]Christopher Dawson, *Dynamics of World History* (Sheed & Ward, 1959), p. 257.

6
History Under the Shadow of Divine Judgment

In our last chapter we concluded with a discussion of the apocalyptic nature of history, the contrast between the apparent meaning of history as seen by the secular historian, and its deeper meaning when viewed from the standpoint of sacred history. This conception is the basis for the interpretation which the Hebrew prophets gave to the historical events of their own day; and it has been inherited by Christianity as one of the key elements in the Christian worldview. In a passage written while he was still an Anglican, this is how John Henry Newman presents the biblical view:

> Men, who are plunged in the pursuits of active life, are no judges of its course and tendency on the whole. They confuse great events with little, and measure the importance of objects, as in perspective, by the mere standard of nearness or remoteness. It is only at a distance that one can take in the outlines and features of a whole country. It is but holy Daniel, solitary among princes, or Elijah the recluse of Mount Carmel, who can withstand Baal, or forecast the time of God's providence among the nations. To the multitude all things continue to the end, as they were from the beginning of the creation. The business of state affairs, the movements of society, the course of nature, proceed as ever, till the moment of Christ's coming. "The sun was risen upon the earth," bright as usual, on that very day of wrath in which Sodom was destroyed. Men cannot believe their own time is an especially wicked time. . . . Thus the world proceeds until wrath comes upon it and there is no escape. "Tomorrow," they say, "shall be as this day, and much more abundant."
>
> And in the midst of this their revel, whether of sensual pleasure, or of ambition, or of covetousness, or of pride and self-esteem, the decree goes forth to destroy. The decree goes forth in secret; angels hear it, and the favored few on earth; but no public event takes place to give the world warning.[1]

Christopher Dawson points out that this prophetic view of history

---

[1]E. Przywara, *A Newman Synthesis* ed. (Sheed & Ward, 1945), pp. 335-336.

was the inspiration of Newman, when he was conducting a valiant campaign to change the religious attitudes of England, during the years of the Oxford Movement. Newman saw this view especially in terms of "the decisive function of individuals—of the few who are called to bear witness against their age and then to change the current of history."[2]

The passage which we have quoted from Newman points to another element which is part of the Jewish and Christian view of history: the theme of the end of history and of divine judgment. The Day of Final Judgment is the fulfillment of the apocalyptic character of history. At that time, the meaning under the surface of historical events is no longer hidden, but is made manifest; divine judgment reveals the reality which was always present though not recognized.

Although it is only the end of history which is to show the fullness of divine judgment, there are throughout the course of history particular judgments being rendered against those nations and powers which war against the sovereignty of God. These judgments are not so clear-cut that they may not be denied and attributed to merely natural causes; and thus they differ from the judgment rendered at the end of history, where the reality of God's Providence and His justice is fully revealed and brought home to all. But it is important to recognize that the Jewish and Christian interpretations of history do look to these particular judgments for the vindication of God, and the reinforcement of their own hope. They fulfill somewhat the same function in the order of historical events that miracles do in the order of nature. And in fact, a great deal of the body of Old Testament prophecy is concerned with the prediction of particular judgments against the heathen nations and their rulers. One of the most eloquent of these is the prophecy of *Isaiah* in chapter 14 concerning the downfall of the ruler of Babylon:

> How art thou fallen from Heaven, O Lucifer, who didst rise in the morning! How art thou fallen to the earth, that didst wound the nations! And thou saidst in thy heart: I will ascend into Heaven, I will exalt my throne above the stars of God, I will sit in the mountain of the covenant, in the sides of the north. I will ascend above the height of the clouds, I will be like the most High. But yet thou shalt be brought down to Hell, into the depth of the pit. They that shall see shall turn toward thee, and behold thee. Is this the man that troubled the earth, that shook kingdoms, that made the world a

---

[2]*The Formation of Christendom*, p. 82.

wilderness, and destroyed the cities thereof, that opened not the prison to his prisoners? All the kings of the nations have all of them slept in glory, every one in his own house. But thou art cast out of the grave, as an unprofitable branch defiled, and wrapped up among them that were slain by the sword, and art gone down to the bottom of the pit, as a rotten carcass.[3]

John Henry Newman, whose mind was so deeply impressed with the Jewish interpretation of history and with its continuance under the Christian dispensation, gives the following reflection upon a particular judgment which was rendered upon a ruler as great as any of those with whom the Hebrew prophets were dealing. Here we have not a prophecy in the sense of the prediction of some future event, but a reflection upon the meaning of what has already happened, the downfall of Napoleon Bonaparte, and seeing this in terms of God's providential intervention in history:

All states of the world, all governments, except so far as they are Christian, except so far as they act upon Christian principles, are scarcely more than robbers and men of blood; and against these God exalts Himself; against these He is ever exalting Himself; against these at this very time is He rising, as in all times; against all states, all governments, all power of man which does not acknowledge Him, and bow before Him. And "the nation and kingdom that will not serve" Him, or rather, as the prophet says, His Church, "shall perish. . . . At Thy rebuke, O God of Jacob, both the chariot and horse are fallen." Do we ask how this is fulfilled now? Have we not seen in our time, or did not our fathers see, a great anti-Christian power in the world, exalting itself against religion, and especially against Christ's Church? And did it not seem sure of success? And yet has it not, after all its threat and triumphs, ceased to be, leaving naught behind it but the Egyptian upon the seashore, and a small dust and ashes, for its worshippers fondly to hang over? And this is but one instance of what takes place in every age, the triumph of the Church over the world.[4]

A similar reflection after the fact might have been made about Assyria, the ruthless conqueror who practiced a policy of *Schrechlichkeat* on the populations against whom she warred. Of Assyria, the Hebrew

---

[3]*Isaiah* 14: 12-19.

[4]John Henry Newman, *Sermons on the Subjects of the Day* (Christian Classics, 1968), pp. 263-264 [from a sermon delivered in December, 1842].

prophets had said that she was to serve as the rod of God's anger against Israel and the other peoples of the Near East; but then she would be cast aside, utterly broken and destroyed when His purposes with her had been served.   Arnold Toynbee implies how these prophecies were fulfilled in the ruined condition of Nineveh, the Assyrian capital, as it was seen some 200 years after the downfall of the Assyrian Empire in 612 B.C. Not only was the city destroyed and deserted, but the people round about had no knowledge of what nation had once lived there.

As the Hebrew prophet Isaiah said. "All flesh is as grass, and all the goodliness thereof is as the flower of the field. The grass withers, the flower wilts, when the breath of the Lord blows upon it."[5]

Here is Toynbee's description of the condition of Nineveh about 400 B.C.:

> The disaster in which the Assyrian military power met its end in 614-610 B.C. was one of the most complete yet known in history. It involved not only the destruction of the Assyrian war machine, but also the extinction of the Assyrian state and the extermination of the Assyrian people. A community which had been in existence for over 2,000 years and had been playing an ever more dominant part in southwestern Asia for a period of some two-and-a-half centuries, was blotted out almost completely. Two hundred and ten years later, when Cyrus the Younger's 10,000 Greek mercenaries were retreating up the Tigris Valley from the battlefield of Cunaxas to the Black Sea coast, they passed in succession the sites of Calah and Nineveh and were struck with astonishment, not so much at the massiveness of the fortifications and the extent of the area they embraced, as at the spectacle of such vast works of man lying uninhabited. Xenophon was unable to learn even the most elementary facts about the authentic history of these derelict fortress-cities. Although the whole of southwestern Asia, from Jerusalem to Ararat and from Elam to Lydia, had been dominated and terrorized by the masters of these cities little more than two centuries before Xenophon passed that way, the best account he is able to give of them has no relation to their real history, and the very name of Assyria is unknown to him.[6]

As Toynbee remarks, the modern reader of history knows far more about Assyria and its achievements than did this leader of the Greek

---

[5]*Isaiah* 40:8.

[6]Arnold Toynbee, *A Study of History*: (Somervell condensation, Volume I, Oxford Univ. Press, 1947), p. 338.

military force passing by Nineveh only two centuries later. The work of archaeologists in the Near East in the nineteenth and twentieth centuries, and their discovery of great libraries of cuneiform tablets in the buried cities of Assyria, have opened a new chapter in our knowledge of the history of the ancient Near East which ratifies the descriptions of that period by the Hebrew Prophets.

A similar fulfillment of a prophetic judgment, this time from the words of Jesus in the Gospel, is suggested by Abbé Constant Fouard's *Life of Christ*, as he surveys the present scene of the western shore of the Lake of Genesareth where were located the chief cities in which Jesus carried on his apostolate in Galilee. Fouard recalls the denunciation of these cities by Christ, as given in St. Matthew's Gospel (11:21-24):

> Woe to thee, Chorozain! woe to thee, Bethsaida! for if Tyre and Sidon had beheld such miracles wrought among them as have been worked in your midst, they would have done penance long since in sackcloth and ashes. This is why I say to you that Tyre and Sidon in the Day of Judgment shall be dealt with more mercifully than shall you. And thou, Capharnaum, wouldst thou lift thyself up to the heavens? Thou shalt be humbled down to Hell; for if the miracles which have been done in thee had been wrought in Sodom, she would perchance be living even to this day. That is why I say to thee, in the Day of Judgment, the land of Sodom shall be dealt with more mercifully than shalt thou.

Fouard draws a picture of the abundant life in this area in the time of Jesus, and how difficult it is today to discover just where any of these cities was located. And he concludes with this description of the region (this was around 1880):

> The green pastures, the vines, and the orchards have disappeared; the flourishing towns are only heaps of ruins; jackals slink about the synagogues of Tell Houm, where Jesus taught; the few thorny thickets do not suffice to temper the great heats within these hollow spaces, and the air which one breathes fairly burns with the dry glow. The lake indeed still shimmers in the sunlight between the long lines of hills, as clear and as calm as it was of old. . . . And yet . . . this sea aforetime so brilliant with life, and now doomed to the desolation of death, must recall great thoughts to all who wander about the solitary stretches of sand along its shores today,—thoughts

which remind us how terrible it is to reject the word of God and incur His Anathema.[7]

---

[7]Abbe Constant Fouard, *The Christ the Son of God*, pp. 158-159.

7

The Redemption as Liberation
from Satan

In our preceding chapter we gave some examples of particular judgments in the course of history which appear to manifest the justice of God against transgressors before the final judgment of mankind at the end of history. The interpretation of historical events in terms of divine judgment is in accord with the principle of Hebrew prophecy, which saw the disasters visited upon particular peoples and empires in the ancient world as divine retribution for their sins against God. The full thrust and direction of Hebrew prophecy, however, was toward the final triumph of God's justice, not merely over particular nations and rulers, but over the entire world order dominated by the pride and injustice of man. The later Hebrew prophets foresaw the replacement of this old order by a new one which would show forth the greatness and the glory of God. Fr. Louis Bouyer speaks of the development by the prophets of this more universal conception of the goal of world history:

> This expectation does not attain its full clarification until after the return from exile. In the prophecies of Ezekiel or of the second part of Isaias, it appears decisively that it is nothing less than the expectation of another world, of a new world, of the world which is coming, in which it is Yahweh Himself who will come, and who will come to reign. . . . One of these worlds is to supplant the other and to take its place by force. This is why the Day of Yahweh, the Day in which His reign begins, is the Day of Judgment, of the "crisis" that is to entangle present history by the conquering invasion of the sovereign power.[1]

Fr. Bouyer points out that the transition from a natural to a supernatural end of history was gradually forced upon the consciousness of the Jewish people, even though, as we see in the time of Christ and for some time thereafter, a great part of the Jewish people continued to identify the supernatural end of history with their own triumph over the Gentiles. Fr. Bouyer writes:

---

[1] *The Meaning of Sacred Scripture*, pp. 159-160.

Israel as a whole was slow to come to a full realization of this fact. Desperately attached to a religion of the immediately present and of the flesh, the Jewish people attempted to find the eternal Jerusalem hailed by the last prophets in the city rebuilt by the liberated exiles and in the reconstructed temple. . . . [But] from the time when the walls of the new temple began to be built, Israel felt that this construction, far from surpassing the old one, did not even equal it. It felt less quickly, but it felt soon enough, that the ordeal of the exile had put an end to any earthly hope in *this* world.[2]

The development of Hebrew thought, under the impulse of this new idea, was toward the creation of a new type of Jewish writing: the apocalypse. One of the key features which distinguished this kind of sacred literature was its emphasis on the contrast between the present aeon or age, and the age which is to come. To the writers of the apocalypses, the present age lies under the dominion of Satan, and it will require the coming of God in power to dispossess him.

Fr. Bouyer suggests that, although this concern with the demonic is a relatively late development in Jewish thought, it is a natural corollary from the earlier Jewish belief in the irreconcilable conflict between Yahweh and the gods of the pagan peoples who surrounded Israel. As the ancient Hebrews identified the pagan peoples with their gods, so now, in this new development, based on a more universal perspective, the Jews saw the whole of the present aeon controlled by heathen world powers which were under the dominion of demons who were worshipped as gods. Consequently, the ultimate apocalypse of history would see the overthrow not only of the earthly kingdoms, but also of the demonic powers who stand behind these kingdoms and whose spirit is incarnated in the practices of their public life. Fr. Bouyer points out:

Thus the work of the "Son of Man," coming on the clouds of Heaven accompanied by the faithful angels, will be to break this domination so that the Kingdom of God may come at last, and with it the salvation of His people.[3]

The ideas present in the apocalypses dominate Jewish thought of the first century B.C. and A.D.; and it was by giving a certain new

---

[2]*Ibid.*, pp. 160-161.
[3]*Ibid.*, p. 171.

direction to these ideas that Christianity made one of its most significant contributions. The Son of Man was indeed the destined instrument for the overthrow of the diabolic powers; but His triumph would be accomplished, not by force of arms in the first instance, but by means of His suffering and death. This meant also that a distinction had to be drawn between the first coming of Christ as the Suffering Servant, and His later coming with His angels in power and glory. Nevertheless, the early Christians shared the basic Jewish conception that the present state of the world was under the dominion of diabolic powers, and that the Messiah was meant to roll back this demonic conquest. Fr. Bouyer describes the Christian view of the cosmic struggle for the soul of man, which gave the Christian doctrine of redemption its vital meaning:

> [A]nd, transformed into demons cast headlong from the celestial kingdom at the time of their revolt, they [that is, the fallen angels] have been able to establish themselves in this world as in a heaven of which they themselves were the gods. Thus is explained the unreserved condemnation that invests nearly every biblical mention of the world, particularly in St. John's writings. Indeed, by this word Scripture no longer means ordinarily the creation as such, but insofar as it has become the home and dwelling of evil spirits. . . .
>
> One of the most significant details in this connection is without doubt the opinion of the Apostles, and more generally of the first Christian generations, concerning idolatry (we might say also that of the prophets, for the New Testament has done nothing in that direction but shed new light on the judgments of the Old). This opinion alone can explain the violent recoil of the Christian martyrs from the slightest compromise with even the apparently least offensive of the pagan rites. . . . If the idol, the piece of wood or stone or metal, is nothing in itself, the devotion paid to it, according to St. Paul, goes through it straight to the demon. St. Paul looks upon Artemis and Ares and Baal and Astarte not as empty dreams but as "false gods," angels fallen indeed, but, since their defection and ours, endowed with an evil power all too real. Have they not succeeded in making themselves adored in this world by men, under cover of the elements that are for the moment subjected to them?
>
> Understood thus, idolatry, far from being an empty cult, assumes a frightening form. It is not a nightmare, but a true revelation of the devil and his angels inasmuch as they have become masters of this world.

Seen in this context, the redemption accomplished by Christ is the liberation of man from slavery to the devil, and from the reign of sin which subjects man to the power of the demons. Even though Christ came in humility as the Suffering Servant, the conflict with the powers of evil is nonetheless real and deadly, and His triumph over Satan nonetheless an accomplished fact. Fr. Bouyer writes:

> But over against the slavery of sin-idolatry, St. Paul presents Christ to us as "the stronger one" . . . who has come to bind the "strong man" in his home, has stripped him of his weapons, and, having made him incapable of doing harm, drives him from his citadel. . . . If there is one point on which the synoptic Gospels are in perfect accord with St. Paul, it is surely in this method of interpreting the Redeemer's mission and work.[4]

The idea of an irreconcilable conflict between the Son of Man and the forces of evil, the latter embodied in the kingdoms of the heathen powers, is given dramatic expression in the Old Testament *Book of Daniel*. The prophet speaks of four great beasts seen in his vision, each representing a particular pagan empire, one succeeding to the other, with the last one having especially great power to oppress those who remain faithful to God. Of the king of this fourth empire Daniel is told by the angel:

> And he shall speak words against the High One, and shall crush the saints of the Most High: and he shall think himself able to change times and laws, and they shall be delivered into his hand until a time, and times, and half a time. And judgment shall sit, that his power may be taken away, and be broken in pieces, and perish even to the end.

The instrument for that destruction of the last and greatest of the heathen powers is identified as the Son of Man.

> I beheld therefore in the vision of the night, and lo, one like the Son of Man came with the clouds of Heaven, and He came even to the Ancient of Days: and they presented Him before him. And he gave Him power, and glory, and a kingdom: and all peoples, tribes and tongues shall serve Him: His power is an everlasting power that shall not be taken away: and His Kingdom that shall not be destroyed.[5]

---

[4]*The Paschal Mystery*, pp. 100-102.
[5]*Daniel* 7:25-26; 13-14.

Christopher Dawson gives the following explanation of the significance of the *Book of Daniel* for both Jews and Christians in New Testament times:

> This Jewish interpretation of history finds its most systematic expression in the *Book of Daniel* which formed a model for the later apocalyptic literature. It no longer takes the form of isolated prophecies and denunciations of particular judgments, but of a synthetic view of world history as seen in the series of world empires which occupy "the latter times." Each empire has its allotted time and when "the sentence of the watchers" has gone forth its kingdom is numbered and finished. And at the same time the transcendent character of the Messianic hope is brought out more clearly than before. The Kingdom of God does not belong to the series of world empires, it is something that comes in from outside and replaces them. It is the stone cut out of the mountain without hands that crushes the fourfold image of world empire to powder and grows till it fills the whole world. It is the universal Kingdom of the Son of Man which will destroy the kingdoms of the four beasts and will endure forever.
>
> This is the tradition that was inherited by the Christian Church. Indeed it may be said that it was precisely this prophetic and apocalyptic element in Judaism to which Christianity appealed. . . . To the primitive Christian it was in the literal sense the Good News of the Kingdom.[6]

If there is one thing, therefore, that distinguishes the early Christian worldview from that of a great deal of so-called Christianity today, it is the belief in the reality of the demonic world and its domination over a world that rejects its Messiah. Much Modernist theology denies altogether the existence of diabolic powers and thus renders quite pallid its idea of the Redemption. Instead of the sharp conflict between the forces of good and evil for control of the cosmos found in early Christianity, we have instead a few high-sounding platitudes about peace and brotherhood. And since this kind of religiosity is so sharply at variance with one's experience of reality, these Modernist theologians readily turn to Marxist ideas of society, based essentially on class warfare, in order to reintroduce the element of conflict with evil which they have eliminated from their religious

---

[6]*Dynamics of World History*, pp. 253-254.

worldview. Only now it is a portion of mankind, the bourgeoisie, which is the incarnation of evil rather than the demonic powers.   And the redemption which is to be achieved is merely from some form of economic exploitation, which may easily be reinstituted under a new and more oppressive form when "the new class" comes to power.

8

The Apocalypse
and the Gospel of Jesus

In the preceding chapter we saw the importance of the *Book of Daniel* in establishing the main themes of the apocalyptic type of literature which was to be so much a part of the environment of thought in which Christianity had its origin and phenomenal first growth. We saw portrayed in this book the irreconcilable enmity between the Kingdom of the Son of Man and the kingdoms of the four beasts which dominate in succession the present world order.

But, we may ask, is not this kind of apocalyptic attitude and expectation the characteristic of Judaism rather than of Christianity? Must we not remember the teaching of Jesus that "the Kingdom of God is within you?" Was it not this apocalyptic conception which led the Jews to challenge the might of Rome on numerous occasions and which eventually resulted in the destruction of Jerusalem in 70 A.D.? And should we not see in Christianity's rejection of the apocalyptic view of history the reason why Christians were able to survive and spread their faith most widely? Even if some Christians were tempted to hold on to apocalyptic hopes and forget that the Kingdom of God is within, did not the destruction of Jerusalem and the disasters suffered by the Jews serve to show Christians the folly of setting one's hopes in a triumph over the kingdoms of this world?

On this view, Christians should be content to preach the Fatherhood of God and the brotherhood of man, and to employ Christianity as the means for bringing that message to all mankind. Christianity would thus be primarily an ethical and moral teaching, and it would be here, as Harnack asserted, that the true essence of the Christian religion is to be found. Anything apocalyptic in it was merely the outworn husk which fell away when the seed had been fully matured.

The first fact we should note, as against this nineteenth century liberal Christianity, is that the last book of the New Testament, the *Apocalypse*, continues in a decisive manner the tradition of the *Book of Daniel*. Here also there is the emphasis upon an irreconcilable hostility between the Kingdom of God and the kingdoms of man. If anything, it is even more uncompromising in its affirmation of that hostility than is the *Book of Daniel* itself. Here is a representative passage expressive of the view of history which we find in the *Apocalypse*:

> And I saw that the Lamb had opened one of the seven seals, and I heard one of the four living creatures, as it were the voice of thunder, saying: "Come, and see. . . ." And when he had opened the fifth seal, I saw under the altar the souls of them that were slain for the Word of God, and for the testimony which they held. And they cried with a loud voice, saying: "How long, O Lord (holy and true) doest thou not judge and revenge our blood on them that dwell on the earth?" And white robes were given to every one of them; and it was said to them, that they should rest for a little time, till their fellow servants, and their brethren, who are to be slain, even as they, should be filled up.
>
> And I saw, when he had opened the sixth seal, and behold there was a great earthquake, and the sun became black as sackcloth of hair: and the whole moon became as blood: And the stars from heaven fell upon the earth, as the fig tree casteth its green figs when it is shaken by a great wind: And the heaven departed as a book folded up: and every mountain, and the islands were moved out of their places.
>
> And the kings of the earth, and the princes, and tribunes, and the rich, and the strong, and every bondman, and every freeman, hid themselves in the dens and in the rocks of mountains: And they said to the mountains and the rocks: "Fall upon us, and hide us from the face of Him that sitteth upon the throne, and from the wrath of the Lamb": For the great day of their wrath is come, and who shall be able to stand?[1]

Speaking of this book of the *Apocalypse*, Christopher Dawson calls it "the first Christian interpretation of history." At the same time, it is the source of practically all future Christian interpretations of history down to the latter part of the eighteenth century. For it was not until then that the rise of liberal Christianity, under the influence of the French Enlightenment, led to a discarding of the apocalyptic elements in the Christian worldview. But this liberal Christianity was not able to supplant but was forced to coexist with a continuance of the original Christian view of history, together with various sectarian interpretations

---

[1]*Apocalypse* 6:1; 6:9-17.

which tried to fix the exact date for the end of the world and the Second Coming of Christ.

Dawson sees the *Apocalypse* as the culmination and inspired expression of the attitude toward history held by the early Christian Church. This was the worldview of the Christians of the first and second centuries who were in continual danger of martyrdom for their Faith.

> It is marked by an historical dualism of the most uncompromising kind; which even accentuates the contrast between the Kingdom of God and the kingdom of man that we find already in the prophets and in the *Book of Daniel*. The city of God is not built up on earth by the preaching of the Gospel and the labor of the saints: it descends from God out of Heaven like a bride adorned for her husband. But before it comes the mystery of iniquity must fulfill itself on earth and the harvest of human power and pride must be reaped. This is the significance of the judgment of Babylon, which appears in the *Apocalypse* not as a conquering military power as in the earlier prophets, but as the embodiment of material civilization and luxury, the great harlot, whose charms bewitch all the nations of the earth, the world market whose trade enriches the merchants, and the ship owners.[2]

If we are to accept the *Apocalypse* as an authentic expression of the early Christian worldview, is there not an absolute dichotomy between this view of God's providence, and the message and teaching of Jesus which emphasizes nonviolence? Should we not recognize that the apocalyptic attitude meant the triumph of the Jewish element in Christianity at the expense of the specifically Christian one? Did not the Christians allow their desire for revenge against their persecutors to overcome the real meaning of the message which Jesus had brought them? For did not Jesus teach us to turn the other cheek, and is not the view which we find in the *Apocalypse* essentially a refusal to do so?

This raises the question of whether the liberal interpretation of the message and character of Jesus is not much too selective, ignoring those elements in the Gospel which cannot be fitted into a preconceived notion of what it is thought Jesus really came to teach. In other words, does it not impose upon the Word of God as it exists in the Gospel, the restrictions of the word of man? Does it not practice a surgery which cuts out of the Gospel those elements it does not wish to hear? But, if

---

[2]*Religion and the Modern State* (Sheed & Ward, 1935), p. 77.

one reads the Gospel itself, it is impossible to ignore the apocalyptic character of Christ's attitude. He makes everything in life subordinate to God's final judgment and the divine reversal of the values of this world. Neither the liberal interpretation of the Gospel, nor the social activist one, often inspired by Marxism, is based upon the Gospel itself; they are preconceived attitudes, fitting in with the *Zeitgeist* of a certain period which seeks to pick and choose from the Gospel whatever it thinks will serve to bolster its own conception. They are not genuinely concerned with Jesus and His teaching, but rather with the things of this world which serve as their final standard of judgment.

Since the resemblance between the teaching of Jesus and that of the Apocalypse is not always clearly perceived, as is evident from the Liberal interpretation of the Gospel, let us set it forth directly, as in this passage of commentary by Christopher Dawson:

> At first sight there may seem little in common between all this lurid apocalyptic imagery and the teaching of the Gospels. Nevertheless the same fundamental conceptions underlie both of them. The dualism of the Kingdom and the world in the Gospels and the Epistles is no less uncompromising than that of the two apocalyptic cities. This is especially true in the case of the fourth Gospel with its insistence on the enmity of the world as the necessary condition of the children of the Kingdom. "I pray not for the world, but for those that thou hast given me." And again—"The prince of this world cometh and in me he has not anything."[3]
>
> So too, the supernatural and catastrophic character of the coming of the Kingdom is insisted on in the synoptic Gospels no less than in the *Apocalypse*. There also, in what may be called the apocalypse of Jesus, we find the same prophecies of coming woe and the same conception of a world crisis which is due to the ripening of the harvest of evil rather than to the progress of the forces of good. "And as it was in the days of Noe, so it shall be also in the days of the Son of Man. They ate and drank, they married and gave in marriage until the day when Noe entered into the ark and the flood came and destroyed them all." (*Luke* 17:7).[4]

This idea that the Gospels themselves are apocalyptic in character is also the position taken by Fr. Louis Bouyer. And he adds that, because of this, the Gospels necessarily involve a reversal in the scale of

---

[3]*John* 17:9, 14:30.
[4]*Religion and the Modern State*, pp. 77-78.

the world's values, so that it is the poor who are especially to be the heirs of the Kingdom.

> One might say that in the mouth of Jesus Himself, the antagonism between the *aion outos* [i.e., the present age] and *aion mellon* [i.e., the age to come] appears so primary that a man's condition in the one seems to be automatically the reverse of his condition in the other. This is, moreover, exactly what appears in the Canticle of Mary.[5]

How, then, are we to distinguish the Christian view of the apocalyptic nature of history from that which prevailed in first-century Judaism, which gave support to the Zealot-led attempt to overthrow the Roman power in Palestine? If Christianity holds to an apocalyptic view of history, how does it protect itself from that kind of zealotry and from a fanatical desire for revolution?

The answer may possibly be found in discovering how Christianity protected itself from that danger in the first century. When the Jewish community from which Christianity first sprang was filled with demands for the overthrow of the Roman power, and inflamed by Zealot-led attempts to get the revolution started, how did Christianity respond to this situation?

There was, no doubt, a revolutionary element in the early Church's view of Gentile society and the Roman Empire; but it expressed itself in a different manner from that which was taken by the Jewish community with its resort to insurrection. According to Christopher Dawson, the Church was ultimately the source of a revolution in Graeco-Roman society; but it was achieved by changing social attitudes from within, by means of conversion of the heart, not by military conquest. Referring to the Roman Empire and the Christian attitude toward it, Dawson writes:

> Yet the whole splendid building rested on nonmoral foundations—often on mere violence and cruelty. The divine Caesar might be a Caligula or a Nero, wealth was an excuse for debauchery, and the prosperity of the wealthy classes was based on the institution of slavery. . . .
> The early Church could not but be conscious that she was separated by an infinite gulf from this great material order, and that

---

[5]*The Meaning of Sacred Scripture*, pp. 172-173.

she could have no part in its prosperity or in its injustice. She was in this world as the seed of a new order, utterly subversive of all that had made the ancient world what it was. Yet, though she inherited the spirit of the Jewish protest against the Gentile world power, she did not look for any temporal change, much less did she attempt herself to bring about any social reform. The Christian accepted the Roman state as a God-given order appropriate to the condition of a world in slavery to spiritual darkness, and concentrated all of his hopes on the return of Christ and the final victory of the supernatural order. Meanwhile, he lived as a stranger in the midst of an alien world.

Yet this attitude, so strikingly in contrast to demands for relevance on the part of modern Christians, had nevertheless profound social consequences:

> Christianity substituted membership of the Church for membership of the city as man's fundamental and most important relationship to his fellows. In the new religious society rich and poor, bond and free, Roman citizen and foreigner all met on an absolutely equal footing. Not only were their earthly distinctions overlooked, they were almost inverted, and it was the poor who were privileged and the rich who were humbled. This world was for the rich, but the new world—the only world that mattered—was above all the inheritance of the poor.[6]

Thus we can see the basic difference in outlook between the Jewish and Christian attitudes toward Gentile society. Messianic Judaism wanted a kingdom of this world, Christianity looked essentially for the Kingdom that was to come. First-century Judaism would rely upon the arm of the flesh to achieve its goals, despite the repeated warnings of the Old Testament Prophets against reliance on man rather than God. And it would have to impose its ideals on Gentile society by force: that was the essential meaning of Zealotry, the coming of the Kingdom of God by the power of armed might. And this is what caused the reign of terror which the fanatical Jewish leaders inflicted upon their own people in Jerusalem during the Roman siege of that city.

Nevertheless, despite this contrast with the Jews, the early Christians were not simply detached in their attitude toward the future;

---

[6]*The Formation of Christendom*, pp. 116-117 (originally published in *Blackfriars*, July, 1924).

they did not practice *apatheia* as the Stoics did, indifference to what might come. They had an intense longing for the coming of the Kingdom, and for the establishment of the reign of God's justice. But they recognized that the time of its coming was in God's hands, not theirs. As Dawson points out:

> It does not follow, however, that the faithful are powerless to affect the course of events. It is their resistance that breaks the power of the world. The prayers of the saints and the blood of the martyrs, so to speak, force the hand of God and hasten the coming of the Kingdom. If the unjust judge listens to the importunity of the widow, will not God much more avenge His elect who cry to Him night and day?[7]

Thus Christians should pray with intense hope for the coming of the Kingdom; but they must not insist that it has to come in their lifetime, nor, above all, identify it with any set of earthly arrangements. They should remember that, whatever changes may take place in society, or whatever hopes may be held for social betterment, Christians have here no abiding city. Neither may the Christian try to fix the time of Christ's coming, or slacken off work in the vineyard because the time is short. John Henry Newman portrays for us what should be the proper attitude in waiting for Christ:

> By the eleventh hour is not meant that Christians have little to do, but that the time is short; that it is the last time; that there is a "present distress"; that they have much to do in a little time; that "the night cometh when no man can work"; that their Lord is at hand, and that they have to wait for Him. . . . Earth and sky are ever failing; Christ is ever coming; Christians are ever lifting up their heads and looking out, and therefore it is the evening. . . . The evening is long, and the day was short; for the first shall be last, and last first. What seems vigorous, perishes; what seems ever expiring is carried on; and this last age, though ever-failing, has lasted longer than the ages before it, and Christians have more time for a greater work than if they had been hired in the morning.[8]

But this greater work can only be achieved if one avoids the pitfalls of Scylla and Charybdis: of revolutionary action which identifies

---

[7]*Religion and the Modern State*, p. 78.
[8]*Sermons on the Subjects of the Day*, pp. 9-10.

the coming of the Kingdom with a particular political solution, or a self-centered religiosity which concentrates only upon attaining one's individual salvation and ignores the social character of the Christian hope.

9

The Church and the Kingship of Christ

We now wish to see what we should expect to be the condition of the Catholic Church in history in the light of two different aspects under which Jesus is portrayed in the Gospels, as the Suffering Servant of Isaiah, chapter 53, and the Son of Man of the Book of Daniel, chapter 7. The idea which the early Christians had of their present condition reflected these opposite elements in the Messianic role of Jesus. But they saw one of them, that associated with the prophecies concerning the triumph of the Son of Man, as being postponed until after the Second Coming. Christopher Dawson describes their outlook upon the Church and its future in the following passage:

> Thus the primitive Christian idea of the Kingdom of God was essentially twofold. On the one hand there was the period of hidden life and growth, the Kingdom in seed; on the other, the state of perfection and glory, the Kingdom in fruit. On the one hand there is the "little flock," persecuted, poor and without honor in face of the triumphant kingdom of this world; on the other the People of God reigning with Christ in a restored universe. In short, to use theological language, the Kingdom of God includes first the Kingdom of Grace, then the Kingdom of Glory.[1]

The early Christian saw the Church as continuing the work of Jesus, animated by His Spirit, and destined to be the means by which humanity would be transformed. At the same time, this worldview emphasized the fact of an apocalyptic contrast between the work of the Spirit carried on invisibly under the surface of things, and the domination of the present age by the powers of evil. Speaking of the teaching of St. Paul, Dawson points out:

> The Kingdom of God is shown to be nothing less than the restoration of the whole creation in and through Christ. The Church is the embryo of a new world, and the Spirit of Christ, which dwells in it, is the principle of its life and the source of its growth. With the death of Christ, the old order came to an end, and His Resurrection,

---

[1] *Enquiries*, pp. 334.

together with the consequent gift of the Spirit to His disciples, inaugurated a new order which will only attain completion at His Second Coming "with power."

The life of the faithful during the present world-age is consequently of a double or intermediate character. They share in the life of two worlds, one dying, the other still in the womb. Their bodies are still "subject to the bondage of corruption," the powers of this world-age are against them, the force of spiritual evil is still unsubdued, but by their membership of the Church they already belong to the new world which is being built up invisibly under the veil of the old, and their possession of the Spirit and His gifts is a "pledge of the world to come," an assurance of the reality of the new life.[2]

It will be noted that Dawson in this passage implicitly identifies the Church with the Kingdom of God and draws a sharp contrast between the period of hidden life and growth which is the Church's present condition—the Kingdom in seed, and the state of perfection and glory—the Kingdom in fruit, which follows upon the Second Coming of Christ. And that raises an important question. Is the Church, in the present intermediate age between Christ's First and Second Coming, meant only to share in His humiliation and suffering, but not to participate in His glory until the end of history? I think the first approach to that question has to be through an examination of what was the example given by Jesus Himself in the Gospels. If Jesus is to be the model for the Church, what do we find to be characteristic of Him in His earthly existence? Do we find that it is only the role of the Suffering Servant, the man of sorrows and rejected of men, which is what is portrayed of Jesus in the Gospels? Granted that He emptied Himself of His Godhead and became man, were there no reflections of that heavenly glory to be found about His Person when He became incarnate among men?

Now it is true that His passion and death, with all the suffering and humiliation which this involved, was carried out in full public sight; and that His Resurrection, by which His triumph over death was shown and the nature of His Kingship manifested, was made known only to a certain private circle of witnesses—it was not manifested in the same public way as the crucifixion had been. The Resurrection was not wholly without public evidence, of course; or the Apostles would not have been

---

[2]*Ibid.*, pp. 334-335.

able to point to the empty tomb in witness to the fact that Jesus was the Messiah who had overcome death by rising from the dead. Nevertheless, on the whole, it is true that the Resurrection did not manifest His glory in the same public and open manner that the crucifixion had shown His humiliation and suffering and death.

However, to stop at this point would be to ignore the witness of the three years of His public life as providing part of the model which His Church might be expected to follow. In His public life, despite the fact that He embraced a life of poverty, and had not a stone on which to lay His head, and that He had no formal position either as teacher or priest or scribe in the hierarchy of Judaism, and was harried and spied upon by the Pharisees: did not His miracles and His teaching bear witness that He was indeed the promised Messiah? Must we not say, that about Jesus of Nazareth, there was both an anticipation and an evidence of the Messianic Kingship which He will only assume in full glory at His Second Coming?

The public life of Jesus afforded the Jewish people good reason to hail Him as the promised Messiah; and the Messiah in their eyes was not the Suffering Servant, but rather the figure of power and majesty portrayed in the *Book of Daniel* and in the Jewish apocalypses, where His Kingdom was to include all tongues and tribes and peoples. Therefore, if we are to draw upon the witness of the public life of Jesus, as distinct from the ultimate public *denouement* in the crucifixion and death, we can scarcely deny that Christ provides His Church with an example in which striking manifestations of divinity and power are present. If the evidence of Christ's character and His miracles and teaching ("Never man spake like this man") are to be a seal for the authenticity of the claim He made, then the same kind of seal may be expected to distinguish His Church.

However, we should remember that the exaltation of the Church depends on her remaining poor in spirit, possessed of meekness and humility of heart, and also upon her having undergone privation and suffering. Even as the triumph of Jesus portrayed in the *Apocalypse*, the Lamb to whom is due power and honor and glory and might, is a result of His having emptied Himself to become man and then having undergone His passion and death, so likewise the Church's triumph in this world comes through her following that pattern. And this is why it is that the saints are the foremost exemplars of the Church's holiness and triumph, and the most efficacious means by which her work is carried on. For it is they who show forth in their lives the pattern of suffering and humility leading to spiritual triumph which Jesus showed forth in His life and death.

Our conclusion, therefore, is that while the Church should expect to encounter persecution and humiliation, and thus to participate in the passion of Jesus, it should also be true that she will show forth to the world something of the coming of the Kingdom of Christ in glory. For by this means she will be recognized as possessing divine authority and power and holiness, even as Jesus Himself could be so recognized by the people of Judea during His earthly existence.

This fact is ignored or denied by many who assail the "triumphalism" of the Church, as though the signs of Christ's triumph over error and evil, so strikingly displayed in His public life, are not meant to characterize the life of His Church as well. Yet if we remove these signs of triumph from the Church, we deprive mankind of one of its strongest reasons for recognizing her as being of divine origin. We level the Church down to a flat uniformity in which any one of the world religions may be found equally acceptable as Catholicism. Whether these critics of "triumphalism" realize it or not, they strive to make men blind to the marks of supernatural origin with which God has endowed the Church—and thus make it more difficult for men to accept her saving truth.

10

The Meaning of the Messianic Age

In an earlier chapter we compared the view of history held by the Oriental world religions with that which was characteristic of Judaism and Christianity. We saw that the Oriental religions tended to empty history of significance by making it the scene of an endless series of repetitions—whether of reincarnations or cosmic cycles. As a result, the goal of the spiritual elite was to escape from history by means of enlightenment or Nirvana. This introduced a basic conflict between the goals of religious striving and the needs of everyday life, including the need to maintain the social structures by which society could be kept in existence. Christopher Dawson has pointed out what are the results of this conflict when the other-worldly idea of the spiritual elite becomes predominant in society. He suggests that the riches of a greater religious understanding of the transcendent were paid for in a decline in social vitality and a loss of what society had earlier achieved. Dawson writes:

> For in religions of pure contemplation there is the danger of a divorce from historical reality and from the social order which deprives it of spiritual efficacy and creativity in the order of culture. The great verse of the Pragnaparamita Sutra, "The verse of the great wisdom, the unsurpassed verse, the verse that extinguishes all pain" is also the epitaph on Buddhism as a living and creative religion:
> "O wisdom gone away, gone, gone to the other shore, landed on the other shore, Svaha."
> In the first chapter I said that religion was like a bridge between two worlds by means of which the order of culture is brought into conscious relation with the transcendent reality of spiritual being. But in these religions of negation and pure contemplation, the bridge is open in only one direction. It is a way of escape from the city into the wilderness and the spirit that goes out does not return again. Thus the world of culture is gradually weakened and finally deserted, like the great Buddhist cities of ancient Ceylon where the jungle has returned and swallowed up palaces and monasteries and irrigation tanks, leaving only the figure

of Buddha contemplating the vanity of action and the cessation of existence.[1]

Jean Danielou also speaks of the basic difference between Christianity and the Oriental religions concerning the meaning of history and he identifies the philosophical premise which leads the latter to regard history with distrust and disdain:

> The other religions, for the most part, view time, the order of reality in which history unfolds, as a degradation with respect to eternity, which they hold to be the only genuine reality; they consider being, in the full sense of the word, as exempt from change, progress, and evolution. For them, time is nothing but a mirror, a degraded reflection of eternity.... For Hinduism, and even more for Buddhism, time represents multiplicity, division, dispersion, whereas what truly exists is unity.[2]

In contrast to this, and possibly in reaction against it, the Jewish conception of history saw time as all important, for it was the scene in which God was working out His providential purposes for mankind. And, so far was it from being abstract and other-worldly in its conception of the goal of history, that it identified those purposes with the destinies of one people among all the peoples of the earth, who were the Chosen People of God. It was through them that the race of mankind was to be blessed, and it was through their exaltation that the rest of humanity would be able to partake of the glories and benefits of the Messianic age. Moreover, the conception which the Jewish people held of the culmination of history with the coming of the Messiah was not something intellectualized and remote and hard to visualize. It was presented in concrete, material terms, as we see in the descriptions of it given by the different Hebrew prophets. Take, as one example of the social and material character of Jewish Messianic expectations, this passage which opens the Catholic liturgical year on the First Sunday of Advent:

> That is what Isaiah, son of Amoz, saw concerning Judah and Jerusalem, in days to come. The mountain of the Lord's house shall be established as the highest mountain and raised above the hills. All nations shall stream toward it; many peoples shall come and say:

---

[1]Christopher Dawson, *Religion and Culture (Sheed & Ward, 1948) p. 193.*
[2]Jean Danielou, *The Salvation of the Nations* (Sheed & Ward 1949), pp. 68-9.

"Come, let us climb the Lord's mountain, to the house of the God of Jacob, that He may instruct us in His ways, and we may walk in His paths." From Zion shall go forth instruction, and the word of the Lord from Jerusalem. He shall judge between the nations, and impose terms on many peoples. They shall beat their swords into ploughshares, and their spears into pruning hooks; one nation shall not raise the sword against another, nor shall they train for war again. O house of Jacob, come, let us walk in the light of the Lord.[3]

Moreover, the close personal relationship which that messianic age would establish between God and His people is suggested by this Reading for the Second Sunday of Advent:

Here comes with power the Lord God, who rules by His strong arm; Here is His reward with Him, His recompense before Him. Like a shepherd He feeds His flock; in His arms He gathers the lambs, carrying them in His bosom, and leading the ewes with care.[4]

This conception of God's action in the Messianic age clearly anticipates the Christian image of Jesus as the Good Shepherd.

However, the manner in which Christianity saw Jesus as fulfilling the Messianic hopes of the Jews led to a sharp conflict with older Jewish conceptions. It required a rethinking of the true purpose and significance of the Messiah. The Jews had expected the transformation of the world into an ideal social order, where all sin and warfare had come to an end. As the Responsorial Psalm for Tuesday of the First Week of Advent expresses it, "Justice shall flourish in His time, and fullness of peace forever."[5]

Yet the Christian Gospel claimed that the Messiah had already come and achieved His divine purposes and ascended into Heaven, while the social order remained the same as before. In fact, in His prediction of what His followers might expect after they had begun to preach the Gospel, Jesus declared that they would encounter more conflict and opposition than they had ever known before.[6]

The basic problem, as Christopher Dawson points out, was that the Jews had expected a new world, and Christ brought a new humanity.

---

[3]*Isaiah* 2: 1-5.
[4]*Ibid.*, 40:10-11.
[5]*Ps.* 72:7.
[6]Cf. *Matthew* 10:16-25; 34-39.

He was the firstborn of many brethren. The leaven which He introduced into the human race, through His suffering and death and glorification by the Father, was now to be introduced into the lives of others also, until the whole of humanity should be leavened. And this leavening process was not something which would occur overnight, by some miraculous transformation; it would require time for its achievement, and the Church must first spread the message and grace of the Gospel to all peoples throughout the world—"in Jerusalem and in all Judea and Samaria and even to the very ends of the earth" (*Acts* 1:8). This is what Jesus replied to His disciples before His Ascension, when He was asked whether He would now establish the expected Messianic kingdom.

That involved a change in the Jewish conception of history and separated the first from the second coming of Christ by an indefinite period of time.

But, one might ask, why was it that the Jews were allowed to believe in the concrete and material and social nature of the Messianic kingdom? Why was it that they were not given from the first to understand its true character? The answer would seem to be similar to the reason why they were not given an understanding of the Trinity; that is, in this latter case, they were surrounded by peoples given to polytheist worship in which the conception of God was defiled with licentious ideas and rites. Thus too early a revelation of the nature of the Trinity could have led them to fit this idea into this highly-sexed polytheism. Even with the severe denunciations of polytheism by the Hebrew prophets, it was still most difficult to maintain the monotheistic idea of God; how much more so if the Jewish people had known of the Trinity?

In like fashion, too early a revelation of the spiritual character of the Messianic kingdom might have led them to the kind of rarefied and abstract spirituality which characterized the Oriental world religions. Looking at the range of pre-Christian religious experience, there existed the danger not only of polytheism, but also of the worship of some non-personal cosmic principle, union with which was possible only to a spiritual elite. Such a development in Judaism would have split the unity of the Jewish people into two different kinds of religion—on the one hand, the great mass of the people following the worship of polytheistic deities unhindered by their spiritual leaders, and on the other hand, those leaders now finding refuge in a purely "spiritual" religion.

Moreover, the Messianic kingdom of Christ the King which is the ultimate goal of history in the Christian conception bears some resemblance to the images in which it is presented in the language of the Hebrew prophets. It will indeed be a social entity: the New Jerusalem, the City of God. And its members will be not disembodied spirits, but spiritually transformed human beings who have been redeemed in both body and soul. The external expression of the social order predicted by the prophets—"Justice shall flourish in His time, and fullness of peace forever"—is a reflection of the internal order of peace and justice in the minds and hearts of those who make up that City. For, as Dante gave expression to the principle which governs the heavenly Kingdom of the redeemed, *"In la sua voluntade é nostra pace"*—"In His will is our peace."

11

The Early Christians
and the Second Coming

In earlier chapters we have seen the contrast between Jewish expectations of the Messiah and the quite different fulfillment of those hopes which Jesus presented. Nevertheless, the reorganizing of Christian thought concerning the nature of the Messiah was not made easily. One sees some reflection of that difficulty in the question given to Jesus by some of His disciples just before His Ascension, "Lord, will you at this time restore the kingdom to Israel?" (*Acts* 1:6.)

It was this continued immersion of the early Christians in Jewish apocalyptic hopes that was apparently responsible for their vivid expectation of Christ's Second Coming in the very near future. Fr. Louis Bouyer describes how the practice of vigils resulted from this sense of the imminence of the advent of Christ. Although it was based on a mistaken conception concerning the actual time of Christ's coming, Bouyer shows how it was nevertheless saved from disappointment by the fact that Christ was, in one sense, already with them, although concealed under the appearances of the sacrament:

> Thus the first Christians used to gather at nightfall for their vigil, saying to one another, "The Lord is nigh." They always began this observance in the conviction that the Lord was going to appear with the first rays of morning, and the miracle is that this expectation, ever renewed, was never disappointed. Every time, at the bread-breaking that closed the vigil, they recognized the One whom they loved without yet seeing Him: in the sacramental mystery, grace, after the manner of faith, revealed dimly the substance of gifts which the light of glory would soon illumine.

Fr. Bouyer points to the fact that the desire for Christ's Second Coming, however long delayed it may be, is essential to any authentic Christianity, as is also, in some way, a sense of its imminence.

> We are in the last night separating us from the dawn after which there will be no evening; we are at the very entrance to the nuptial banquet; the Spirit sighs in us for the moment when the door

will open. Therefore we must watch, with loins girt and lighted
lamps in our hands, so that, at the longed-for moment when the cry
shall resound, "Behold the Bridegroom, go out to meet Him," we
may enter with Him and take our place in the company of Abraham,
Isaac, and Jacob. There we shall join all those who belong to Him
and whom He will gather from the ends of the earth to the messianic
banquet . . .[1]

That the advent of Christ might be expected in the very near
future was not derived from the words of Jesus Himself, but was instead
a gloss or interpretation which the early Christians had added on to
them. Thus it was to some degree the Jewish cultural environment, with
its desire to fix the exact time for apocalyptic occurrences, which was
responsible for this idea. The way in which Christ Himself conceived
and spoke of His Second Coming laid emphasis rather on its
unexpectedness, its breaking in upon a world that no longer gave any
attention to the realities of the judgment. And it is the very fact of the
length of the waiting which makes people settle down into an easy
acceptance of the present order of things, and thus they are caught by
the suddenness of the Second Coming. Making use especially of the
parables, Karl Adam shows what was the nature of Jesus' attitude
concerning the end of the world:

> The wicked steward maltreats the servants and squanders the
> property entrusted to him under the pretext that "My lord is long
> acoming." (*Matt.* 24:48.) The bridegroom "tarries" so long, that the
> virgins awaiting Him, the wise as well as the foolish, slumber and
> sleep. (*Matt.* 25:5.) The industrious servants were able to double
> the talents committed to them, before their lord returned "after a
> long time" (*Matt.* 25:19.). . . . If we judge all the eschatological
> utterances of our Lord according to their true meaning . . . we shall
> find that they are nothing but a vivid and imperative summons to
> constant watchfulness and readiness for the Day of the Lord, come
> when it may. . . . The point that Jesus emphasizes is this, that His
> coming cannot be calculated beforehand, that it breaks in suddenly,
> as unexpected as a thief in the night (*Luke* 12:39), as instantaneous
> as a flash of lightning (*Luke* 17:24), as quick as the snare that
> entraps an animal (*Luke* 21:35) . . . [T]he Apostles and evangelists
> were aware that our Lord Himself had not said that He would come
> soon, but that He would come suddenly.[2]

---

[1]*The Paschal Mystery*, pp. 5; 4.
[2]Karl Adam, *The Spirit of Catholicism* (Macmillan, 1944), pp. 87-88.

Despite these words of Christ, it seems to have been only gradually that the early Christians came to recognize that the coming of their Lord was not imminent and might be indefinitely postponed. Jean Danielou, analyzing several texts from the New Testament, identifies one essential precondition of that Coming. He quotes this statement of Jesus: "And this Gospel of the Kingdom shall be preached in the whole world, for a testimony to all nations, and then shall the consummation come." (*Matt.* 25:14.) And he adds:

> The First Christians . . . lived in expectation of Christ's coming in glory to establish His Kingdom for all eternity. That is the ultimate goal of Christian hope, of which we see only the beginning at the present time. Now, in order that this may come about, in order that our hope may attain its goal, there is only one condition, but it is indispensable: The Gospel must have been preached to all the nations of the world, to the entire universe.[3]

While the expectation of the imminence of Christ's coming preserved an important element in the Christian attitude toward history which is apt to be lost in our own day—that one should always be waiting for the Master's return, and not allow ourselves to fall into sloth and slumber—it also involved a certain danger. That danger was that history would no longer seem of any great importance, that everything of significance was over and done with, and therefore that what happened in secular society and history had no relevance for the Christian In speaking of the apocalyptic elements which were so prominent in the early Christian view of history, Dawson observes:

> Consequently the existing order of things had no finality for the Christian. The kingdoms of the world were judged and their ultimate doom was sealed. The building had been condemned and the mine which was to destroy it was laid, though the exact moment of the explosion was uncertain. The Christian had to keep his eyes on the future like a servant who waits for the return of his master.[4]

Lying behind this view of history was the understanding that the fullness of time had already been realized, that the Messiah in whom is

---

[3]*The Salvation of the Nations*, p. 78.
[4]*Dynamics of World History*, p. 297.

contained the fullness of God's Providence for mankind, had already come, achieved His salvific purposes, and ascended again into Heaven, whence He would shortly come to judge both the living and the dead. John Henry Newman expressed this understanding in an Anglican sermon of 1840, which was more Evangelical Protestant than Anglican in outlook:

> But when once the Christ had come, as the Son over His own house, and with His perfect Gospel, nothing remained but to gather in His saints. No higher Priest could come—no truer doctrine. The Light and Life of men had appeared, and had suffered, and had risen again; and nothing more was left to do. Earth had had its most solemn event, and seen its most august sight; and therefore it was the last time. And hence, though time intervened between Christ's First and Second Coming, it is not recognized (as I may say) in the Gospel scheme, but is, as it were, an accident. For so it was, that up to Christ's coming in the flesh, the course of things ran straight towards that end, nearing it by every step; but now, under the Gospel, that course has (if I may so speak) altered its direction, as regards His Second Coming, and runs, not towards the end, but along it, and on the brink of it; and is at all times equally near that great event, which, did it run towards, it would at once run into: Christ, then, is ever at our doors . . . [5]

If this view were to have prevailed, not balanced by other considerations, it could have led to an emptying out of the significance of the secular history of mankind. The effects upon social effort might not have been too much different from the effects upon society of the view of history held by the Oriental world religions. There were, however, certain important factors which distinguished it from the Oriental worldview. These included:

First, the fact that it was a whole people which was involved, not merely gifted individuals or solitary ascetics seeking spiritual enlightenment. Thus it maintained the sense of corporate solidarity which had characterized the Jews as the People of God.

Second, this was reinforced by the vivid awareness the Christians had of a sharp conflict between the Church and the world, each with its own principle of organization and its own set of values and purposes. This also was similar to the contrast which the Jews had drawn between

---

[5] John Henry Newman, *Waiting for Christ* in *Parochial and Plain Sermons*, Volume VI (Christian Classics, 1968), pp. 240-241.

themselves and Gentile society.

Third, despite their hostility toward the values of secular society, the early Christians possessed a very strong missionary drive which led them to evangelize in that society and add to the number of the brethren called to salvation. Josef Jungmann's estimate of the success of that evangelization, after almost three centuries of effort, is given in this statement: "In spite of the persecutions, by the time that Constantine appeared at least one fourth of the population in the Roman Empire and also in the city [of Rome] must have been Christian."[6]

Moreover, there were other counterbalancing elements in the Christian worldview which recognized a certain value in what was present in pagan society, and which held that the history of non-Christian peoples also had a providential purpose to play in the salvation of mankind. With Greek philosophy, this could even go too far, as in the case of early Church Fathers like Origen and Clement of Alexandria, who lived in the first half of the third century. St. Justin Martyr, however (died 165), gave an earlier and more balanced answer. Of this answer Etienne Gilson observes that, to Justin, the Prologue of *St. John's Gospel* showed that:

> [T]he Word enlightens every man who comes into the world; consequently, and on the testimony of God Himself, we must admit a natural revelation of the Word, universal and antedating the Revelation given when He took flesh and dwelt amongst us. Moreover, since the Word is Christ, in participating in the light of the Word all men participate in the light of Christ. Those who lived according to the Word, whether pagans or Jews, were therefore, properly speaking, Christians; while on the other hand, those who lived in error and vice, neglecting what was taught them by the light of the Word, were really enemies of Christ before He came ... [W]here the Apostle [Paul] invoked against the pagans a natural revelation which condemns them, St. Justin gives them the benefit of a natural revelation which saves them. ...
>
> From this decisive moment, therefore, Christianity accepts the responsibility for the whole preceding history of humanity; but then it also claims the benefit ... all truth is as by definition, Christian.[7]

The attitude of catholicity shown here is also open to exaggeration and distortion, as we see today in the arguments in favor of "anonymous

---

[6]Josef Jungmann, *The Early Liturgy* (Univ. of Notre Dame Press, 1959), p. 74.
[7]Etienne Gilson, *The Spirit of Medieval Philosophy* (Scribner's, 1940), p. 27.

Christianity," with the consequence that there is no need for evangelization. But, in its proper form, this conception, together with the sense of the imminence of Christ's coming, forms a necessary element in the Christian view of world history.

ᴣ

12

The Christian Leap
into the Graeco-Roman World

In several chapters in this book, we have discovered certain significant differences between Judaism and Christianity in their views on the meaning of history and its ultimate goal. It was especially in their conception of the role of the Messiah and what the Messiah was intended to do, that such disagreement was most apparent and led to the rejection of Jesus by the majority of the Jewish people. Moreover, this rejection was not simply a matter of the Jews being able to ignore the Christians and go their own way. Because both religions were anxious to spread their ideas and to win converts, there developed active conflict and opposition. And it must be recognized that the first Christian efforts at conversion were directed at members of the Jewish communities either in Palestine and Samaria, or later, in the Hellenistic cities of the Roman Empire, where the Jews had established themselves as an important part of the population.

So extensive was this spread of Judaism beyond Palestine that John Henry Newman, in emphasizing a basic continuity between Israel and Christianity, can point to the fact of a certain "catholicity" which Judaism had already achieved before the rise of Christianity. He writes:

> Consider again the state [i.e., the condition] of Israel . . . when Christ came, partly settled in a part of Canaan, partly in Alexandria, with a rival temple, and partly scattered all over the face of the earth, like a mist, or like the drops of rain. And let it be observed, as this last instance suggests, its change when Christ came, from a local into a Catholic form, was not abrupt, but gradual. What was first a dispersion, became a diffusion; during the last centuries of Judaism, the Church was in great measure Catholic already. Besides Jerusalem and Alexandria, it had a number of centers or metropolitan posts scattered over the Roman empire, as we read in the *Book of Acts;* and about these were collected a number of proselytes from the heathen, waiting for the promised Paraclete to make the dead bones live. And, in matter of fact, these centers did become the first channels of the Gospel, and starting points of its propagation. . . .

The line of continuity, surely, was not less definite when the Church became Christian. Christ and His Apostles were all Jews; the first converts were Jews; the centers of conversion throughout the Roman empire were composed of Jews. In one place, we are even told, that "a great company of the priests were obedient of the faith" *Acts* 6:7.[1]

Consequently, as Newman observes, the Jewish synagogues became the first centers for Christian evangelization. In general, the "proselytes from the heathen" responded more favorably to the Gospel than did the Jews themselves. These proselytes were Gentiles who had adopted the moral code and some ritual practices of Judaism (e.g., observance of the Sabbath), but had not become full converts to the Jewish religion—sometimes, where the Gentile men were concerned, because they regarded the rite of circumcision as a kind of mutilation. Thus the Gentiles, who had first become aware of the Old Testament and the Messianic promises through their contact with Judaism, were now becoming Christians, while most of the Jews did not.

Naturally this resulted in a great deal of hostility and adverse reaction from the Jewish communities, who did what they could to impede the spread of the Gospel. *Acts* records a number of instances where the Jews in the cities of Asia Minor, where St. Paul was preaching Christ in the synagogues, called on the Roman authorities to put an end to his preaching as a disturbance of the peace, or themselves inflicted corporal punishment upon him and his fellow apostles. This was a natural enough reaction on the part of Jewish communities who saw their previous unity in teaching and practice now seriously threatened.

From the standpoint of the Christians, this conflict could not be helped, and it was in fact what they had been led to expect from the predictions of Jesus, and from how He Himself had finally been dealt with by the leaders of the Jewish community in Jerusalem. Since the Christians believed Jesus to be the promised Messiah of Israel, they felt impelled to spread this saving truth among the Jews and do whatever they could to have Him accepted by the Jews as the fulfillment of the Messianic promises.

Eventually, as we know, the Christian Apostles turned to the Gentiles and reaped there the fruits of their apostolic preaching. As one

---

[1] *Sermons on the Subjects of the Day*, pp. 190-193. Sermon delivered in 1842.

result, the Jewish Christian community in Jerusalem and Palestine, which had provided the basis for the first growth of the Christian Church, gradually became isolated from their Gentile fellow-Christians in the rest of the Roman Empire, and declined into relative unimportance.

In chapters 9 to 11 of his *Letter to the Romans*, we see St. Paul's response to the tragic division between Jew and Christian, and his explanation of how the rejection of their Messiah by the Jewish people was the means by which God's grace and salvation were made available to the Gentiles. And it is striking that, from what we know of the first generation or so of Christian evangelization—from Pentecost to the execution of Sts. Peter and Paul in Rome in the middle 60s—it was the converts to Christianity from Judaism who did most to spread the message of the Gospel in the Gentile world. This was not done without a great deal of soul-searching concerning the rights and privileges of the Jews as the Chosen People of God, and also as to whether Jewish law should become normative for the early Christian community and thus ultimately for the entire history of the Christian Church. Eventually, the leaders of the Christian Church rejected the claim of certain Jewish-Christian converts that Christianity should be a kind of Messianic Judaism, maintaining the law, the practice of circumcision, dietary regulations, etc. It was of course St. Paul who did most to force the issue, and his view of the matter, the belief that Christ had brought Christian freedom from the Jewish law, was accepted by the Council of Jerusalem which met in 49 A.D.

It is the view of the Anglican scholar, Dom Gregory Dix, that the leaders of the Christian community meeting in this council were well aware of the revolutionary consequences of the decision which they were making, and that it would irrevocably lead to the divorce of the Jewish people from Christianity. Speaking first of the beneficial effects of the decision, so far as Gentile Christianity was concerned, he writes:

> There can be no question that the sudden bound forward of Gentile Christianity in the decade after A.D. 50 is due to a much wider influence than the preaching of St. Paul. The proportion of Gentiles to Jews in the Church changed greatly with every year at this time. The dissociation of "the Gospel" from the Syriac rite of circumcision and the Jewish association of the law took it at once right out of the emotional antipathies of the Gentiles, and left it free

to make its way among them by its own inherent spiritual force and attractiveness.[2]

Dom Gregory then speaks of the results of the council's decision on evangelization among the Jews, and declares that the Jewish leaders of the Council at Jerusalem recognized that this would necessarily be the case:

> This was one effect of the Jerusalem decision. But the other was that it permanently antagonized the Jew....
> When one considers the actual situation of the Jewish-Christian Church in A.D. 49, it is one of the miracles of Church history that it decided as it did. As always, it is St. Paul who best interprets for us the soul of the Jewish Church in the agony of that decision. The terrible lament over "my brethren, my kinsmen according to the flesh" and their rejection of their own vocation in the Messiah which fills *Rom.* 9-11 is perhaps the most moving sustained passage which he ever wrote.... The Jewish Church at the Council of Jerusalem in A.D. 49 finally accepted the fact that the Old Israel as such had lost its Covenant and in the pathetic phrase of the *Epistle to the Hebrews,* "They went forth unto Jesus without the camp, bearing His reproach" (*Heb.* 13:13). The same historical situation which had forced Jesus Himself to choose between the cross and the betrayal of the truth of the Old Covenant had speedily brought the Jewish-Christian Church to the same choice between ensuring its own rejection by Israel and a betrayal of the truth of the New Covenant. It chose His solution.[3]

Dom Gregory in a following passage gives us a sense of the Providential development of the Christian Church in that first apostolic generation, when it had to move by a spiritual conquest into the Gentile world, before its base in Palestine was destroyed by the on-coming all-out conflict of the Jews with the Romans:

> The deepest impression left by the study of the apostolic generation is of the hurtling swiftness of its exodus. Jesus of Nazareth Himself springs from, indeed is, the very heart of the whole Syriac world, now preparing for its own Thermopylae against the Greeks. In ten short years His Syriac "Gospel" is forcing the gates of the Greek world at Antioch. Ten more, and it has followed Xerxes into Athens itself, in a victorious thrust that would meet no

---

[2]Gregory Dix, *Jew and Greek* (Dufour, 1958), p. 53.
[3]*Ibid.,* p. 53-54.

Salamis. Only ten more and it is already so deeply planted in the whole Hellenic world that all the struggles of the Hellenistic Empire to eradicate this Syriac thing from its own vitals will fail. There was need of swiftness! The Syriac roots of "the Gospel" were about to be cut by the collapse of the Jewish forlorn hope of Syriacism in A.D. 66-70. If "the Gospel" was to survive, it must be rooted afresh before that happened. The astonishing "leap" of Christianity from one world to the other between A.D. 50 and 60 was made only just in time.[4]

This spiritual conquest was achieved, in the first Christian generation, largely among the lower classes in the Hellenistic cities—as St. Paul tells the Corinthians, "[T]here were not many wise according to the flesh, not many mighty, not many noble." But since Christianity is a true wisdom, it would eventually make a conquest of the mind of the educated classes as well. Dom Gregory claims that it was St. Athanasius who completed that conquest, some three centuries later:

It was he who finally formulated the doctrines of the Incarnation and the Trinity in the only Greek terms which could fully express Jewish-Christian messianism and monotheism while satisfying Greek intellectualism and rationality. But all this later achievement was only made possible by the daring "leap for life" accomplished in the single apostolic generation.[5]

---

[4]*Ibid.*, pp. 54-55.
[5]*Ibid.*, p 55.

13

"The Contagion of Divine Fire"

Any study of the conception of history held by the Catholic Church would be vastly incomplete without mention of her missionary character, that quality which Dawson called the "contagion of divine fire." This led uncountable numbers of her members to devote their lives to prayer and penance in order to save souls as well as to bring the message of salvation to far off and dangerous lands, witnessing before pagan societies the eternal truth of Christ the King. These activities manifest the Church's prophetic element in action.

In the study of the missionary work of the Church, the transcendent element in Christianity must be clearly recognized. It must not be allowed to become submerged in, or identified with, the process by which the Church becomes incarnate among men. The Church, in carrying out the commission given her by Christ, ever reaches out to new peoples and cultures, so that they also may become part of the sanctified people which Jesus is offering to His Father. And while it is important to have a certain sympathy for the natural gifts and achievements of particular peoples, it is no less important to see that the Church comes to purify their way of life and thus to reject certain elements in the culture of those peoples to whom the Gospel is being preached. As the late Jean Cardinal Danielou put it, in a small book written back in the 1940s, in a chapter entitled, "What Must Live and What Must Die":

> It was Constantine who seemed to be Christianizing the world, but in reality it was Anthony who was tearing it away from the powers of evil. Anthony buried himself in the desert, that he might be in the thick of the fight. Indeed, Our Lord has told us that souls are to be won away from the Devil by fasting and vigils, and that the great battle is fought in the heart of the desert, in the depths of solitude, on the summit of Carmel, before it is fought through the ministry of preachers, on the great highways and in the villages.
>
> We must tear souls away from Satan first of all through prayer, penance, and sacrifice. That is the most crucial combat, and we can take part in it even now. As for the rest, that is Christ's concern, and He sends forth His laborers when He will. But first there is a mystical battle, a spiritual conflict, more bloody than any human battle. God's real combats are fought in the interior world. There,

we fight furiously, trying to free ourselves from all the wretched desires within us; there, saints suffer the assault of Satan himself, of the powers of evil.[1]

It is necessary for us to grasp this principle of penance and purification, for today we are mostly Constantinian in our viewpoint, even while we denounce the Constantinian era of Christianity. Because of the widespread and superficial character of modern culture, its employment of the mass media and mass politics to gain its ends, we are likely to be impressed with how much we could achieve if only we controlled the mass media or made some effective use of them. But that is to ignore the superficial character of the conversion and conviction which results from the kinds of surface influence of which the mass media are capable. In fact, the ineffectiveness of much of the religion teaching in our Catholic education, where we do possess such an instrument for reaching people in these multitudinous schools and colleges and universities, is a testimony to the failure of the Constantinian approach when it is not balanced and supported by the spirit of sacrifice of St. Anthony of the Desert.

With regard to the significance of this for the understanding of the missionary work of the Church, here is Danielou's conclusion to the selection we have quoted:

> Our conclusion, then is that a full-fledged missionary spirituality must not see only the evil in other civilizations, nor be so unduly optimistic as to see only the good. It must be at once a spirituality of incarnation and a spirituality of redemption.[2]

There is a second means open to us for making known the prophetic element in the history of the Church. This lies in a recognition of the inspiration which the life of Christ and His teachings had for the motivation of the lives of the great saints and missionaries of the Church. Only if we hear the echoing of the words of Christ and see the imitation of His example in the lives of the saints who brought the fact of the supernatural home to the ordinary Christian, do we comprehend the essential continuity in the life of the Church.

I would conclude, therefore, that, we must strive to see the history

---

[1]*The Salvation of the Nations*, p. 43.
[2]*Ibid.*, p. 47.

of the Church from within rather than simply from without. It is this which should distinguish our approach from what has too often in the past been the nature of the study of Church history. This is our own history which we are studying, and we can know it with an intimacy not possible with much of secular history. For it is the history of Christ and the Gospel as it has been realized in successive ages of His Church of which we are now members. The statement that the Church is the continuation of the Incarnation is not just an expression of a doctrinal fact; it should be a living experience of our own. And hence the great importance of the study of the sources in each age of the Church, to make us familiar with the inner life of the Church and not only its external triumphs and vicissitudes.

In conclusion, I think we must recognize that the history of the People of God is so much a part of the Christian Revelation that it is impossible to understand Christianity without it. Unlike the Oriental world religions, which are essentially based on certain books of spiritual wisdom, Christianity is founded upon history, the history of God's dealings with His people. To assume therefore that Christianity can somehow be better taught by ignoring the center of it, the history, of God's Chosen People under both the old and the new dispensations, is to cut right across the grain of what constitutes the nature of Christianity. If the study of Church history is said to be not necessary, then we should conclude that an understanding of the inner meaning of Christianity is not necessary either. That would mean that we can make up our own religious beliefs to suit whatever we think is the particular need of the moment.

Christian Revelation is best understood when it is seen to be historical in its inmost nature, from the Creation to the Last Judgment. It is, therefore, through history that Revelation can be communicated in great depth and fullness. In sacred history of the Old Testament we have a rich series of narratives of heroic and commanding figures, whose flesh-and-blood reality can inspire interest and dedication. Here are deep and moving accounts of the Patriarchs and Kings and Prophets, in their wrestling with God and being tested by Him to determine their fitness for carrying out His purposes.

And in the new dispensation of God's mercy, inaugurated by the fulfillment of the Messianic promises, sacred history overflows with the lives of apostles, martyrs, and saints in whom the teachings of the Gospel find realization. A Church history fully aware of its resources would give to the student the great and dramatic events in the history of the Church—St. Paul and the striking and colorful events of his missionary journeys, with the perils he endured and the triumphs for the Church which he achieved; the martyrs in the arena confronting the might of the great pagan empire of Rome; the Christians celebrating Mass in the catacombs and burying their dead in the walls there; the first monks of the desert going out to seek a new way of Christian life and perfection, the later monks going out to convert the barbarians of Northern Europe; St. Francis of Assisi finding his way to Egypt to try to convert the Sultan to Christianity; the multitude of missionaries that went out in the sixteenth and seventeenth centuries to convert the Indians of the Americas and the peoples of the Indies in the East. And then there are St. Joan of Arc and St. Thomas More standing firm for their religious convictions against the overwhelming power of the State, and innumerable other saints and ordinary faithful who suffered persecution and obloquy rather than give up the Faith of the Church of Christ. All of these things lend themselves admirably to the kind of thinking which is concrete, empirical, the finding of universal truth in the particularities of place and time—in other words, the whole sacramental order of the eternal finding expression in the temporal, which is the special genius of the Christian Faith.

And the Gospel itself, with the story of Our Lord in His birth and the moving events which surrounded it, the dramatic events and confrontations of His public life, the culmination of that life in His trial and Passion and Death; and then His triumphant Resurrection and Ascension into Heaven, leaving His apostles with a commission to spread His teaching to all the peoples of the earth: what kind of events could be more suited than these to enkindle zeal and inspire dedication in the minds and hearts of all?

Let us, then, restore the study of Church history in all of its direct and personal reality, adopting once again the mode of teaching which God Himself made use of to instruct His people in both the Old Testament and the New. There is no better way to learn the inner meaning of the doctrines we profess than to see them in action, as they motivate the great heroic figures of the Christian Tradition whose commitment to Christ so greatly advanced the eternal salvation of the People of God.

CHRISTIANITY AND THE CHALLENGE OF HISTORY

PART II: The Challenge of the Philosophers of History

1

Karl Jaspers and Christopher Dawson on the Axial Age in History

One of the most striking phenomena in world history is the period in the first millennium B.C. which saw the rise of the Oriental world religions and philosophies, the flowering of Greek philosophy, the origins of Zoroastrianism, and the work of the Hebrew Prophets. The latter preceded the others by a century or two.

Christopher Dawson dealt with this movement in his book *Progress and Religion*, (1929), in a chapter called "The Rise of the World Religions," and also in two chapters of *Christianity and the New Age*, published in 1931. Karl Jaspers, a representative of German existentialist philosophy, who studied world history from that standpoint, also discussed this development. This was in a volume entitled *The Origin and Goal of History*, published in German in 1949, and in an English translation in 1953. Both writers are impressed with the striking originality shown in these parallel developments taking place in different centers of culture. But Dawson finds a closer link between the movement and what preceded it in mankind's earlier experience than does Jaspers, who sees it more in terms of an absolute break with the past.

It should be noted that Jaspers, in his discussion of writers who have earlier dealt with this development, does not mention Dawson, whose work preceded his by twenty years. Jaspers confines himself to four German writers. It is possible that Dawson raises issues, especially concerning the relationship of Christianity to the axial period, which Jaspers does not wish to discuss.

Of great importance is the fact that Jaspers brings the period to an end before the rise of Christianity. For he gives as his limits for this period the centuries between 800 and 200 B.C. Dawson, on the other hand, sees the Jewish prophetic movement as finding its fulfillment in Christianity in the early centuries A.D. Jaspers gives his reasons why he believes it legitimate to exclude Christianity, a movement so important for the development of world history, from his consideration of the axial age. These reasons, as we shall see later, do not seem very convincing.

The term axial period is used to indicate that, after this time, the whole axis of world history was changed, and there was established a new direction for history which lasted down until the twentieth century. It is clear that, for Jaspers, the rise of Christianity does not form part of this movement, which affected all subsequent history.

Let us first consider the points of agreement between Jaspers and Dawson, before we examine the parting of the ways between them.

Here is Jaspers' description of the axial age as it appeared in *The Origin and Goal of History*, as translated into English in 1953:

> The most extraordinary events are concentrated in this period. Confucius and Lao-tse were living in China, all the schools of Chinese philosophy came into being, including those of Mo-ti, Chuang-tse, Lieh-tsu and a host of others; India produced the Upanishads and Buddha and, like China, ran the whole gamut of philosophical possibilities down to skepticism, to materialism, sophism and nihilism; in Iran Zarathustra taught a challenging view of the world as a struggle between good and evil; in Palestine the prophets made their appearance, from Elijah, by way of Isaiah and Jeremiah to Deutero-Isaiah; Greece witnessed the appearance of Homer, of the philosophers—Parmenides, Heraclitus and Plato—of the tragedians, Thucydides and Archimedes. Everything implied by these names developed during these few centuries almost simultaneously in China, India, and the West, without any one of these regions knowing of the others.
>
> What is new about this age, in all three areas of the world, is that man becomes conscious of Being as a whole, of himself and his limitations. He experiences the terror of the world and his own powerlessness. He asks radical questions. Face to face with the void he strives for liberation and redemption.[1]

Two points should be noted here. One is the existentialist cast of thought, with his emphasis upon man and his seeking, rather than upon God. And the other is the way in which, after mentioning Zarathustra in Persia and the Hebrew prophets in Israel, he ignores these in his summary statement in which he refers to "China, India, and the West." This may be because he finds the element of Divine Revelation too strong in the Jewish development. He prefers to seek an explanation of the phenomenon of the axial period on a purely human level.

---

[1] Karl Jaspers, *The Origin and Goal of History* (Yale Univ. Press, 1953), p. 2.

Here is the manner in which Dawson refers to this intellectual advance which Jaspers has called the axial age:

> Nevertheless in the first millennium B.C. a cultural change of the most profound significance passed over the world, a change that was not confined to any one people or culture, but which made itself felt almost simultaneously from India to the Mediterranean and from China to Persia. It was, however, a change of thought rather than a revolution of material culture. It was due to the first appearance of new spiritual forces which have been active in the world ever since and which still influence the minds of men today. The teachings of the Hebrew prophets and the Greek philosophers, of Buddha and the authors of the Upanishads, of Confucius and Lao Tzu, are not the half-comprehended relics of a vanished world, like the religious literature of Egypt and Babylonia; they are of perennial significance and value. They have the same importance in the intellectual and spiritual life of mankind that the material achievements of the Archaic Civilization possess in the sphere of material culture. Like the latter, they have laid a permanent foundation on which all later ages have built, and on which our own intellectual and religious tradition is based.[2]

Despite some measure of agreement between Jaspers and Dawson on the breakthrough to a higher level of understanding represented by the axial age, the relationship of this age to what went before it is seen in a different light by each of them. Jaspers emphasizes the radical nature of the break with the past; Dawson sees elements of continuity in which the earlier civilizations had provided certain conceptions of the universe which were now given a more profound meaning. Here is how Jaspers speaks of the unprecedented character of the Axial Period:

> The step into universality was taken in every sense. As a result of this process, hitherto unconsciously accepted ideas, customs and conditions were subjected to examination, questioned and liquidated. Everything was swept into the vortex. In so far as the traditional substance still possessed vitality and reality, its manifestations were clarified and thereby transmuted. . . .
> (1) The *thousands of years old ancient civilizations* are everywhere brought to an end by the Axial Period, which melts them down, assimilates them or causes them to sink from view, irrespective of whether it was the same peoples or others that

---

[2]Christopher Dawson, *Progress & Religion* (Sheed & Ward, 1929), pp. 119-120.

became the bearers of the new cultural forms. . . .

To sum up: The conception of the Axial Period furnishes the questions and standards with which to approach all preceding and subsequent developments. The outlines of the preceding civilizations dissolve. The people that bore them vanish from sight as they join in the movement of the Axial Period. The prehistoric peoples remain prehistoric until they merge into the historical movement that proceeds from the Axial Period, or die out. The Axial Period assimilates everything that remains. From it world history receives the only structure and unity that has endured—at least until our own time.[3]

Jaspers refers here to elements being assimilated from the earlier civilizations, but his primary emphasis is upon liquidation and dissolution of what has come down from the past. Nor does he identify what elements he has in mind which he believes entered into the new developments. His concern is to bring out how much the axial age is a completely new development which has left the past behind in its forward advance.

Dawson, on the other hand, does identify a definite link between the older sacred civilizations, with their emphasis on ritual observances, and the conceptions of the new world religions. He sees these older Archaic cultures, as they were subjected to nomadic invasions, beginning to question the sacred character of their present societies and to look back to an idealized past. Dawson points out:

In contrast to this idealization of the past, the present appeared as an age in which the divine order was no longer observed, and evil and wrongdoing ruled supreme. And thus there arose a sense of moral dualism, an opposition between that which is and that which ought to be, between the way of man and the way of the gods. Men compared the world they knew with an ideal social and moral order and passed judgment upon it accordingly.

In this way, the central belief that underlies the archaic culture—the conception of a sacred order which governs alike the way of nature and the life of man—continued to exercise a vital influence on the mind of the new age, but it was at the same time remolded and transformed. The idea which the previous age had expressed in a ritual form became moralized and spiritualized. The sacred order was no longer a ceremonial system, but a moral law of justice and truth.

---

[3]*Origin and Goal*, pp. 4, 6, 8.

> Thus the ancient conception of a sacred ritual order was everywhere the starting point from which the new religious development proceeded.[4]

From a Christian standpoint, the major difficulty with Jaspers' idea of the axial period is his attempt to make the religious philosophies of the axial period superior to Christianity. For that reason he ends the period at 200 B.C. Here we have a writer who is emphasizing the achievement of universality by the axial period and, at the same time, excluding the worldwide spread of Christianity to the far parts of the earth. It surely must be a crippled kind of universality which he has in mind, especially as he is forced to admit that the universality he claims for the axial period was very soon lost. He writes:

> Secondly, the three parallel movements [i.e. India, China, and the West] are close to each other only during those centuries. The attempt to prolong the parallels beyond the axial period ... becomes increasingly artificial. The lines of subsequent development do not run parallel, but rather diverge. Though originally they appeared like three roads directed toward the same goal, they finally became deeply estranged from one another.[5]

In the light of these facts, how does Jaspers seek to justify his putting Christianity aside from the historical movement toward universalism? How is he able to ignore such obvious universalizing influence as Christianity has exerted, and still claim that history, through the Axial Period, has achieved universality? His explanation is based on the idea that Revelation has to be excluded from historical consideration, that it is only what man can achieve on his own through philosophy and science, that is worthy of a scholar's attention. Here is how he presents it:

> (a) Really to visualize the facts of the Axial Period and to make them the basis of our universal conception of history is to gain possession of something *common to all mankind*, beyond all differences of creed. It is one thing to see the unity of history from one's own ground and in the light of one's own faith, another to think of it in communication with every other human ground, linking one's own consciousness to the alien consciousness. In this sense, it

---

[4]*Progress and Religion*, pp. 120-121.
[5]*Origin and Goal*, p. 12.

can be said of the centuries between 800 and 200 B.C. that they are the empirically evident axis of world history for all men.

The transcendental history of the revealed Christian faith is made up out of the creation, the fall, stages of revelation, prophecies, the appearance of the Son of God, redemption and the last judgment. As the contents of the faith of an historical human group it remains untouched. That which binds all men together, however, cannot be revelation but must be experience. Revelation is the form taken by particular historical creeds, experience is accessible to man as man. We—all men—can share the knowledge of the reality of this universal transformation of mankind during the Axial Period. Although confined to China, India and the West, and though there was to begin with no contact between these three worlds, the Axial Period nonetheless founded universal history and, spiritually, drew all men into itself.[6]

Certain comments seem in order here. First, by excluding Revelation from serving as a basis for universalism, he not only excludes Christianity, but also Judaism and Islam. It is certainly a most attenuated and anemic universalism which he is willing to accept. Second, the concept of a mission from God seems to have been part of the way in which Confucius conceived his work. The same thing would seem to be true of Mo-ti, another important Chinese philosopher of the Axial Period. And in Greece, this same idea seems to have motivated Socrates and to have played a considerable part in the teaching of Plato. Thus their views were not simply philosophic, but religious. Even some of the early Greek philosophers, such as Xenophanes and Heraclitus, saw their efforts as being religious in character, not simply philosophic. It is upon this element found in some of the pre-Socratic philosophers that Werner Jaeger based his Gifford Lectures, *The Theology of the Early Greek Philosophers*, given in 1936, and published in 1947. (Was this a German thinker whom Jaspers could not afford to recognize?)

Third, does it not seem a special philosophic bias to claim that philosophy alone is capable giving a universal experience? Surely the religious experience, rooted in Divine Revelation . . . is deeper and more encompassing than what may be attained by philosophy. And reference to dogmas and creeds as opposed to experience is a prejudice which ignores the fact that doctrine serves as a protection for the original Revelation, so that it maintains its integrity and allows man to enter into

---

[6]*Ibid.*

communication with God instead of with some fantasy of his own mind. Doctrine serves the same purpose as do the banks of a stream as they keep it fresh and vigorous, instead of having it run to waste in swamps and backwaters.

Fourth, the history of philosophy does not afford us much evidence of a sharing in certain universal ideas among philosophic thinkers; rather, the opposite is true.

Fifth, although Jaspers claims that the breakthrough to universality is the special achievement of the axial period, that which makes it unique, by offering an experience which is open to all men equally regardless of their religious beliefs, he is nevertheless forced to admit that although "the old mythical world sank slowly into oblivion, [it] nevertheless remained as a background to the whole through the continued belief of the mass of the people (and was subsequently to gain the upper hand over wide areas)."[7]

Are the mass of the people of no importance when it comes to this existentialist philosopher's conception of universalism? And if the world of mythology subsequently spread over wide areas of the world, despite the achievements of the axial age, how much is this age's universalism really worth?

And, in another passage, he recognizes, it would seem, that axial age universalism is largely a philosophical construct, not a historical reality. He writes:

> The highest potentialities of thought and practical expression realized in individuals did not become common property, because the majority of men were unable to follow in their footsteps.[8]

Sixth, if one begins with the intention of excluding Revelation, how can one possibly include, as Jaspers does, the Hebrew Prophets as part of the Axial Age? They gave us a universal vision of the purposes of Divine Providence in history, and their achievement falls well within the limits—800 to 200 B.C.—which Jaspers has decided upon for his definition of the axial age. He does at first include them, but thereafter, as we have noticed, he leaves them out of consideration, speaking only of China, India, and the West. But once the Hebrew Prophets are

---

[7]*Ibid.*, p. 3.
[8]*Ibid.*, p. 5.

recognized as part of the new developments which characterized the axial age, then Christianity should be seen as developing and bringing to fulfillment the vision of universal history taught by the Prophets.

As Christopher Dawson has pointed out in his Harvard lectures:

> To the Old Testament we owe a whole series of religious traditions which are characteristic of Christianity and have no place in the purely ethical interpretation of Christianity of Renan, Strauss and the other nineteenth-century Liberals. Not the least important is the Christian interpretation of history, which was in fact the creation of the Hebrew prophets and was handed on without essential change to St. Paul, St. John and St. Augustine.
>
> In the Old Testament, especially in the Prophets, we find first the guiding idea of divine providence and divine intervention in history—the conception that the great events of history are all integrated in a divine plan leading to a divine judgment.
>
> There is also a historical dualism—there are two principles at work in history. True history—sacred history—is not the same as apparent history or secular history. The spiritual meaning and value of history are hidden under the veil of outward political and economic change.
>
> There is the vital role of individuals who are called by God, often against their will or without their knowledge, to carry out a particular mission. This is seen in the calling of Abraham and Moses and in the prophetic vocation of Elias and the great writing prophets.[9]

Seventh, in a passage towards the end of his chapter on the axial age, Jasper makes clear what he believes the purpose of the axial age to have been. It was intended to forestall "the claim to exclusive possession of the truth" on the part of any one creed. From what he has said earlier, it is evident that he has Christianity in mind. And, in implying that Christianity is the source of the fanatical ideologies of the twentieth-century, such as Communism and Nazism, he is following the path also taken by Arnold Toynbee in his later volumes of *A Study of History.*

Here is the passage in which Jaspers sent forth the most important purpose of the axial age:

> [It] is the best remedy against the erroneous claim to exclusive possession of truth by any one creed. For a creed can only be

---

[9]Christopher Dawson, *The Formation of Christendom* (Sheed & Ward, 1967), p. 81.

absolute in its historical existence, not universally valid for all in its predications, like scientific truth. The claim to exclusive possession of truth, that tool of fanaticism, of human arrogance and self-deception through the will to power, that disaster for the West—most intensely so in its secularized forms, such as the dogmatic philosophies and the so-called scientific ideologies—can be vanquished by the very fact that God has manifested himself historically in several fashions and has opened up many ways toward Himself. It is as though the deity were issuing a warning, through the language of universal history, against the claim to exclusiveness in the possession of truth.[10]

Thus, in his analysis of the axial period in history, Jaspers intends to provide us with an important object lesson for today: distrust Christian doctrine and rely instead upon existentialist philosophy.

Let us first consider his denunciation of "the erroneous claim to exclusive possession of truth by an one creed." If he has Catholic Christianity in mind, he has shot wide of the mark. From the very beginning, the Church has recognized important truths found, for example, in Greek philosophy, which prepared the Gentiles for receiving the message of the Gospel. The same attitude governed the Church's attitude toward Roman society and culture. It was a matter of discerning which elements could be reconciled with Christian teaching and which could not.

What Jaspers really objects to in Catholic Christianity is not a claim to exclusive possession of the truth, but a claim to having received the fullness of Divine Revelation, which it must safeguard and protect. Thus Jaspers is setting up a straw man by the use of the term "exclusive." The real question, which he evades by this procedure, is whether all religions are to be held equally valid and equally in possession of the truth. And, in that case, what is to be said when one of these religions contradicts a basic truth held by another one? In trying to denounce exclusive possession of the truth, Jaspers has ignored what the basic nature of truth demands.

And since he states that "scientific truth [is] universally valid for all its predications," what his position really amounts to is a certain disregard for religious truth as such. For, to him, this kind of "truth" exists on a much lower level of reality.

---

[10]*Origin and Goal*, pp. 19-20.

An excellent example of his carelessness with regard to religious truth is to be found in this key statement of his position: "The claim to exclusive possession of the truth ... can be vanquished by the very fact that God has manifested Himself historically in several fashions and has opened up many ways toward Himself." To use the term God, as Jaspers does here, to cover two different conceptions of the Absolute Being—the impersonal and the personal—which are at opposite ends of the spectrum, shows a lack of clarity of thought. Or, more likely, it shows a lack of concern for whether there is any truth in religion at all. One simply cannot use the term God with such indiscrimination; nor can one speak of how "God has manifested Himself historically" when in fact one is referring to an impersonal Absolute principle such as we find in Hinduism and Taoism. Or, in the case of primitive Buddhism, we have the rejection of any such ultimate principle at all and its replacement by a discipline of salvation, a salvation which man is able to achieve on his own.

The whole concept of a historical manifestation by God belongs to the Judaic type of religion—Judaism, Christianity, and Islam—where God is conceived of as a Person with definite will and purposes, and, in the case of Christianity, is so intensely personal that "the Word was made flesh and dwelt amongst us." (*Jn.* 1:14.) So Jaspers is confusing two different approaches to the nature of the Absolute Being; his desire to prove his point about the need for tolerance has led him into striking theological error. And into philosophic error also, for one does not need to be a theologian to perceive the basic difference between a personal and impersonal concept of the Supreme Being.

Here is the way Dawson identifies the mistake involved in ignoring such essential facts in the history of the world religions. This is directed at Arnold Toynbee's position, which, like that of Jaspers, accords tolerance a higher value than that of truth.

> These [world] religions ... represent at least two alternative and contradictory solutions to the religious problem.
> On the one hand the religions of the Far East—Hinduism and Mahayana Buddhism—adapt themselves well enough to Dr. Toynbee's ideal of religious syncretism, but they do so by denying the significance of history and creating a dream world of cosmological and mythological fantasy in which eons and universes succeed one another in dazzling confusion and where the unity of God and the historical personality of Buddha are lost in a cloud of

mythological figures: Buddhas and Bodhisattvas, gods and saktis, demigods and spirits. On the other hand, the three higher religions of the West—Judaism, Christianity, and Mohammedanism—have followed quite a different path. Their very existence is bound up with the historic reality of their founders, and with the establishment of a unique relation between the one God and His people.

Thus any syncretism between religions of these two different types would inevitably mean the abdication of the monotheistic religions and their absorption by the pantheistic or polytheistic ones.[11]

When we recognize this vital distinction between the two alternative approaches to the religious problem, we see that Revelation is only possible in the case of the living God of Scripture, and cannot be posited of an impersonal abstract principle. For this reason, Jaspers' argument from the axial period about several historical manifestations of God simply falls apart.

What also needs to be considered here is that, in trying to use history to drive home a particular belief to which the philosopher himself is committed, Jaspers is repeating the mistake of Hegel. Jaspers claims to be finding in history only what is empirically evident there; but, as we have seen, his empiricism overlooks basic elements in the religious facts he is studying. Consequently, what Dawson remarked of the nineteenth century philosophers of history seems to apply equally well to Jaspers:

> Now it is true enough that history leads us to wider knowledge, but only to a knowledge of historical phenomena. It does not create truth or moral values.... The philosophers of history have judged differently because they had their philosophy of history already and applied it to history, like Hegel, who saw history as the progressive revelation of the Absolute Spirit, because he had a metaphysical conviction that whatever is real is rational, and whatever is rational is real. And so one does not feel that Hegel actually learnt much from history; he discovered his principle of historical dialectic by a process of philosophical speculation, and he then applied the principle (not always very happily) to the facts of history as he saw them.[12]

---

[11]Christopher Dawson, *Dynamics of World History* (Sheed & Ward, 1957), p. 398.

[12]Christopher Dawson, *Religion and World History* (Image Books, 1975), p. 272.

The second major question concerns the influence of the axial age. Is it indeed unique in the movement of world history, so that no other period can be found of anywhere near its significance?

While recognizing the importance of this period, Dawson would question Jaspers' view that the axial period is the only age when decisive influences were exerted on the direction of world history. For example, when Dawson was serving as a Catholic consultant for a multi-volume world history project which was being planned in the mid-1950s, he identified for the editor of the project a number of periods that were of crucial significance for world history. These were times when historical events led to the opening up of more extensive areas of communication and the wider diffusion of both ideas and institutions. Among several such periods which Dawson pointed out, we may note the following:

(1) The creation of the Hellenistic *oecumene* in the fourth century B.C. and its subsequent extension by the Roman Empire to include Western Europe.

(2) The rise of Islam and the formation of a new world unity based on Islamic religion and culture, extending from the Mediterranean and North Africa to Central Asia and North-west India.

(3) The age of Enlightenment and the First Scientific Revolution, which led on to the establishment of European world hegemony.

And of course he notes that the twentieth-century is pre-eminently a period of such world-historical change, as the entire earth becomes subject to the influence of modern Western culture and technology.[13]

The way in which the first mentioned of these periods, the Roman-Hellenistic one, permanently altered the future of a large part of mankind, Dawson describes in the following passage. Here he is disagreeing with Spengler's idea that "civilization" is the final period of a culture marked by decline and decay:

> The true significance of the Roman-Hellenistic period, for example, is not decay, but syncretism. Two different streams of culture, which we describe loosely as "Oriental" and "Western," as "Asiatic" and "European," flowed for several centuries in the same bed, mingling with one another to such a degree that they seemed to

---

[13]From a memorandum to Professor Ralph Turner concerning the projected Unesco World History, dated Jan. 24, 1954).

form a new civilization.   And this intermingling of culture was not merely of importance for the past as the conclusion of the old world, it had a decisive influence on the future. . . . The West was molded by a religion of the Levant, the East carried on for centuries the tradition of Hellenic philosophy and science. Aristotle and Galen traveled to India with the Moslems, to Scotland and Scandinavia with the Christians. Roman law lived on, alike with the medieval canonists and the Ulema of Islam . . .

And as East and West, each in its own measure, have received the inheritance of Hellenic culture, so too is it with the tradition of Israel. Without that tradition, neither Christendom nor Islam is conceivable; each claims it as its peculiar birthright. It is interwoven with the texture of the Koran; it lives on in modern Europe; . . . And it was in the same age of syncretism, the period of the Hellenistic-Oriental culture, that the Jewish tradition acquired these new contacts and opportunities for expression.[14]

Thus, the Judaism of the Hebrew Prophets, a religion which Jaspers does recognize as having arisen in the axial age, did not exercise its most widespread influence until this later time. And it did this, not in itself, but in the form of the new religions—Christianity and Islam—which were its offspring. And these came into existence after the particular centuries which Jaspers identifies as the axial period.

This indeed would be Dawson's analysis for all of the religious conceptions and movements which arose in the axial period: that it was not until a later period that their development into world religions actually took place.   The ideas and insights generated by the philosophers and prophets of the axial age only took on sociological embodiment at a period subsequent to that in which they first found expression.

However, in the case of the religious philosophers and sages of the Orient, this crystallization into definite religious forms failed to preserve the integrity of their ideas and the purposes they intended to achieve. Instead, there occurred a process of accommodation with the idolatrous nature worship of the earlier archaic cultures. That is, with the kind of religion which we find in ancient Egypt and Mesopotamia and in Palestine when the Hebrews first settled there, and which was also characteristic of India and China before the axial age.

Thus, while the great Oriental religious thinkers and sages had

---

[14]*Progress and Religion*, pp. 42-43.

been inspired by the desire to throw off the yoke of polytheism and nature worship, and to go beyond the visible phenomena of nature in order to be united with the transcendent principle which governs the universe, this later development frustrated these intentions. For it involved the acceptance of a working compromise with polytheism and idolatry.

Dawson declares that this process was taking place in both the East and the West, that it occurred in the Roman Empire in the early centuries of the Christian era but came somewhat earlier than this time in the religion cultures of the Orient. In the West, however, Christianity intervened to prevent this mixing of philosophy and polytheism from becoming the accepted solution to the religious problem.

From this standpoint, therefore, Christianity, instead of being pushed into some historical backwater, as Jaspers asserts, coming on the scene only after all the important religious issues had been settled, was in fact at the very heart of the struggle. It was decisive at the period when East and West were making opposite decisions concerning their religious future; and in the West it assured the triumph of monotheism over various rationalized forms of polytheism, when the Roman Empire seemed ready to go the same way as the Oriental cultures.

The following passage gives Dawson's view of how the religious contributions of the axial age were greatly altered by subsequent developments in world history.

(1) Rise of the World Religions: First Century B.C. to Third Century A.D.

This period witnessed the reawakening of the East, and at the same time the process of cultural and religious syncretism attained its highest point of development... It was still an age of great secular empires.... but under the surface there was an intense process of religious fermentation going on, and the great world religions were being born or renewed.

In the Mediterranean world, the great fact was the rise of Christianity, the most complete and most typical of all the world religions; but at the same time the pagan cults were being remolded in a spiritualist and universalistic sense, while the evolution of Greek philosophy finally culminated in the semi-religious synthesis of Neoplatonism. In India it was the time of the great Hindu revival, when the religion of India was transformed by a fusion of philosophic Brahmanism and popular paganism in theistic cults, like that of Krishna in the Bhagavad Gita—a process which closely resembles the fusion of Greek philosophy with the pagan cults of the Roman Empire.... At the same time Buddhism was being transformed from a moral discipline, analogous to Stoicism, into a theology and even a mythology of salvation, and it was in this new Mahayana form that it began to conquer China and the other lands of the Far East.[15]

One reason for Dawson's difference of view from Jaspers on this subject of the axial period is that Dawson is considering not only the great religious thinkers and prophets, but also the actual religious developments by which the ideas of these thinkers influenced subsequent world history.   For example, what could be more contradictory of the ideas and spirit of original Buddhism than the development of the Mahayana form of it which reintroduced as a means of salvation the gods and mythological figures against which Buddha himself had arisen in revolt?   Thus to speak of Buddha's founding a world religion without adverting to the massive changes which Buddhism underwent at a somewhat later time, which indeed altered its essential character, is to give a most misleading impression.   It allows the writer to ignore the fact that the axial period did not of itself determine the future religious consciousness of mankind.   Almost always there were new factors brought into the religious situation, which substantially changed the purposes which the axial thinkers and sages had striven to achieve. Jaspers' weakness in this matter lies in the fact that he is basically only a philosopher, and not also a sociologist and historian.

---

[15]From "Cycles of Civilization," a lecture delivered in 1922, and published in *Enquires* (Sheed & Ward, 1933), pp. 82-83.

2

Friedrich Nietzsche and Christopher Dawson on Classical Civilization

On the Early Greek Philosophers

Let us consider Nietzsche's view of history from the perspective of two of those cultures of which Western civilization is the spiritual offspring, that is, the cultures of Greece and Rome. For Nietzsche finds in the Greeks and the Romans, but especially the Greeks, the highest peaks of human achievement. And he sees in the society of the pre-Socratic philosophers of ancient Greece the most valuable part of the history of Greek culture. He characterizes the thought of these philosophers as essentially different from the later intellectualism of Socrates, Plato, and Aristotle. Here is a representative passage in which Nietzsche exalts the achievement of the early Greek philosophers. (At this time, about 1874, he still included Socrates among those whom he admired; it was not until a later stage of Nietzsche's thought that Socrates became for him a symbol of abstract rationalism based on a skill in dialectics.)

> Every nation is put to shame if one points out such a wonderfully idealized company of philosophers as that of the early Greek masters, Thales, Anaximander, Heraclitus, Parmenides, Anaxagoras, Empedocles, Democritus, and Socrates. All those men are integral, entire, and self-contained, and hewn out of one stone. Severe necessity exists between their thinking and their character.... They all stand before us in magnificent solitude as the only ones who then devoted their life exclusively to knowledge. They all possess the virtuous energy of the Ancients, whereby they excel all the later philosophers in finding their own form and in perfecting it.... Thus they form what Schopenhauer, in opposition to the Republic of Scholars, has called a Republic of Geniuses; one giant calls to another across the arid intervals of ages, and, undisturbed by a wanton, noisy race of dwarfs, creeping about beneath them, the sublime intercourse of spirits continues.[1]

---

[1]Friedrich Nietzsche, *Philosophy in the Tragic Age of the Greeks* (in *The Philosophy of Nietzsche* ed. by Geoffrey Clive, The New American Library,

This, we may note, is little more than a panegyric rather than any definition of what their thinking consisted. In his later discussion of the ideas of these different philosophers, however, Nietzsche accords a special value to Heraclitus, and does so because he believes that Heraclitus eliminates the permanence of Being and leaves only the ever-changing process of Becoming. Everything solid and substantial is dissolved and nothing is left except flux, as Nietzsche interprets Heraclitus' contribution to Greek thought. Apparently to Nietzsche, Becoming was in some way allied to the instinctual life, while Being represented the dominance of the intellect. Nietzsche identifies the special characteristic of all these early Greek philosophers as being guided by Instinct rather than by the abstract conceptions of the Reason. It is this fact which for him constitutes their nobility. Following are two passages in which Nietzsche describes the thought of Heraclitus:

> The eternal and exclusive Becoming, the total instability of all reality and actuality, which continually works and becomes and never is, as Heraclitus teaches—is an appalling and awful conception. . . . It required an astonishing strength to translate this effect into its opposite, into the sublime, into happy astonishment. Heraclitus accomplished this. . . .

And again:

> Out of the war of the opposites all Becoming originates . . . the wrestling continues to all eternity. Everything happens according to this struggle, and this very struggle manifests eternal justice. It is a wonderful conception, drawn from the purest source of Hellenism. . . . The Things themselves in the permanency of which the limited intellect of man and animal believes do not "exist" at all.[2]

In one of his later works, written more than a decade later, Nietzsche expresses a different view of Socrates, who is now classed with Plato as a striking indication of the degeneration of Greek culture. Nietzsche writes, "I recognized Socrates and Plato as symptoms of decline, as instruments of the disintegration of Hellas, as pseudo-Greek, as anti-Greek." He later explains why he makes this radical rejection of

---

1965), pp. 154-155.
    [2]*Ibid.*, pp. 168-169.

the thinkers who are usually regarded, along with Aristotle, as the greatest philosophers produced by ancient Greece. He asserts:

> Socrates was a misunderstanding. *The whole of the morality of amelioration—that of Christianity as well—was a misunderstanding.* The most blinding light of day: reason at any price; life made clear, cold, cautious, conscious, without instincts, opposed to the instincts, was in itself only a disease, another kind of disease, and by no means a return to "virtue," to "health," and to happiness. To be obliged to fight the instincts—this is the formula of degeneration; as long as life is in the ascending line, happiness is the same as instinct.[3]

Here we find two reasons for Nietzsche's rejection of Socrates and Plato: they exalted reason above instinct, thus destroying the basis for happiness; and they prepared the way for Greek acceptance of Christianity. In his later period Nietzsche always portrays the Christian religion as anti-life, as opposed to the creative vitality which can only come from giving full expression to the instinctual life. Nietzsche writes:

> From the very first Christianity was, essentially and thoroughly, the nausea and surfeit of Life for Life, which only disguised, concealed, and decked itself out under the belief in "another" or "better" life. The hatred of the "world," the curse on the affections, the fear of beauty and sensuality, another world, invented for the purpose of slandering this world the more, at bottom a longing for Nothingness.[4]

Now, Dawson believes that rationalism divorced from the life of the emotions and the senses is a wholly inadequate guide for human life and leads to a sense of psychological frustration. In fact, one of Dawson's chief criticisms of the nineteenth century is that its culture was based on a shallow and arid rationalism, which thus prepared the way for the revolutions of the twentieth century. In this view of modern culture, he is at one with Nietzsche.

Dawson, however, disagrees sharply with Nietzsche's view of religion, and specifically of Christianity, as being based upon a rationalistic conception of existence. In the following passage, he is

---

[3]Friedrich Nietzsche, *The Twilight of the Idols*: "The Problem of Socrates," Sections 2 & 11 (in Clive ed. volume, pp. 189; 191).

[4]Preface to *The Birth of Tragedy*, written in 1886 to make the earlier work correspond to Nietzsche's increasingly anti-Christian views.

contrasting religion with the Nazi attempt to reinvigorate culture by an appeal to racial mysticism. Since the Nazi ideal was, however, greatly influenced by Nietzsche's thought, Dawson is also providing a response to Nietzsche.

> The real ally of life and the only true source of spiritual power is to be found in religion. All genuine forms of religious experience and religious action—repentance, asceticism, sacrifice; prayer, contemplation, communion, ecstasy—are vital acts and experiences. They are a turning away from external centrifugal non-vital activity to the heart of life and the source of spiritual power. This is the case with primitive religion which is essentially a cult of the forces of life in nature and man and a consecration of the social order and the work by which men live to the divine powers that rule the world. It is still more the case with Christianity, which transcends the sphere of nature and brings human life into immediate contact and communion with the divine source of supernatural life. Christianity is at once the revelation of the inadequacy of human knowledge and human civilization and the communication of the divine life by which alone human nature can be healed and restored.[5]

And in another volume he states:

> In no other religion is the conception of *life* so central and so characteristic as in Christianity.... Christianity defeated its rivals, because it was felt to be an historical and social reality, capable of transforming human life. Primitive Christianity is instinct with a triumphant sense of spiritual vitality that has no parallel in the history of religion.[6]

To return to the achievement of the early Greek philosophers, whom Nietzsche set in opposition to Socrates and Plato, how does Dawson view these pre-Socratic thinkers? His ideas concerning them are set forth in an essay entitled "Rationalism and Intellectualism." He distinguishes between two types of rationalism, the one superficial and dealing only with the appearances of things, the other using the mind to try to penetrate the mysteries of existence. It is the historical development of this latter kind of rationalism, more properly called intellectualism, which Dawson sees as the central tradition of Greek

---

[5]Christopher Dawson, *Religion and the Modern State* (Sheed & Ward, 1935), pp. 111-112.
 [6]Christopher Dawson, *Enquiries* (Sheed & Ward, 1933), pp. 296-297.

philosophy. It extended from the earliest of the Greek philosophers down to Socrates and Plato and Aristotle and even beyond them. Thus, instead of putting the pre-Socratics in opposition to Socrates and Plato, as does Nietzsche, Dawson perceives them as linked to these later thinkers by a basic continuity in their purpose. He writes concerning this second type of rationalism:

> It may be defined as a belief in the supremacy of reason; the conviction that the human mind is capable of understanding the world and consequently that reality is itself intelligible and in a manner rational. The whole development of Greek thought from the Ionians to the Alexandrians was dominated by this rationalist ideal. It was responsible not only for the rationalization of nature by science and mathematics, but also for the rationalization of human conduct by scientific ethics, and for the rationalization of religion by philosophy. Inasmuch as Greek rationalism tended to replace traditional religion, however, it became itself a religion, and a religion of a very high order. Greek rationalism finds its ultimate expression in Logos worship—in the deification of intelligence as the supreme cosmic principle.

Dawson then applies this interpretation of the whole range of Greek philosophy to the specific subject of the pre-Socratic thinkers:

> This tendency is to be found in Greek thought from its beginnings. We see it in the Pythagoreans, in Xenophanes and Parmenides, in Heraclitus and Empedocles. All of them were not only philosophers and scientists, but religious reformers and prophets of the Logos. Their criticism of the anthropomorphism and superstition of the popular religion was not merely destructive. They substituted a philosophical theism for the traditional cults of Greek paganism.[7]

It is evident that this conception of the early Greek philosophers using reason to create a new philosophic religion is completely incompatible with Nietzsche's view of them as representing the forces of instinct rather than reason.

In his first volume of Gifford Lectures Dawson deals with Heraclitus and provides a number of quotations from his work. The last of these reads:

---

[7]*Ibid.,* pp. 141-142.

Wisdom is common to all things. Those who speak with intelligence must hold fast to the common, as a city holds fast to its laws and even more strongly. For all human laws are fed by one law, the Divine; it prevails as much as it will and suffices for all things and something to spare.[8]

This passage suggests that Nietzsche neglected an important element in the thought of Heraclitus, and that the latter can scarcely be regarded as the philosopher of Becoming rather than Being, who denies any permanent reality to existing things.

After giving this quotation from Heraclitus, Dawson adds: "Heraclitus was himself a religious thinker—a theologian in the Greek sense of the word—who revealed the mystery of the divine word in cryptic oracular utterances which are prophetic rather than rationalistic in character."[9]

And in another part of this same volume Dawson points out the high regard which Heraclitus had for the Delphic Oracle and his respect for prophecy as an instrument by which the divine powers might have made known their will to men.

This interpretation by Dawson implies that Nietzsche has misjudged the basic character of the development of Greek philosophy. There was no such break between the thought of the early Greek philosophers on the one hand, and, that of Socrates, Plato, and Aristotle, on the other—as Nietzsche's conception of Hellenic philosophy requires there to be. Nietzsche has failed to see that the driving force behind Greek philosophy was to understand the nature of the cosmos in its totality, and thus to gain a comprehensive view of both man and the universe. And, in attaining to that goal, it was not the life of the instincts which governed its progress, but the mind seeking to know the true nature of reality. This resulted in what may be called a theology (Werner Jaeger entitles his Gifford lectures *The Theology of the Early Greek Philosophers*) which found a more complete and balanced expression in the thought of Socrates, Plato, and Aristotle. And, by this achievement, the whole of Greek philosophy became a preparation for the coming of Christianity some four or five centuries later.

---

[8]*Religion and Culture* (Sheed & Ward, 1948), p. 147.
[9]*Ibid.*, pp. 147-148.

On Greek and Roman Civilization

In our preceding section we concluded with the contrast between Dawson's view and that of Nietzsche concerning the early Greek philosophers. Now, we wish to consider how Dawson compares with Nietzsche concerning Socrates and Plato. Although he disagrees with Nietzsche by seeing the whole course of Greek philosophy as developing a rational interpretation of reality, he does agree with Nietzsche on one important point. That is, in seeing Socrates and Plato as preparing the way for the coming of Christianity; but he gives this fact a much more positive evaluation.

> Its victory [i.e. of Christianity] over Hellenism was an internal victory which took place within the spiritual experience of Hellenic culture. Ever since the days of Socrates the development of Greek philosophy had tended towards the spiritualization and "interiorization" (if I may use the word) of the idea of culture. Already with Plato the representative of the higher tradition of culture had broken with the ancient religion of the city state and had begun to envisage the idea of an absolute philosophic religion which would be a service of God in spirit and in truth. . . . It prepared the way for Christianity by its insistent assertion of the spiritual need which found its ultimate satisfaction in the Christian Faith.[10]

And speaking of the whole later development of Greek philosophy, Dawson noted the way in which it helped the spread of the Christian Gospel:

> The Greeks and the Romans had been prepared for Christianity by centuries of ethical teaching and discussion. Plato and Aristotle, Zeno and Epictetus and Marcus Aurelius had familiarized men with the idea of man's spiritual nature, the immortality of the soul, divine providence and human responsibility.[11]

As we take an overall view of Nietzsche's conception of Greek culture, we find that it is singularly limited from the standpoint of world

---

[10]Unpublished manuscript on Christianity and Hellenism by Christopher Dawson.

[11]Christopher Dawson, *The Crisis of Western Education* (Sheed & Ward, 1961), p. 10.

history. For it is confined to Hellenic culture as such, and ignores the achievements of the Hellenistic age, when the culture of the Greeks exerted worldwide influence and created an *oecumene* in which Greek institutions and the Greek language extended from the Nile to the borders of India. But, in addition to this limitation of his perspective, Nietzsche denounces as non-Greek some of the greatest figures in Greek philosophy—Socrates and Plato, and by implication Aristotle, who owes so much to both of them—as well as Euripides, the Greek tragic dramatist who to Nietzsche represents the spirit of Socrates. And he has no time at all for the Stoics and the Epicureans and other later developments in Greek philosophy. In other words, the influences which were strongest when Greek culture was spreading over the civilized world and making its influence felt on many different peoples in both the East and the West, are to Nietzsche so many negative and subversive factors, when seen from the standpoint of one particular period in Greek culture.

On Nietzsche's interpretation, Greek culture seems to have suffered a catastrophic breakdown, and a reversal of its basic values, some time in the later fifth century B.C., when the spirit of Socrates and concern for transcendent realities invaded and overcame the earlier Greek ethos. Now, apart from the fact that concern with the transcendent certainly was not absent from earlier Greek thought, there is a striking resemblance between Nietzsche's conception and that of Arnold Toynbee, who dates the breakdown of Greek culture to 431 B.C., the year of the opening of the Peloponnesian War between Athens and Sparta. This, of course, offers a different reason from Nietzsche, but they both agree on an early period for the breakdown.

What Nietzsche and Toynbee both do is to box themselves in, so that the great developments of classical antiquity in philosophy, history, mathematics, and science, as well as in Roman law and government, have to be regarded as essentially symptoms of cultural degeneration. Practically all of Roman history, and especially the period of decisive interaction between Greek and Latin culture, occurs after the period which Nietzsche and Toynbee identify as the time of the breakdown of Hellenic society. And since the Romans are so heavily indebted to later Greek culture for their own literature and philosophy, this means that Rome fed upon a culture already corrupted and fallen away from its true values—if we are to believe Nietzsche and Toynbee.

Because of Nietzsche's hostility to anything related to an order of transcendent realities, he is led to make that kind of condemnation of some of the most important developments in Greek history and culture.

Nietzsche's ignoring of the Hellenistic age and its importance for the spread of Greek culture to other peoples is shown when one consults the Index volume of the 18-volume Oscar Levy-edited translations of the works of Nietzsche. There is not a single reference to either the Hellenistic Age or Hellenistic culture in any of the volumes of this collected edition. This betrays a certain blindness which makes Nietzsche unfitted to deal with the wider issues of universal history.

Nietzsche's neglect of the Hellenistic age was not something peculiar to him, it was characteristic of the general attitude which prevailed among classical scholars in the nineteenth century. They, also, had their conception of an ideal age of Greek culture, the age of Pericles, which was set up as a model for all future ages to be measured by. What was ignored by this idealization of Greek culture of a particular period is the fact that Greek culture was not something static, not something fully finished and achieved, but that it was in the process of developing new ideas and new areas of achievement and influence, even at a time when it was undergoing social breakdown on its native soil.

For example, as Henri Marrou points out in his *History of Education in Antiquity,* it was the program of education in oratory and literature developed by Isocrates in his Athenian school in the fourth century B.C. which became the basis for Greek education—*paideia*—in the Hellenistic age, in the many Greek cities in the East. This was carried on by the Romans under a somewhat different form under the name of *humanitas*, and transmitted to both medieval and modern Europe. This particular achievement, of outstanding importance for the culture of the West, as well as that of classical Rome,[12] Nietzsche has no room to recognize, for it was developed in a period which he looked down upon as non-Greek.

In comparison with this, what is Dawson's view of the significance of the Hellenistic age in the history of Greek culture? On the one hand, he recognizes a definite decline in the quality of Greek culture which

---

[12]Henri Marrou, *A History of Education in Antiquity* (New American Library, 1964). See Part Two, chapters I and XI and conclusion. A Classical Humanism, and Part Three, chapters II, VI & VII.

began even before the conquests of Alexander had opened the Hellenistic age. He ascribes this to the social changes which undermined or destroyed the rural foundations of earlier Greek society. As he expresses it, "the decline of the culture was due to a process of social degeneration—the passing of the Greek people from the land that had fed and nursed it into the melting pot of urban cosmopolitanism."[13]

Nevertheless, looking at the broad picture of the Hellenistic age and the age of the Roman Empire which succeeded it (for Rome simply protected and extended the culture which the Hellenistic monarchies had inaugurated), Dawson points out its key importance for world history:

> The Hellenistic age has been the Cinderella of history both in ancient and in modern times. The historians of Greece have regarded it as a deplorable anti-climax to the glories of the classical age, while the historians of Rome treat it merely as a preface to the imperial achievements of Rome. And yet it is the key to the understanding of ancient civilization. Not only does it supply the link of continuity between the civilization of Athens and that of Rome, it is the basis of the whole cultural development of the ancient world from the age of Alexander to that of Mohammed.
>
> Without it we can understand neither the Roman Empire, nor the rise of Christianity, nor the survival of the ancient tradition of culture in the Byzantine and medieval world. Even from the narrower standpoint of classical Hellenism, it is impossible to understand Greek civilization unless we study the period which saw the full development of Greek science and the establishment of Hellenism as a universal standard of culture. For the age which the classical scholars despised was the real creator of classical scholarship, and though they did not realize their debt, later generations have always seen classical culture through the eyes of Hellenistic scholars and artists and thinkers.
>
> But though this neglect is inexcusable, it is nevertheless easy to explain. For the age of Alexander was one of the great points in the history of humanity. It was the abrupt and spectacular creation of a new world. If ever an individual has changed the history of the world, that man was Alexander. He tore the Hellenic world from its traditional moorings and launched it on a new course across an unknown sea.

This statement has reference to Greek culture, and how the

---

[13]*Progress and Religion*, p. 45.

Hellenistic achievement must be seen as an essential part of it.   In another statement he shows how the Hellenistic period coincided with the expansion of Roman power in the Mediterranean world:

> The last 30 years of the fourth century B.C. are one of the great turning points in the history of humanity, and the whole future development of the ancient world hangs upon their achievement. At the same time that the Romans were painfully building up their compact state in central Italy, Alexander and his generals were conquering the East: founding cities and sowing the seeds of Hellenic culture from the Nile and the Orontes, to the Oxus and the Indus.   Thus a single generation created two new social organisms, the Italian confederation and the Hellenistic monarchy, utterly dissimilar from one another in spirit and in organization, but destined to be so drawn together, that ultimately they absorbed one another and passed into a common unity.[14]

From this passage it is clear that Dawson is more attuned to the cultural realities of world history than is Nietzsche.   At a time when a new meeting between East and West has been taking place for almost two centuries, Nietzsche's thought is far too limited, far too provincial. For he turns away from the movement of world change which challenges the present age, in order to discover in the past a period of ideal stability and balance, protected from alien influences and outside disturbance.

When we arrive at Nietzsche's attitude toward Rome, we find his favorable evaluation of the Roman Empire and its achievements quite surprising.   For we have already seen his condemnation of later Greek culture, by which Rome was so greatly influenced.   It is possible that Nietzsche regarded the Romans as less concerned than the Greeks with problems of the spiritual life and life after death, and more fixed upon the construction of a practical social order in the present world.   Thus they would correspond, as Nietzsche saw it, to the kind of attitude which he enjoined upon his followers: "I beseech you, my brothers, *remain faithful to the earth,* and do not believe those who speak to you of otherworldly hopes."[15]

At any rate, Nietzsche bestowed great praise on the Romans. Here is a passage from Fr. Frederick Copleston's book where he gives

---

[14]From "Christopher Dawson on the Hellenistic Age" by John Kyran in the Dawson Newsletter, Volume VIII, No. 2.

[15]*Thus Spake Zarathustra,* part I, sec. 3.

certain key passages from Nietzsche which show the latter's high regard for the achievements of Rome:

> Nietzsche recognizes, therefore, the genius of Rome, and in *The Genealogy of Morals* he speaks of the Romans as "the strong and aristocratic; a nation stronger and more aristocratic has never existed in the world, has never even been dreamed of; every relic of them, every inscription enraptures, granted that one can divine *what* it is that writes the inscription." Moreover, when it comes to the question of style, Nietzsche definitely prefers the Romans to the Greeks: "I am not indebted to the Greeks for anything like such strong impressions; and to speak frankly, they cannot be to us what the Romans are. One cannot learn from the Greeks—their style is too strange, it is also too fluid to be imperative or to have the effect of a classic. Who would ever have learned it without the Romans!"[16]

As to the Roman tradition in education, to which Nietzsche is referring when he speaks of learning how to write, Dawson also thinks this tradition of the highest importance for the education of the West. But he makes no such sharp division between the Greeks and the Romans as Nietzsche does. Dawson writes:

> Though it is so closely linked with the Roman tradition, Rome was not its creator, but rather the agent by which it was transmitted to the West from its original home in the Hellenic world. The classical tradition is, in fact, nothing else but Hellenism, and perhaps the greatest of all the services that Rome rendered to civilization is to be found in her masterly adaptation of the classical tradition of Hellenism to the needs of the Western mind and the forms of Western speech, so that the Latin language became not only a perfect vehicle for the expression of thought but also an ark which carried the seed of Hellenic culture through the deluge of barbarism.
>
> And thus the great classical writers of the first century B.C., above all, Cicero, Virgil, Livy, and Horace, have an importance in the history of Europe that far outweighs their literary value, great as this is, for they are the fathers of the whole Western tradition of literature and the foundations of the edifice of European culture.[17]

---

[16]Frederick C. Copleston, *Friedrich Nietzsche, Philosopher of Culture* (1942), p. 67.

[17]Christopher Dawson, *The Making of Europe* (Sheed & Ward, 1932), p. 49.

A comparison of these two passages by Nietzsche and Dawson concerning the Romans makes clear the importance of a certain scholarly objectivity and balance which Nietzsche definitely does not have. There is too much of self will and self assertion in Nietzsche's evaluation of cultural reality to allow him to grasp the truth of a matter—or even to want to do so. He is not concerned with arriving at the truth, which requires a certain fidelity to the facts, and a willingness to modify one's preconceptions. Instead, he wishes to impose his own will upon the facts, to bend them to the purposes he wishes to achieve. Consequently, he is not a reliable guide in matters of historical understanding. Some insights that he arrived at become the only views that matter to him; everything else is cast aside as of no real importance. In this he resembles his German predecessor, Martin Luther, whom Dawson describes in these words:

> The authority of the church, the witness of tradition, the religious experience of others, the dogmas of the theological schools, counted for nothing, or less than nothing, when they did not agree with his personal intuitions and convictions.[18]

In contrast to this, what one sees in Dawson's writing is his reliability, his desire to see both sides of a question and to do justice to each of them. At the same time, Dawson does possess depths of insight and eloquence of language by which to give his ideas effective expression. What is particularly significant is that Dawson has greater depth, both spiritually and intellectually, than Nietzsche's self-will ever allows him to achieve.

Christianity and Classical Culture

In our previous section we saw the high regard which Nietzsche had for the Romans. Now we wish to see what he thought of the conversion of the ancient world to Christianity. It is here that he reaches his supreme heights—or depths—of moral denunciation. True, these passages come from *The Antichrist*, the volume written the year before he

---

[18]Christopher Dawson, *The Dividing of Christendom* (Image Books ed., 1967), p. 70.

went mad, and they may therefore reflect something of the lack of psychological balance which led to his mental collapse. Nevertheless, they do but express in sharper and more extreme form Nietzsche's fundamental animosity against Christianity, and indeed any philosophy or religion which focuses on transcendent realities and makes this life a preparation for a life to come. For that reason, Christianity, whatever might be the nature of its achievements in the realm of culture, was bound to arouse Nietzsche's hostility.

For as Dawson has remarked:

> It is true that if we regard culture as the fruit of a natural process of adaptation by which society finds a way of life perfectly fitted to its natural environment, Christianity brings a sword of division into human life, and closes the gate which leads back to the dream of a social utopia and a state of natural perfection.[19]

And thus it struck at Nietzsche's desire to bring about an ideal society in some utopia, whether through conversion to the worldview of the early Greek philosophers, or by the advent of the Superman.

Here, then, is the passage of passionate outburst against Christianity and the damaging effects it had upon the culture of classical antiquity, as Nietzsche delivered this historical judgment on the meaning of the fall of Rome:

> In a grand organization of society, eternal,—Christianity found its mission in putting an end to such an organization, *precisely because life flourishes through it.* The harvest is *blighted* in a single night. That which stood there, *aere perennius*, the *imperium Romanum*, the most magnificent form of organization, under difficult conditions, that has ever been achieved, and compared with which everything that preceded, and everything which followed it, is mere patchwork, gimcrackery, and dilettantism,—those holy anarchists made it their "piety," to destroy "the world"—that is to say, the *imperium Romanum*, until no two stones were left standing one on the other,—until even the Teutons and other clodhoppers were able to become master of it.
> ...Christianity was the vampire of the *imperium Romanum*,—in a night it shattered the stupendous achievement of the Romans.
> ...*All this in vain!* In one night it became merely a

---

[19]*Dynamics of World History*, pp. 108-109.

memory!—The Greeks!   The Romans!   Instinctive nobility, instinctive taste, methodic research, the genius of organization and administration, faith, the *will* to the future of mankind, the great *yea* to all things materialized in the *imperium Romanum*, become visible to all the senses, grand style no longer manifested in mere art, but in reality, in truth, in *life*.—And buried in a night, not by a natural catastrophe!   Not stamped to death by Teutons and other heavy-footed vandals!   But destroyed by crafty, stealthy, invisible anemic vampires!   Not conquered,—but only drained of blood! . . .[20]

What response might Dawson make to Nietzsche?   We find it based on an analysis of sociological factors which Nietzsche ignored in his exaltation of the achievements of Rome.   It so happened that Ernest Renan, some twenty years or more before Nietzsche's *Antichrist*, was writing his *History of the Origins of Christianity*.   In one of his volumes he uses the same metaphor of Christianity as a vampire which we have seen Nietzsche employing to describe the new religion's baneful effects upon the vitality of the Roman Empire.   Dawson, then, in commenting upon Renan's view, is at the same time replying to Nietzsche:

> Are we, then, to conclude with Renan that the rise of Christianity was the real cause of the decline of the Empire—that "Christianity was a vampire which sucked the lifeblood of ancient society and produced that state of general enervation against which patriotic emperors struggled in vain?" (Renan: *Marc Aurele*, p. 589).   Certainly the victory of Christianity does mark a most profound and vital aspect of the decline of the old culture, but it does not follow that it was directly responsible for it.   The cosmopolitan urban culture of the later Empire broke down through its own inherent weaknesses, and even before the victory of Christianity it had already failed to justify itself on sociological and economic grounds . . .
>
> The Roman Empire and the process of urbanization which accompanied it were, in fact, a vast system of exploitation which organized the resources of the provinces and concentrated them in the hands of a privileged class.   The system worked well so long as the Empire was expanding, for there was no lack of new territory to urbanize and new masses of cheap slave labor with which to cultivate it.   But the close of the period of external expansion and internal peace at the end of the second century put an end to this state of things and the Empire was left with diminishing resources to

---

[20]Friedrich Nietzsche, *The Antichrist* (1889) (Oscar Levy trans), vol. 16, pp. 221-225, sec. 58-59.

face the growing menace of external invasion and internal disruption.[21]

Thus Rome was undermined, not by Christianity, but by "its own inherent weaknesses"—its system of exploitation of the peasantry and of its subject peoples.

Nietzsche is equally one-sided when he portrays the attitude of the early Christians toward Greece and Rome. The Fathers of the Church drew heavily upon the resources of Greek thought, and Plato in particular was a thinker of the greatest importance for them, and they accorded his work a high degree of admiration. Of the general culture of the Fathers of the Church, Dawson makes the following observation:

> From the time of Clement of Alexandria and Tertullian to that of St. Jerome and St. Augustine and Theodoret, the Fathers were men who were steeped in the literary and philosophic culture of the classical world and they had to adapt the sacred literature of the Church to the needs of a public which accepted the standards and values of classical culture. Thus the educated Christian belonged to two worlds, and had inherited the cultural traditions of both of them [Dawson is here referring to the world of the Christian Faith rooted in Judaism and to that of the classical tradition embodied in Greek and Latin literature].[22]

And while the Roman Empire as the persecutor of the Christians was often denounced as the second Babylon, such as we still find in St. Augustine's *The City of God*, there was at the same time growing up, after the conversion of the Empire to Christianity, a strong sense of loyalty to Rome and an appreciation of her achievements, so that she was regarded as the providentially ordained instrument for the spread of the Christian Faith. No doubt this view of Rome would do nothing to mollify the severity of Nietzsche's judgment against Christianity, but it does show that many Christians had an admiration for Rome which is scarcely inferior to that of Nietzsche himself. Following is a passage from Dawson in which this Christian loyalty to Rome is portrayed. Speaking

---

[21]Christopher Dawson, *Medieval Essays* (Sheed & Ward, 1954), pp. 38-40.
[22]Christopher Dawson, *Christian Culture in the Patristic Age* in *Folia* magazine, Vol.VIII, No. 2, p. 63. Reprinted in *The Dawson Newsletter* in Vol. IX, No. 3, under the title "Christian Culture in the Ancient World," p. 3.

of the Spanish poet Prudentius, who has been called the Christian Virgil and Horace, Dawson writes:

> He yields to none of the pagan poets in his civic patriotism and his devotion to the great name of Rome. He does not look on Rome with the eyes of Tertullian and Augustine as a mere manifestation of human pride and ambition. Like Dante, he sees in the Empire a providential preparation for the unity of mankind in Christ. The Fabii and the Scipios were the unconscious instruments of the divine purpose, and the martyrs gave their lives for Rome no less than the legionaries. The last words of St. Lawrence in the *Peristephanon* [a work of Prudentius] are a prayer for Rome: "O Christ, grant to thy Romans that the city by which thou hast granted to the rest to be of one mind in religion should itself become Christian." . . . Now this prayer had been fulfilled; the Rome of the consuls and the Rome of the martyrs had become one.[23]

It was as a result of this reconciliation between Christianity and the Roman tradition that the Latin language and its great classical writers became the means for Christian education, both in later classical antiquity and in the Middle Ages. Far from being a vampire, Christianity infused new life into the traditions of Latin culture.

It is an appreciation of the unifying power of the Christian Faith in reconciling peoples of different cultural traditions within a common spiritual community which makes Dawson a much more perceptive interpreter of the movement of world history than is Nietzsche. The latter essentially retreated from the cosmopolitan developments which were bringing into being a new age of world history, and sought instead a refuge in some ideal age of the past. And even his Superman and the promise of the future it holds forth are based upon a sweeping of the earth clean of its present societies and cultures, in order to bring into existence some supposedly ideal culture of the future. It is essentially a rejection of history.

Nietzsche was living in an age in which there had been a tremendous increase in historical studies, so that mankind was gaining a much greater knowledge of its past than it had ever had before. Yet, Nietzsche saw this increased knowledge primarily in terms of the danger it presented to maintaining confidence in one's own tradition of culture.

---

[23]Christopher Dawson, *The Making of Europe* (Sheed & Ward, 1932), pp. 58-59.

He felt that Western man would be lost in the midst of all the new information about past cultures and civilizations which was now coming into his possession. And for this reason he tended to condemn historical studies as counterproductive to genuine culture.

Dawson notes this pessimism of Nietzsche concerning the great achievements of Western man in the field of history. In illustration of it, he quotes from one of Nietzsche's works—*Beyond Good and Evil*—before presenting his own more positive view of the significance of this great increase in humanity's knowledge of its past:

> No doubt, as Nietzsche pointed out, the acquisition of this [historical] sense is not all pure gain, since it involves the loss of that noble self-sufficiency and maturity in which the great ages of civilization culminate—"the moment of smooth sea and halcyon self-sufficiency, the goldenness and coldness which all things show that have perfected themselves." It was rendered possible only by the "democratic mingling of classes and races" which is characteristic of modern European civilization. "Owing to this mingling the past of every form and mode of life and of cultures which were formerly juxtaposed with or superimposed on one another flow forth into us," so that "we have secret access above all to the labyrinth of imperfect civilizations and to every form of semi-barbarity that has at any time existed on earth."

Christopher Dawson then makes this response to Nietzsche:

> Yet it is impossible to believe that the vast widening of the range and scope of consciousness that the historical sense has brought to the human race is an ignoble thing, as Nietzsche would have us believe. It is as though man had at last climbed from the desert and the forest and the fertile plain onto the bare mountain slopes whence he can look back and see the course of his journey and the whole extent of his kingdom. And to the Christian, at least, this widening vision and these far horizons should not bring doubt and disillusionment, but a firmer faith in the divine power that has guided him and a stronger desire for the divine Kingdom which is the journey's end.[24]

Thus, while Nietzsche could accurately diagnose the ills which result from a cosmopolitanism which has lost its roots in the culture from which it has sprung, he was not capable of moving forward to a new

---

[24]*Dynamics of World History*, pp. 270-271.

synthesis for which that cosmopolitanism was in fact preparing the way. He lacked the amplitude of vision and depth of perception which is the gift of Christianity to those who follow its light in interpreting the meaning of history.

3

Francis Schaeffer, St. Thomas Aquinas, and Secular Humanism

St. Thomas Aquinas and the Criticism of Francis Schaeffer

In connection with the issue of Christianity and humanism, there has been presented recently in Protestant Evangelical circles an interesting criticism of the thought of St. Thomas Aquinas. The claim is made that he imported philosophic humanism into the purity of Christian Revelation and thus prepared the way for the secular humanism of our own time. This criticism has been voiced by Francis A. Schaeffer, an Evangelical thinker whose books have sold widely in the United States, and who participated in a film at one time defending the sanctity of human life against abortion and euthanasia. Schaeffer's book in which the criticism of Aquinas appears is entitled: *How Should We Then Live?*, subtitled "The Rise and Decline of Western Thought and Culture." The book was also made into a ten-part film for wider presentation of its message. Its criticism of Aquinas has been taken up in a book by Tim LaHaye, *The Battle for the Mind*; LaHaye is a well-known lecturer in Protestant Evangelical circles. Both Schaeffer and LaHaye are concerned with preserving the Christian heritage of Western culture as they perceive it, but they seemingly hope to do this without the cooperation and help of the Catholic Church. For of Catholicism they are made distrustful by their Protestant interpretation of the history of the West.

Schaeffer is not unsympathetic to St. Thomas Aquinas in some respects, and he has a number of good things to say about the Middle Ages in their attempt to create a Christian society, although he has a definite Protestant reserve concerning the nature of their achievement. His attitude toward the Middle Ages—and toward Aquinas—is thus considerably different from that of earlier Protestant controversialists, who saw in the Catholic Middle Ages simply the time of the great apostasy from the Gospel, from which mankind had to be rescued by the Protestant Reformation. Schaeffer's more ambivalent attitude toward the medieval period, striving to retain the essentials of the older Protestant condemnation of it while being open to some re-evaluation of the Middle Ages, is shown well in this passage:

> Nevertheless, the pristine Christianity set forth in the New Testament gradually became distorted. A humanistic element was added. Increasingly, the authority of the Church took precedence over the teaching of the Bible. And there was an ever-growing emphasis on salvation as resting on man's meriting the merit of Christ, instead of on Christ's work alone. While such humanistic elements were somewhat different in content from the humanistic elements of the Renaissance, the concept was essentially the same in that it was man taking to himself that which belonged to God. Much of Christianity up until the sixteenth century was either reaction against or reaffirmation of these distortions of the original Christian, biblical teaching.
>
> These distortions generated cultural elements which mark a clear alternative to what we could otherwise call a Christian or biblical culture. . . . It would be a mistake to suppose that the overall structure of thought and life was not Christian. Yet it would be equally mistaken to deny that into this structure were fitted alien or half-alien features—some of Greek and Roman origin, others of local pagan ancestry—which at times actually obscured the outlines of the Christianity underneath.[1]

Schaeffer's attitude toward St. Thomas Aquinas manifests the same sense of ambivalence. On the one hand, Aquinas restored an awareness of the value of creation (in this view, Schaeffer accords with the ideas about St. Thomas which we find in Chesterton's book on Aquinas):

> Aquinas' teaching had a positive side in that before his time there was little emphasis on the normal, day-to-day world, that is, the world and our relationship to it. These things do have importance because God created the world. . . . Thanks to Thomas Aquinas, the world and man's place in the world was given more prominence than previously.

On the other hand: "The *negative* result of his teaching was that the individual things, the particulars, tended to be made independent,

---

[1] *How Should We Then Live?* "The Rise and Decline of Western Thought and Culture" by Francis Schaeffer (Fleming H. Revell Co., 1976), p. 32.

autonomous, and consequently the meaning of the particulars began to be lost."[2] This charge seems to ascribe to the work of Aquinas what was in fact the revolt of later medieval nominalism against the teaching of St. Thomas, the nominalist view being that the universals are mere empty concepts, and that only particular things have any reality.

The main thrust of Schaeffer's criticism of Aquinas, however, is that through his emphasis on Aristotle, St. Thomas became the historical source for modern secular humanism. In Schaeffer's view, Aquinas planted the seeds for a non-Christian humanism that would come to flower only at the time of the Renaissance, when a clearly identifiable pagan humanism showed what had already been implicit in the thought of St. Thomas. And from the Renaissance this humanism was passed on to the Enlightenment and developed to its full anti-Christian potentiality in the twentieth century. Here is Schaeffer's account of the historical significance of St. Thomas Aquinas:

> (In the Renaissance) There was a change in thinking about man, a change which put man himself in the center of all things.... The Renaissance is normally dated at the fourteenth, fifteenth, and early sixteenth centuries, but to understand it we must look at events which led up to this, especially its philosophical antecedents during the Middle Ages. And this means considering in a bit more detail the thought of Thomas Aquinas (1225-1274).... He was the outstanding theologian of his day and his thinking is still dominant in some circles of the Roman Catholic Church. Aquinas' contribution to Western thought is, of course, much richer than we can discuss here, but his view of man demands our attention. Aquinas held that man had revolted against God and thus was fallen, but Aquinas had an incomplete view of the fall. He thought that the fall did not affect man as a whole but only in part. In his view the will was fallen or corrupted but the intellect was not affected. Thus people could rely on their own human wisdom. This meant that people were free to mix the teachings of the Bible with the teachings of the non-Christian philosophers ...
>
> As a result of this emphasis, philosophy was gradually separated from Revelation—from the Bible—and the philosophers began to act in an increasingly independent, autonomous manner. Among the Greek philosophers, Thomas Aquinas relied especially on one of the greatest, Aristotle (384-322 B.C.). In 1263 Pope Urban IV had forbidden the study of Aristotle in the universities;

---

[2]*Ibid.*, p.55.

Aquinas managed to have Aristotle accepted, so the ancient non-Christian philosophy was re-enthroned.[3]

The first thing we might note about Schaeffer's case against St. Thomas is that it does not give us any texts from Aquinas to support it, but relies upon interpreting the significance of certain paintings of late medieval and Renaissance times in which St. Thomas is presented. (Painting and art is a field of special interest to Schaeffer.) Such a method will not commend itself to anyone with a serious interest in the thought of St. Thomas, who has a desire to understand what Aquinas really stands for.

Since one of the chief elements in the Schaeffer criticism of St. Thomas is that he exalted the intellect of man, and encouraged "people [to] rely on their own human wisdom," let us consider these texts from St. Thomas:

> Even regarding truths accessible to the reason, men need to be instructed by divine Revelation, otherwise few would know them, and then only after a long time, and jumbled with errors. Yet their entire salvation, which lies with God, depends on the knowledge of these truths, and is more expeditiously and safely promoted when they are also taught by divine Revelation. (*Sum. Theol.*, Ia. I.1.)

> There are other truths which theoretically lie within the grasp of reason, but to begin with even these demonstrable truths about God must be accepted by faith. The Rabbi Moses [Maimonides] suggests five reasons why this should be so. First, the depth and subtlety of these truths, and their remoteness from workaday experience. Second, the inherent weakness of the human mind. . . . How serviceable, then, is the way of faith, open to all at all times, that they may draw nigh to salvation. (*Disputations*, XIV.)

> Truths about God open to reason have been subtly discussed by many pagan philosophers, though some have erred and others have barely reached the truth after long and laborious study. But they were unable to touch the truths delivered to us by Christianity, which through faith instructs us beyond human sense. (*Comp. Theol.*, 36.)

> Before Christ's coming no philosopher by his entire sustained effort could have known as much about God and the truths

---

[3]*Ibid.*, pp. 51-52.

necessary for salvation as can a humble old woman now that Christ
is come. (*Exposition, Apostles' Creed*)[4]

Such representative passages obviously do not bear out Francis
Schaeffer's claim that, as a result of the work of St. Thomas, "the ancient
non-Christian philosophy was re-enthroned."

Second, with regard to the nature of the Renaissance, especially
the Italian Renaissance, there was certainly a strong element in it of the
man-centered individualism to which Schaeffer refers. In some of the
Italian humanist writers of the 15th and early 16th century, this became a
dedication to paganism and hedonism. The effect of this element in the
Renaissance upon the Papacy and the Papal court was to produce a
decided moral decline in the character of the occupants of the Papal
throne.

Nevertheless, this was not the only element in the Renaissance,
and in both Italy and the North, there was the development of a new
type of Christian humanism. In Italy this found expression in the
institution of new forms of education, based on literature rather than
philosophy, which sought to use the ancient classics to serve the purpose
of Christian formation. Christopher Dawson describes the goals of a
group of these Christian humanist educators who were active in Italy in
the 15th and early 16th centuries:

> Moreover, it must be emphasized that the goal of humanist
> education was in no sense a revival of paganism, for all the
> Renaissance writers on education ... entirely accept the traditional
> Christian view of the place of religion in education. Liberal
> education was the education of a Christian gentleman or citizen and
> in no way rejected the supremacy of Christian ethics and theology.
>
> The great humanist educators, like Leonardo Bruni, Guarino
> of Verona, Vittorino da Feltre, and Vergerio, were themselves
> devout Christians who wished to unite the intellectual culture of
> Hellenism with the spiritual ideals of Christianity.[5]

We might note that a somewhat similar view of the linking of
Christianity and the Graeco-Roman classics is at the base of Cardinal
Newman's *The Idea of a University,* written well over three centuries later.

---

[4]*St. Thomas Aquinas: Theological Texts* ed. by Thomas Gilby, O.P. (Oxford
Univ. Press, 1955), pp. 11-12, 13, 44, 184.
[5]*The Crises of Western Education*, pp. 47-48.

In northern Europe there was another influential development of the ideals of Christian humanism, promoted by John Colet and Thomas More in England and by Erasmus on the Continent. Of this development Dawson writes:

> Thus Erasmus, the greatest humanist that northern Europe had produced, became the exponent of a form of Christian humanism very different from the contemporary humanism of Italy. This movement, which has been called "Biblical humanism," sought the reform of religion by a return to the sources, above all to the New Testament in the original Greek, and secondly to the study of the writings of the Fathers of the Church. As the Italian humanists had made classical antiquity the pattern of culture and the only standard of literary and artistic merit, so now Erasmus and his friends and disciples set up the ideal of Christian antiquity as its counterpart in the spiritual realm and made it the standard of moral and religious values.[6]

Thus, neither with St. Thomas Aquinas, nor with important Renaissance humanist educators in Italy and in the North, was there any attempt to subordinate Christianity to the newly discovered Greek classics. The Greek classics were those of philosophy and science for Aquinas and the medieval scholastics, and of Greek literature and the Greek Christian Fathers of the East in the case of the Renaissance. The goal was to make use of these Greek texts in order to widen the intellectual and aesthetic horizons of Christian culture.

St. Thomas Aquinas and the Defense of the Human Person

At the conclusion of our preceding section we gave certain texts from St. Thomas Aquinas which showed that, contrary to Professor Francis Schaeffer's belief, St. Thomas did not exalt human reason above Revelation, nor hold that man's mind could attain to a knowledge of supernatural truth apart from Revelation.

There was a second part to the Schaeffer criticism, which implied that St. Thomas exercised no discrimination in incorporating Aristotelian philosophy into Christian thought. As Schaeffer put it, "This meant that people were free to mix the teachings of the Bible with the teachings of

---

[6]*Ibid.,* p. 57.

the non-Christian philosophers. . . . Aquinas managed to have Aristotle accepted, so the ancient non-Christian philosophy was re-enthroned."[7] The apparent result would be an indiscriminate eclecticism which had no sense of the governing reality of Christian truth.

Now this claim is quite wide of the mark; it is not based on the facts of what St. Thomas actually achieved. It so happened that Aristotle's thought, as it was made known to Western Christendom in translations from the Arabic and with commentaries from Arab philosophers explaining its meaning, contradicted some of the basic beliefs of the Christian Faith. Of the nature of what was at stake in the invasion of the West by Arab Aristotelianism, Christopher Dawson writes:

> The impact of this great mass of new knowledge on the Western mind could not but produce startling effects. It raised the whole question of the relations between religion and science, and between reason and faith, in a very sharp and accentuated way . . . As the theologians of Islam had long ago realized, Hellenic science was not the obedient servant of revealed religion but an independent and rival power. It was a danger alike to Christianity, to Judaism, and to Islam, since it challenged the fundamental dogmas that were common to the three religions: the doctrine of creation, the doctrine of personal immortality, and the belief in a personal Deity who governed the world by His providence and the free exercise of His omnipotent will.[8]

On each of these issues, Aquinas decisively rejected the Arabic-Aristotelian position and provided a philosophical and theological defense for the Christian teaching which stands in opposition to it. And in fact in the whole line of his presentation, his defense was based on the value and importance of the human mind against the Aristotelianism which effectively destroyed the nature of its capabilities. The situation was not one in which Aquinas had "man taking to himself that which belonged to God," as Schaeffer claimed. Instead, Aquinas had to reclaim the dignity and importance of man from an Arabic form of Aristotle, which in fact took from man what belonged to him of right, in his integrity as a human person. The humanism which Aquinas thus defended was rooted in Christian Revelation; and it was asserted against

---

[7]*How Should We Then Live?*, p. 52.
[8]*Medieval Essays*, pp. 142-143.

an inhumanism derived from certain powerful elements in Greco-Roman paganism. No more than modern secular humanism is truly human in its fundamental attitudes and values, as is shown in its anti-life acceptance of abortion and euthanasia, was the basic worldview of Arab Aristotelianism really humanist either. Here is the way Dawson describes the conception of man and the universe against which Aquinas had to do battle:

> Science always tends towards determinism, and Aristotelian science was perhaps the most thorough-going system of determinism that has ever been invented, since it embraced spirit as well as matter in the working of its mechanism.... In fact, so far from eliminating the idea of God as an unnecessary hypothesis [as does modern science], God is, for Aristotle, the mainspring of his whole system of physics, and the motor that drives the world machine.

Extending this principle to the world of men as well:

> [T]he Arabs, following the traditions of later Greek thought, taught that mankind no less than the celestial spheres derived its activity from a spiritual principle—the active intelligence. In other words, reason was not a faculty of the human soul but a cosmic principle—the lowest in the hierarchy of spiritual substances—and man attained to rational activity only insofar as his passive and mortal intelligence became temporarily actuated by this immortal and impersonal power. This doctrine struck at the very heart of religious faith, since it involved the denial of personal immortality.... It was, in fact, to remain a burning question for three hundred years and more....[9]

Dawson then describes how St. Thomas, drawing upon Aristotle's idea that the soul is not just inhabiting the body as a temporary dwelling place, but is in fact the substantial form of the body and closely conjoined to it, makes this fact the basis for refuting Arab Aristotelianism. The depth of man's involvement in the material world of the senses, even while he is possessed of a spiritual soul which animates the body, gives man a key position in the divine order of creation.

Not only did St. Thomas accept the cardinal principles of

---

[9]*Ibid.,* pp. 143; 146.

Aristotelian physics, but he applied them resolutely to the nature of man, teaching that matter is the principle of human individuation, and that the soul is the form of the body. Hence man is not, as the Platonists believed, a spiritual being temporarily confined in the prison of the flesh, a stranger in an alien world; he is part of nature—that dynamic order which embraces the whole series of living beings from man to plant, as well as the things that are without life but not without their principle of form. And so the human intelligence is not that of a pure spirit which exists only for the contemplation of absolute reality. It is consubstantial with matter, subject to the conditions of space and time, and it can only construct an intelligible order out of the data of sensible experience, systematized by the scientific activity of reason. Thus while on the one hand, human reason is distinctively animal, the lowest and most obscured form of intelligence, it is on the other hand the one principle of spiritual order in nature, and it is its essential function to reduce the unintelligible chaos of the material world to reason and order.

This theory of the human intelligence is the essential doctrine of Thomism and the keystone of the Christian Aristotelian synthesis. Hitherto both the Averroist and the Christian Platonist had regarded the spiritual principle of intelligence as something superhuman and divine. It was not *in* man as a part of his personality; it was a power which illuminated his mind from outside, whether it be regarded with the Christian Platonists as the ray of divine light that illuminates the immortal human soul, or whether, as Averroes taught, it was the power of a universal intelligence actuating the successive, transitory, and mortal minds of men. To St. Thomas, on the other hand, the active intelligence is the very essence of the soul and the root of human responsibility and liberty.[10]

Since the teaching of the Arab philosopher Averroes was that the active intelligence is a principle lying outside men's minds and therefore separate and distinct from them, and this led to the denial of the immortality of the soul, it is of interest to see what argument St. Thomas used to respond to this. First, we have this passage from the *Summa Theologica* in which he makes use of the ideas of Plato and Aristotle on the nature of the human mind to show that the concept of Averroes is in contradiction to them. As the translator, Thomas Gilby, remarks, "Here St. Thomas writes with unwonted informality and vigor."

---

[10]*Ibid.*, pp. 150.

That a unique mind should be shared by all men is quite out of the question. If Plato's doctrine be adopted, namely, that man is his mind, then it would follow that, if there were one mind for Socrates and for Plato, there would be one man there, and they would not be distinct from one another except by something outside their essence: the difference between them would be no more than that between the man in a tunic and the same man in a cloak.

The thesis is also impossible on Aristotle's doctrine that the mind is a part or power of the soul, which soul is man's substantial form. For there cannot be a unique form of several things numerically diverse, as it is impossible for them to possess one being. Indeed, it is an unworkable thesis howsoever the union of mind with this or that man be stated.[11]

St. Thomas is even more direct and challenging in stating the case in his work, written against the Parisian Averroists. Nowhere else in his work does he sound this note of vibrant indignation which is present here. In order to understand the precise situation which St. Thomas was confronting at the University of Paris when he returned there in 1269, five years before his death, we need to know that Siger of Brabant and his followers at the university had proclaimed the thesis that philosophy had no need to consider its relationship to theology, and that philosophic reasoning is superior to truths received on faith, that philosophy is indeed a doctrine of salvation.

Moreover, these Latin Averroists, as they have been called, were in temporary possession of the University of Paris before the return of St. Thomas, and it appeared to many that Siger and St. Thomas, both writing from an Aristotelian standpoint, were in fact presenting the same philosophic doctrines. Josef Pieper gives this account of the situation which faced St. Thomas when he set out to refute the Averroists with whose ideas his own teaching was being identified:

This radical view was received with open arms at the University of Paris.... An English historian has [said]: If the group around Siger of Brabant had continued to hold the intellectual leadership unhindered, without meeting resistance, the authorities would have been compelled to close the university.[12]

That, then, is the background for the deliverance of this challenge

---

[11]*Sum. Theol.* I, a. lxxvi. 2.

[12]Josef Pieper, *Guide to Thomas Aquinas*, pp. 113-114. Mentor-Omega ed.

by Aquinas to the Latin Averroists, and for the power and strength of the words in which it is expressed:

> Of all errors the most indecent attack our heritage of mind. One such has sprung from the words of Averroes, who announced that there is a universal and unique mind for all men. We have already argued against this doctrine elsewhere, but our purpose is to write again and at length in refutation, because of the continued impudence of those who gainsay the truth on this head.
>
> Not that we shall be at pains to show that it is contrary to the Christian faith, for this is sufficiently apparent to all. Since mind is the only deathless part of the soul, were the diversity of minds to be fused, the upshot would be that a unique mind alone remained after death, and so there would be no prospect of rewards and punishments. What we intend to do is to show that this error is no less opposed to the principles of philosophy. (Then follows argument similar to that given in the passage from the *Summa Theologica* we have already quoted.)
>
> These, then, are the points we have made to destroy this error, not by the documents of faith, but in the light of Aristotle. If anyone who falsely glories in the name of philosopher still wishes to oppose what we have written, let him not mutter in corners with adolescents who lack discrimination in such arduous questions, but let him come out into the open, and write if he dares. I am the least, but he will find others beside myself who are servants of truth and who will resist his errors and instruct his ignorance.[13]

Christian Humanism and the Incarnation

We now return to an examination of the theological basis for a Christian humanism. The keystone to the Catholic conception of humanism is to be found in the doctrine of the Incarnation, the teaching that God became man. Not a being halfway between God and man, as the Arians taught, or a man whom God adopted as His son, as Modernist theologians would have us believe, or God merely taking on a human appearance, as held by the heresy of ancient Docetism, but Jesus the Christ, truly God and truly man, the only begotten of the Father who nevertheless took on full human nature from the womb of the Virgin Mary.

---

[13]*St. Thomas Aquinas: Philosophical Texts*, ed. by Thomas Gilby, O.P. (Oxford Univ. Press, 1951), pp. 206-207. "Against the Parisian Averoists."

The doctrine of the Incarnation, including Christ's triumph over sin and death by His Passion, Death and Resurrection, is closely linked with the doctrine of creation. God who created all things from nothing at the beginning of the world, now came to restore creation from the ravages wrought in it by sin and to reconstitute human nature, so that man could become a new creature and an adopted son of God. How central this conception is to Catholic thought may be glimpsed from the fact that the Mass of the Vigil of Easter celebrated on Holy Saturday evening, contains a series of readings from the Old Testament intended to illustrate the significance of Christ's Death and Resurrection. The first of these readings is the account from *Genesis* of the creation of the world—and of man.

Christopher Dawson, drawing upon St. Paul's teaching, shows how the Catholic Church looks upon the Incarnation:

> This restoration or recreation of humanity is the essential doctrine of Christianity. Jesus Christ is to the Catholic not a prophet and teacher nor even is He only the divine revealer of God to man; He is the restorer of the human race, the New Man, in whom humanity has a fresh beginning and man acquires a new nature. His work was genetic and creative in an absolutely unique sense, for it brought into the world a new kind of life which has the power to absorb and transmute into itself the lower forms of physical and psychical life which exist in man . . .
>
> This higher life was of course not entirely absent from humanity before Christ, but it existed rather as a potentiality awaiting realization than as a force dominating the whole nature of man. For it is only through Christ, the second Adam, and in organic connection with Him, that the new humanity is to be built up. By the vital activity of the Spirit of Christ working through the Church and the sacraments, mankind is remolded and renewed; the disorder and weakness of human nature is overcome, and the domination of charity in spiritual love is substituted for the blindness of physical impulse and the narrowness and evil of selfish desire.[14]

St. Thomas Aquinas relates the Incarnation and its effects to the Creation by showing that it was the creation of man as an intelligent being which made possible the greater dignity bestowed upon man when he became an adopted son of God.

---

[14]*Enquiries*, pp. 327-328.

> Man is made to the image of God, because he is created with intelligence. Only intelligent beings are said to be made to His image; they only can be called His sons, and can be adopted through grace. Adoption goes further, for a right to the inheritance is implied. God's heritage is His own happiness, of which only intelligent creatures are capable, though they have no strict title to it from the fact of their creation; such happiness is a gift, the gift of the Spirit. Sharing of possessions is not enough: there must be a sharing of the heritage. And so the adoption of creatures means their communion in divine happiness.[15]

Although St. Thomas speaks here of the importance of the intelligence in man, a good part of his life was spent in making certain that the counterbalancing element in man of the body and the senses was not ignored or neglected. Why there was a need for this Thomistic emphasis on the bodily reality of man goes back to the time of the Fathers of the Church. Throughout the early centuries of Christianity, the understanding and acceptance of the Incarnation in its full reality was especially threatened by the influence of Oriental thought, which was quite strong on the worldview of the peoples of later antiquity. This Oriental influence led to a contempt for the body and to seeking salvation by liberating the soul from its bodily prison, to rejoin the world of the spirit from whence it had come. Moreover, in Greek philosophy this idea was represented by Plato and Platonism, although in not so extreme a form as by Manicheanism and Gnosticism. Thus the Christian teaching of the Incarnation, that the Son of God had become fully man, both body and soul, ran counter to the prevailing religious climate of that time. (In our own time, the danger comes from the opposite side, that of disbelief in spiritual reality, and thus of trying to reduce Christ to a merely human level.) Moreover, Platonic thought exercised its influence from within Christianity, for Plato had provided so many clear explanations of the world of the spirit, and also effective arguments against idolatry, that the Fathers of the Church found him an invaluable philosophic ally in their struggle against paganism. This Platonic influence on patristic thought led to an undue stress on the spiritual elements in Christianity at the expense of man's corporeal reality. This was especially true of the Church Fathers in the East, because they were the first to attempt a full-scale effort to harmonize Greek philosophy

---

[15]Gilby, *Theological Texts of St. Thomas Aquinas,* no. 292, pp. 155-156.

with Christianity. Gilson points out why Plato's thought seemed a natural preparation for Christianity, and why its neglect of man's corporeal nature could be overlooked:

> At first sight it might well seem that Platonism would be the philosophy, and very especially the anthropology, most naturally adapted for Christian purposes. The Fathers of the Church, needing a doctrine of the spirituality of the soul, found it in the Phaedo [a Platonic dialog], found also along with it several demonstrations of the soul's immortality and the conception of a future life, complete with rewards and punishments, Heaven and Hell.[16]

Thus, until the recovery of Aristotle by the West in the thirteenth century, this Platonic character of Christian theology gave very strong emphasis to the spiritual elements in Christian belief, and tended to regard man as a disembodied spirit—not in formal doctrine, but in underlying attitude. When Aristotle was recovered, there developed an opposite movement—to deny the immortality of the soul and any personal relationship between God and man.

It was the task of St. Thomas to make use of Aristotle in order to give new emphasis to the body and the senses, as these were present both in the nature of man and in the nature of Christ in the Incarnation. At the same time St. Thomas met the opposite danger by providing effective refutation of those Arabic-Aristotelian doctrines which rejected the reality of the human intellect, the immortality of the soul, and the Providence of a personal God. Moreover, just about the time of St. Thomas and for a century or so before, Christianity was under attack not only from the side of Arabic Aristotelianism, but also from the side of an extreme kind of spirituality—a resurgence of the ancient Manichean heresy which had asserted the evil of whatever was connected with the body. This new version of Manicheanism was in the form of Albigensianism—or Catharism—in the south of France, which especially condemned marriage because it was the means for the begetting of children and thus carrying forward the evil of bodily existence to the next generation. (The Albigensians were more lenient toward forms of sexual gratification which did not result in offspring.) It is against this background that we can perceive the significance of the work of St. Thomas in defending the full reality of man's bodily nature through his

---

[16]E. Gilson, *The Spirit of Medieval Philosophy*, p. 169.

use of Aristotle, and linking this up with the doctrine of the Incarnation, that God has become fully man, body as well as soul. As Chesterton has pointed out:

> There really was a new reason for regarding the senses, and the sensations of the body, and the experiences of the common man, with a reverence at which great Aristotle would have stared, and no man in the ancient world could have begun to understand. The body was no longer what it was when Plato and Porphyry and the old mystics had left it for dead. It had hung upon a gibbet. It had risen from a tomb. It was no longer possible for the soul to despise the senses, which had been the organs of something that was more than man. Plato might despise the flesh; but God had not despised it. . . . Those revolving mirrors that send messages to the brain of man, that light that breaks upon the brain, these had truly revealed to God Himself the path to Bethany or the light on the high rock of Jerusalem. These ears that resound with common noises had reported also to the secret knowledge of God the noise of the crowd that strewed palms and the crowd that cried for crucifixion. After the Incarnation had become the idea that is central in our civilization, it was inevitable that there should be a return to materialism; in the sense of the serious value of matter and the making of the body. When once Christ had risen, it was inevitable that Aristotle should rise again.[17]

And in this passage from St. Thomas, we find him explaining the connection between the Incarnation and the sacraments of the Church, showing how both involve the principle of making spiritual reality known to man through bodily forms perceptible to the senses. This principle common to both is related to the fact that the Incarnation is the source of the grace which the sacraments communicate to man. St. Thomas also makes note of the fact that this sacramental principle corrects the error of despising the body, as in Manicheanism and Albigensianism, although he does not mention either by name.

> These remedies, which are the Sacraments of the Church, come to us in portions and are bound up with what we can experience.
> . . . God provides for all things according to their condition. To be led forth from the physical world in order to seize the spiritual

---

[17]G.K. Chesterton, *St. Thomas Aquinas* (1933) (Image Books ed., 1956), pp.118-119.

world is our human destiny, and therefore these sacramental reliefs come in sensible guise. Secondly, instruments are adapted to their principal cause, and this, as regards human well-being, is the Word Incarnate. How fitting then that He should come to men in bodily fashion, and that divine virtue should continue to work invisibly in them through visible appearances. Thirdly, men lapse into sin through indulging in what their senses offer them. Lest it should be reckoned that these objects are evil in themselves, or that sin lies in being attached to them, some have been hallowed, and their inherent goodness, created by God, proclaimed. The harm comes when we are inordinately committed to things of sense, not when we take them as we should.

Hence we disavow the heretical error of banishing them from the sacramental life of the Church, an error which is logical enough on the supposition that physical things are bad and produced by the author of evil. What is there awkward about visible and bodily things ministering to spiritual health? Are they not the instruments of God, who was made flesh for us and suffered in this world?[18]

That You May Become Partakers of the Divine Nature

The central issue between Protestants and Catholics concerning a Christian humanism arises from the fact that Catholic theology teaches that the Incarnation transforms human nature, and is not restricted merely to making atonement for man's sin. We have already seen that, in Catholic belief, the Incarnation makes redeemed man into a new creature. But Catholic teaching goes beyond that, and declares that all who share in this new creation have become adopted sons of God and participate in His divine nature.

No doubt some Protestants may say that this is simply importing the ideas of paganism and Greek philosophy into the Christian Faith. For Plato, for example, speaks in these terms of the purpose of human life: "So we ought to escape from earth to Heaven as quickly as we can; and to escape is to become like God, as far as this is possible; and to become like Him is to become holy, just, and wise." (Theaetetus, 176.)

But must we believe that this Platonic conception of the purpose of human life is completely in error, and that Christianity, in contradiction to it, convinces man that he must always remain a sinner,

---

[18]Theological Texts of St. Thomas Aquinas, pp. 353-354. Chap. III.Section 4: pp.118-119.IV.

and that his salvation lies not in any transformation of his nature, but simply in the bare act of belief in Christ as his Savior? Has the arm of the Lord been shortened, so that He cannot really make men righteous, but can only substitute the righteousness of His Son for their continued sinful nature? Granted that there is a war in man's members between evil and good, as St. Paul testifies, is that war always foredoomed to defeat for the good, even when the grace of God is given? Or does God's grace strengthen and reinforce the impulses toward good in human nature by bestowing upon man the new reality of divine life?

From the Catholic standpoint, Plato's error and that of Greek philosophy in general was not in their vision of the goal of human life—"to become like God"—but in believing that man can attain it by means of his own unaided efforts.

That this belief in man's sharing the life of God is not simply the transference of Greek ideas into Christianity can be seen from the testimony of St. Paul himself, in his idea of redeemed mankind as forming one Mystical Body with Christ, of which Christ is the Head and they are the members. It is also given expression in St. Peter's *Second Letter:*

> For indeed His divine power has granted us all things pertaining to life and piety through the knowledge of him who has called us by his own glory and power—through which he has granted us the very great and precious promises, so that through them you may become partakers of the divine nature, having escaped from the corruption of that lust which is in the world. (II *Pet.* 1:3-4). (Emphasis added. The King James version of the Bible gives these texts as providing the same teaching: II: *Cor.* 3:18; *Eph.* 4:24; *Heb.* 12:10; I *John* 3:2).

This same general idea is suggested by the metaphor in St. John's Gospel (15:1-8) in which Jesus speaks of Himself as the Vine and His disciples as the branches, for the vine communicates its own life to its branches. And with Jesus this is a divine life.

All of these clear implications of what II Peter brings out explicitly are overlooked if one takes only certain texts from St. Paul and concentrates on them to the exclusion of what is found elsewhere in Pauline teaching. A truly faithful attention to the teaching of Scripture would have avoided this one-sided interpretation, which arose out of one man's attempt to meet the needs of his own particular spiritual problem, and to meet it in a way which failed to do justice to God's saving power.

Moreover, as Dawson has pointed out, this teaching concerning man's participation in the divine nature was continued and developed by the Fathers of the Church, beginning with St. Irenaeus and finding its most influential expression in the classical age of patristic theology in the fourth century. First , St. Irenaeus in the second century:

> God arranged everything from the first with a view to the perfection of man, in order to deify him and reveal His own dispensations, so that goodness may be made manifest, justice made perfect, and the Church fashioned after the image of His Son.

On the same subject we have some of the greatest of the Greek Fathers of the Church:

> For the writings of the latter [Dawson has just mentioned Eusebius of Caesarea, Theodoret, Basil, and the two Gregories], in spite of their avowed hostility to the Greek religious tradition, were characterized by a genuine spirit of humanism. . . . Their whole apologetic is dominated by the conception of man as the center and crown of the created universe. The first book of the Theophany of Eusebius is a long panegyric of humanity—man the craftsman and artist . . .—man a God upon earth, "the dear child of the Divine Word."
>
> So, too, St. Gregory of Nyssa sees in man not only "the godlike image of the archetypal beauty," but the channel through which the whole material creation acquires consciousness and becomes spiritualized and united to God. This created nature, however, is essentially changeable. It continually passes through a process of evolution, which may become a movement of degeneration and decline, if once the will should become perverted.
>
> This is what has happened in the actual history of humanity, and therefore it has been necessary for the divine nature to unite itself with mankind in a second creation which will restore and still further develop the original function of humanity. Thus the Incarnation is the source of a new movement of regeneration and progress which leads ultimately to the deification of human nature by its participation in the divine life.[19]

A thousand years later St. Thomas Aquinas was expressing that same teaching, this time on the effect of the grace received from the

---

[19]*Progress and Religion,* pp. 158-159, summarizing certain themes in the *Catechetical Discourse* of St. Gregory Nyssen.

Incarnation, and communicated through the Sacrament of the Eucharist:

> Among the innumerable benefits God's goodness has bestowed on Christian people is a priceless dignity.... The only-begotten Son of God, intending to make us partakers of the divine nature (II *Pet*, 1:4), took our nature on Himself, becoming man that He might make men gods.[20]

What had taken place in the theology of Western Christendom in the thirteenth century was a development of doctrine. That is, bringing into clearer focus the implications of a doctrine, where previously more attention had been paid to some other aspect of it. Just as the recovery of Aristotle had allowed St. Thomas to present a better understanding of the corporeal reality of Jesus in the Incarnation, and how this was also manifested in the sacraments, so at the same time this other development was providing a deeper insight into the effects of grace on human nature. Of the cause and the results of this development Dawson writes:

> In addition to this main stream of Aristotelian and Arabic influence there were also a number of translations of the works of the Greek Fathers which had a direct influence on Western theology.... It led the scholastics—above all, St. Bonaventure and St. Thomas—to revise and complete the Augustinian doctrine of grace in the light of the teaching of the Greek Fathers and thus to create a synthesis of the two great theological traditions of the East and the West. While preserving the broad lines of the Augustinian doctrine, they laid a much greater emphasis on the ontological character of the supernatural order. While Augustine conceives grace primarily as an act of divine power that moves the human will, Thomas considers it, above all, under its essential aspect of the new spiritual principle which transforms and renews human nature by the communication of the divine life: in other words, the state of deification of which the Greek Fathers habitually speak. It is not merely a power that moves the will but a light that illuminates the mind and transfigures the whole spirit. This combination of the Augustinian tradition with the characteristic doctrine of the Greek Fathers is perhaps the greatest theological achievement of the scholastic period, though it is usually little noticed in comparison with their philosophical synthesis.[21]

---

[20]Gilby ed., *Theological Texts of St. Thomas Aquinas,* p. 365.
[21]*Medieval Essays,* p. 102.

And it was this doctrine, common now to both East and West, the accepted teaching of the Orthodox Church in schism from Rome as well as the Roman Catholic Church, which came under attack at the time of the Protestant Reformation. That was because Luther's excessive emphasis on man as a sinner drove out this balanced element in Christian teaching. It is one of the great tragedies of Christendom that the failures and spiritual deficiencies of the later medieval Church should have led to such a break from a teaching that is not merely medieval, not merely Patristic, but firmly rooted in Scripture itself.

The importance of this issue of Scriptural support for a Christian humanism is one that is central to the ideological struggle of our day. Most modern ideologies claim to be fulfilling the true needs of mankind, and declare that, for this to be achieved, God and Christianity must be eliminated. No matter how inhuman such ideologies are in the results they produce—we have seen this in our own country in secular humanism's support for the killing of one and a half million unborn infants yearly—they still blazon upon their banners the title of humanism. Now what Evangelical Protestants have to decide, as they face this situation, is whether they will willingly acquiesce in handing over to their ideological adversaries the name of humanists. Do they really believe that the issue between them and the secularists is that the latter are concerned with man in all of his humanity, his hopes and fears and aspirations, while Evangelicals can only sternly reject any idea of humanism because of man's inherently sinful nature?

There is nothing in the Christian tradition which requires Christians to choose between belief in the sinfulness of man and belief in a Christian humanism which has been transfigured by the power of grace. Going back to the New Testament itself, both of these beliefs co-exist in the content of the Christian tradition. We cannot therefore sacrifice one of them in order to give exclusive emphasis to the other, without being unfaithful to the teaching of sacred Scripture.

Once that fact is recognized, the term *humanism* will no longer mean for orthodox Christians today only the goals of some secular ideology, aimed at creating a world from which the idea of God has been banished. Christians will then perceive that God who created man in His own image by that fact laid the essential foundations of Christian humanism. And when God Himself became man, He provided a greater charter for the dignity of human nature than any modern secular humanism can possibly provide. As the Offertory prayer for the celebration of the Eucharist expresses this divinely intended goal of human life: "By the mystery of this water and wine, may we come to share in the divinity of Christ, who humbled Himself to share in our humanity."

4

Henry Adams and the Virgin

The article by Paul Likoudis on Henry Adams and the latter's praise for the achievements of medieval culture, especially as shown in the Gothic cathedrals of France in the thirteenth century, points to a much-neglected Catholic resource. That is, the praise which so many non-Catholic thinkers and writers have bestowed upon the Catholic Middle Ages. The Romantic movement in Germany and France in the late eighteenth and in the nineteenth century first made this discovery of the cultural achievements of the medieval past. As Christopher Dawson has remarked, "Romanticism was a *vita nuova*—the opening up of a new world of spiritual experience. It had found this new world by a rediscovery of the Christian Middle Ages—their art, their poetry, and their thought."[1]

In the generation following upon the rise of the Romantic movement, this intense interest in medieval culture also spread to England, so that some of the best-known poets and essayists of Victorian England chose medieval themes as their subjects. There was, for example, John Ruskin, who wrote a multi-volumed work on the nature and meaning of Gothic architecture; and the interest in Dante's *Divine Comedy* was so widespread that it received numerous translations. Moreover, Alfred Lord Tennyson, poet laureate of England, wrote his great epic poem, *Idylls of the King*, about the ideals of medieval chivalry, as reflected in the stories of King Arthur and the Knights of the Round Table.

Henry Adams, therefore, was entering into an already rich inheritance when his *Mont Saint-Michel and Chartres* was published in 1905. From the standpoint of the defense of authentic Catholicism, what makes the witness of men like Adams and Tennyson, and other nineteenth-century poets and writers on both sides of the Atlantic so impressive is that all of these writers were non-Catholic. They were drawn to praise of the Catholic achievement by the power which its art and literature exerted upon their minds and imaginations. It so happens that human beings are more favorably impressed by praise coming from

---

[1]Lecture of Christopher Dawson at Harvard Divinity.

those outside of a cultural tradition than by those who are within it. The latter are often suspected of being too partisan.

Thus Likoudis, as he brought to bear the testimony of Henry Adams, shows us what can be done by way of effective Catholic witness.

Despite the importance which I attribute to Paul Likoudis' article, however, there were two points to which I think he might have given more attention than the passing reference they received. One of these was his reference to Adams as "a detached skeptic," the other had to do with whether Adams, in his admiration for the Virgin in medieval art and architecture, did not misrepresent the real center of Catholic life and worship.

It is true that the eloquence of Henry Adams' tribute to Gothic architecture may lead us to overlook its ambivalent character. Consider, for example, this statement from the final pages of his work, *Mont Saint-Michel and Chartres*:

> Truth, indeed, may not exist; science avers it to be only a relation; but what men took for truth stares one everywhere in the eye and begs for sympathy. The architects of the twelfth and thirteenth centuries took the Church and the universe for truths, and tried to express them in a structure which should be final.... One idea controlled every line; and this is true of St. Thomas' Church as it is of Amiens Cathedral. The method was the same for both, and the result was an art marked by singular unity, which endured and served its purpose until man changed his attitude toward the universe. The trouble was not in the art or the method or the structure, but in the universe itself which presented different aspects as man moved.[2]

This is what is meant by calling Adams a detached skeptic, as Likoudis does. Note such sentences as: "Truth, indeed, may not exist; science avers it to be only a relation." And, toward the end of the passage, the way in which he speaks of St. Thomas and his Church, "which endured and served its purpose until man changed his attitude toward the universe." St. Thomas believed in the reality of truth which man's intellect could arrive at and hold on to permanently; Henry Adams did not. To Adams, truth was merely relative and changed to falsehood when man adopted a different attitude toward the universe. There was

---

[2]Henry Adams, *Mont Saint-Michel and Chartres* (Houghton Mufflin Co., 1905), pp. 376-377.

no permanent substance to it; all was ultimately flux, as he brings out strongly in *The Education of Henry Adams*.

Notice also the difference between admiring Gothic architecture as an expression of a vibrant faith in truths which God has revealed, and Adams' view that the Gothic is merely an expression of "what men took for truth." Now that, in the twentieth century, this supposed truth is seen to have been quite mistaken, it "begs for sympathy" in the form of the art it has left behind it. There is a world of difference between the Christian understanding of Gothic architecture and that view of it which Adams here gives us.

The tribute which Henry Adams pays to Gothic architecture on the last page of *Mont Saint-Michel and Chartres* shows the same conflict between aesthetic appreciation and intellectual rejection. Adams writes:

> Granted a Church, St. Thomas' Church was the most expressive that man has made, and the great Gothic cathedrals were its most complete expression.
> Perhaps the best proof of it is their apparent instability. Of all the elaborate symbolism which has been suggested for the Gothic cathedral, the most vital and the most perfect may be that [of] the slender nervure, the springing motion of the broken arch, the leap downward of the flying buttress—the visible effort to throw off a visible strain—never let us forget that faith alone supports it, and that, if faith fails, Heaven is lost. The equilibrium is visibly delicate beyond the line of safety; danger lurks in every stone. The peril of the heavy tower, of the restless vault, of the vagrant buttress; the uncertainty of logic, the inequalities of the syllogism, the irregularities of the mental mirror—all these haunting nightmares of the Church are expressed as strongly by the Gothic cathedral as though it had been the cry of human suffering, and as no emotion had ever been expressed before or is likely to find expression again. The delight of its aspiration is flung up to the sky. The pathos of its self-distrust and anguish of doubt is buried in the earth as its last secret. You can read out of it whatever else pleases your youth and confidence; to me, this is all.[3]

In this moving passage, we are apt to be diverted from recognizing the real nature of the outlook on life which Adams ascribes to the Gothic. Where others, his predecessors in admiration for the Middle Ages, have seen the immense structure of the Gothic as a magnificent

---

[3]*Ibid.*

witness to the reality of the faith which subsumes so many different elements in man's life and gives unity and meaning and purpose to them, Henry Adams presents us with a quite different picture. To him the Gothic cathedral gives expression to a faith which has covered over the reality of doubt and skepticism which underlies it, and which, for a brief moment in human history, it has managed to overcome. Or, consider the finality of his judgment on what the Gothic has hidden away from human sight: "The pathos of its self-distrust and anguish of doubt is buried in the earth as its last secret. You can read out of it whatever else pleases your youth and confidence; to me, this is all."

In this last sentence of his book, Adams implicitly dismisses the work of all those who have accepted the Gothic on its own terms, in the spirit of "youth and confidence" which Gothic architecture so strikingly manifests. These, according to Adams, have failed to understand its real message, which lies hidden at its base, and which Adams alone has been able to uncover. Thus, for Henry Adams, the governing principle of his work has been that the Virgin of Chartres is no more than a poetic fiction, a consoling dream for men unaware of the real nature of existence, which could only be believed in and served by the naive mind of the Middle Ages.

The other point on which I would find myself in some disagreement with Likoudis is his belief that the Adams position concerning women in French medieval culture provides us with an effective barrier against the advance of modern radical feminism. The basic problem with Henry Adams in this matter is that, like many other non-Catholics who become attracted to Catholicism, he tends to overstate the role of the Blessed Virgin in Catholic devotion. In reading the following statements of Adams concerning medieval Catholic worship, it is important to recall what his friend, Henry Osborn Taylor, said in reviewing the book for *The American Historical Review in 1913:* "We are left in doubt whether we have gone the round of the twelfth and thirteenth centuries, or gone the round of the mind of Henry Adams." In other words, what we have in *Mont Saint-Michel* is a good deal of Adams' own fanciful construction, which he then imputes to the medieval Catholic. Note, for example in the following passage, his view that the Virgin is "a higher power" than the Trinity, to which men can appeal. Here are some of these statements, reflecting the poetic license which the creator of this volume felt entitled to indulge in:

The Trinity feared absorption in her, but was compelled to accept, and even invite her aid, because the Trinity was a court of strict law, and, as in the old customary law, no process of equity could be introduced, except by direct appeal to a higher power. She was imposed unanimously by all classes. . . . Whatever the heretic or mystic might try to persuade himself, God could not be Love. God was Justice, Order, Unity, Perfection . . . nor could the Son and Holy Ghost be other than the Father. The Mother alone was human, imperfect, and could love.[4]

It is obvious that here the Person of Jesus, who became man for love of sinful mankind, and was crucified and died for our sins, is replaced by the figure of the Virgin, whom the Trinity stands in need of in order to give men the love which God Himself is incapable of giving. But, really, does one have to be a heretic or a mystic to believe that God is Love? The New Testament teaching on this matter is quite clear:

Anyone who fails to love can never have known God, because God is love. God's love for us was revealed when God sent into the world his only Son so that we could have life through Him; this is the love I mean: not our love for God, but God's love for us when He sent His Son to be the sacrifice that takes our sins away. (I *John* 4:8-10.)

Apparently the kind of heretic Adams has in mind is one who fails to share the beliefs of Henry Adams, not the religious beliefs of the Catholic Church. In the religion of Adams, Christ is no longer the Mediator between God and man, but the Virgin instead has taken over this position. This is truly a religion of the mother-goddess type, which is quite in line with the ideas of goddess worship now being revived by modern feminists from the relics of ancient paganism. Adams makes this even more explicit elsewhere in this volume, when he says:

The scientific mind is atrophied, and suffers under inherited cerebral weakness, when it comes in contact with the eternal woman—Astarte, Isls, Demeter, Aphrodite, and the last and greatest deity of all, the Virgin.[5]

---

[4]*Ibid.*, pp. 260-261.
[5]*Ibid.*, p. 196.

One would never know from this *deconstruction* of medieval Catholic religion by Henry Adams that the true center of Catholic life and devotion is not the Virgin, but Jesus Christ. In all of those cathedrals erected in medieval France in honor of Mary, the basic act of worship performed there was the Eucharistic Sacrifice of Jesus to the Father, accomplished through the ministry of His priest, an *alter Christus*. Anyone who ignores that fact, or passes it by without any concern for its existence, is simply playing with images and art objects. He is definitely not dealing with the basic realities of the Catholic faith which caused these many cathedrals to be built. He is creating indeed a religion of culture in place of the religion of the Catholic Church.

In fact, at the very time that there was an increased veneration of the Blessed Virgin in medieval Catholicism, there was also occurring a greater devotion to the humanity of Jesus. Christopher Dawson describes the nature of this development:

> Byzantine religion had developed the transcendent side of Christianity. It had emphasized the divine nature of Christ, the Uncreated Word, rather than the Divine Humanity. That is why the greater part of Oriental Christendom ... fell away from orthodoxy by a denial of the Human Nature of Christ and adopted the errors of Monophysitism.
>
> Medieval Catholicism, on the other hand, concentrated its attention on the Humanity of Jesus, on the contemplation of His Life and Passion, and on the practice of the imitation of Christ. These are the characteristic notes of medieval religion from the time of the reforming movement [of eleventh century monasticism] down to the Protestant Reformation, from St. Anselm and St. Bernard to St. Francis and St. Bonaventure, to the Yorkshire hermit, Richard , and to Thomas a Kempis. St. Bernard is perhaps the greatest of these "doctors of the sacred Humanity," and no single personality is more characteristic of medieval religion, both in thought and action. It is, however, in St. Francis that medieval religion finds its most sublime expression, and which makes a unique appeal not only to the medieval mind but also to that of modern times. And the secret of this appeal is to be found precisely in the Christocentric character of the life and doctrine of St. Francis.[6]

Thus, no matter how eloquent and moving are Henry Adams'

---

[6]Christopher Dawson, *Medieval Christianity* (Comparative Religion series, Catholic Truth Society, London, 1935). Reprinted in *The Dawson Newsletter*, Vol. X, 1, p.7.

praises of Gothic architecture and the cult of the Blessed Virgin in the Middle Ages, he has gone quite astray on the essential meaning of the medieval religious development. Christocentric piety was at the heart of it, as in fact it still is in the Catholic faith today, in a society apparently ruled by the technology of the Dynamo envisioned by Henry Adams.

Cardinal Newman, writing in the middle of the nineteenth century, gives us the true picture of what is the position of the Blessed Virgin in Catholic devotion. He writes:

> This energetic, direct apprehension of an unseen Lord and Savior has not been peculiar to prophets and Apostles; it has been the habit of His Holy Church, and of her children, down to this day. Age passes after age, and she varies her discipline, and she adds to her devotions, and all with the one purpose of fixing her own and their gaze more fully upon the person of her unseen Lord . . .
>
> And so, again, if the Church has exalted Mary or Joseph, it has been with a view to the glory of His sacred humanity. If Mary is proclaimed as immaculate, it illustrates the doctrine of her Maternity. If she is called the Mother of God, it is to remind Him that though he is out of sight, He, nevertheless, is our possession, for He is of the race of man. If she is painted with Him in her arms, it is because we will not suffer the Object of our love to cease to be human, because He is also divine. If she is the Mater Dolorosa, it is because she stands by His cross. If she is Maria Desolata, it is because His dead Body is on her lap. If, again, she is the Coronata, the crown is set upon her head by His dear hand.[7]

In meeting the attacks of the radical feminists on Catholic faith and history, are there not more reliable guides in the great Catholic writers of our time like Newman and Dawson, rather than in Henry Adams, whose poetic appreciation of Catholic art and architecture is nevertheless flawed by his basic philosophic nihilism?

---

[7]John Henry Newman, *Sermons Preached on Various Occasions* (Westminster, MD., Christian Classics, 1968), pp. 40-41.

5

The Protestant View of History and its Consequences

"When All Our Fathers Worshipped Stocks and Stones"

We have elsewhere discussed the unfavorable attitude toward Christianity, and especially toward medieval Catholicism, found in the Liberal interpretation of history. Examples of that are found in the writings of Jacob Burckhardt and John Addmington Symonds, one a Swiss, the other an English Liberal historian. Burckhardt claimed that medieval man was unable to grasp objective reality, and that his religion set up a veil of illusion which left him a victim of childish prepossessions. Symonds asserted that not only did religion keep man in ignorance of the facts by this make-believe world of faith, but it praised ignorance as a proof of one's submission to God. (It is regrettable that Symonds never got to read the *Summa Theologica* of Aquinas, with its considering of a thousand and one objections against the theses St. Thomas was preparing to prove.)

The first thing we have to recognize is the fact that this derogatory idea of the medieval period expressed by Burckhardt and Symonds is not peculiar to the nineteenth century. It had its origins centuries earlier, in the very idea of the Renaissance itself, and in the ideas which the Protestant Reformers held about the state of the Catholic Church in the Middle Ages. And these two currents of rejection of medieval Catholic culture and religion were reinforced and given a new emphasis by the *philosophes* of the eighteenth century Enlightenment, by men like Voltaire and Rousseau and Diderot in France, and Edward Gibbon and David Hume in Great Britain.

The Renaissance looked down upon the Middle Ages because, to the man of the Renaissance, medieval man possessed no real appreciation of ancient classical literature and art. In their newfound intoxication with the beauties of ancient Greek and Roman culture, Renaissance men could see nothing of value in the achievements of the Christian centuries of the Middle Ages; and it was they who applied the term "Gothic" to medieval architecture, as an indication that it was a kind of architecture suitable only for untutored barbarians, who were unacquainted with classical standards of beauty and form. And this contrast between the classical revival of the Renaissance and the Gothic barbarism of the Middle Ages naturally involved the rejection of the cultural achievements of the medieval period. In fact, the whole idea of the Renaissance led to this conclusion. As Wallace K. Ferguson points out:

> Several important studies in recent years have demonstrated, with a wealth of examples, how frequently the humanists of both Italy and the northern countries employed the metaphors of rebirth, revival, or resuscitation, all of which imply a previous death, or the contrasting metaphors of darkness and light, to denote their conception of the history of literature, learning, and the fine arts from antiquity, through the Middle Ages, to their own time.[1]

Thus it was only natural to think of the medieval period as the Dark Ages, once one had accepted this idea of the Renaissance.

But for countries which became Protestant and therefore for the English-speaking world as a whole, a more powerful influence for painting the Middle Ages in dark colors arose from the Protestant revolt against Catholicism. In order to justify separation from the Papacy and the tearing apart of the unity of Christendom, the Protestant Reformers and their disciples developed a new conception of Church History in which the cardinal article of faith was the identification of the Pope as Antichrist; and the Middle Ages were seen as the time when his power over mankind was at its greatest. This was of course a revolutionary attitude involving a great deal of bitterness and hostility against the Catholic Church and all its works. Christopher Dawson notes the influence of this on education in Protestant countries, and he quotes the nineteenth-century German historian Dollinger to the effect that the new generation in the schools and universities of the Reformation period "were taught to despise past generations and consequently their own ancestors as men willfully plunged in error" and to believe "that the Popes and bishops, the theologians and the universities, the monasteries and all the teaching corporations had formed for centuries past a vast

---

[1]Wallace K. Ferguson, *The Renaissance in Historical Thought* (Houghton-Mufflin, 1948), p. 2.

conspiracy to deform and suppress the teaching of the Gospel."[2]

Since *pietas* and respect for one's ancestors are so very important in providing the psychological foundation for a culture, one wonders what the impact of this attitude must have been on the generation being brought up in this new manner of education. May it not have been responsible for the proliferation of different Protestant sects, as one group after another made use of the revolutionary principle of rejection of the past in order to revolt against the particular form of Protestantism held by their predecessors? Moreover, would not this revolutionary attitude spread from religion to other areas of culture as well?

Professor Ferguson describes the conception of history held by the Protestant Reformers, and shows how it necessarily resulted in a condemnation of the Middle Ages:

> The major premise of the reformers, that they were restoring the pure evangelical doctrine of the early Church, which had been deformed by the Church of Rome, demanded historical proof. The early reformers stated the doctrine and in the following generations the historians supplied the data to uphold it. The Protestant interpretation of medieval history was thus oriented by the necessity of demonstrating that the light of the gospel had been progressively obscured under the malign influence of the popes and their agents with the result that Western Christendom had remained for a thousand years sunk in barbaric ignorance, superstition, and spiritual sloth.[3]

Moreover, the idea which the Renaissance had of itself as a rebirth of learning, cultural light after darkness, was incorporated into the Protestant conception. It was only when men's ignorance and superstition had been dispelled by the revival of learning, brought about by the Renaissance, that men were ready to accept the preaching of the pure message of the Gospel which Protestantism offered them. In the English-speaking world, this conception achieved its widest currency through John Foxe's *Book of Martyrs*, written in 1563, and Ferguson quotes from Foxe to show how Protestants regarded the Renaissance:

> "And here began the first push and assault to be given against the ignorant and barbarous faction of the Pope's pretenced church."

---

[2]Christopher Dawson, *The Crisis of Western Education*, p. 35.
[3]Ferguson, *op. cit.*, p. 49.

For after these [i.e., the Renaissance humanists] by their learned writings "had opened a window of light unto the world... immediately, according to God's gracious appointment, followed Martin Luther with others after him, by whose ministry it pleased the Lord to work a more full reformation of His Church."[4]

A striking reflection of the Protestant conception of the Pope and the Middle Ages is to be found in one of the great sonnets of English literature, written by John Milton almost a century after Foxe's *Book of Martyrs* appeared. It is called *On the Late Massacre in Piedmont,* and refers to a massacre of Protestant Waldensians conducted by the Catholic Duke of Savoy, but which Milton finds more poetically appropriate to blame on the Pope. It reads:

Avenge O Lord, Thy slaughtered saints, whose bones
Lie scattered on the Alpine mountains cold;
Even them who kept Thy truth so pure of old
When all our fathers worshipped stocks and stones,
Forget not; in Thy book record their groans
Who were Thy sheep, and in their ancient fold
Slain by the bloody Piemontese, who rolled
Mother with infant down the rocks; their moans
The vales redoubled to the hills, and they
To heaven. Their martyred blood and ashes sow
O'er all the Italian fields, where still doth sway
The triple Tyrant; that from these may grow
A hundredfold, who, having learnt Thy way,
Early may fly the Babylonian woe.

The triple Tyrant has reference to the Pope and his triple tiara; and the seat of his power, Papal Rome, is of course Babylon, the city which is the center of the power of Antichrist in the Apocalypse. The Waldensians who were slain by the Duke of Savoy were a group who had first separated themselves from the Catholic Church in the thirteenth century and thereafter lived in a certain isolation in one of these Alpine valleys. During this period of the later Middle Ages, they alone "had kept Thy truth so pure of old," while the rest of the medieval Catholic

---

[4]*Ibid.,* pp. 54-55.

world, in Milton's Protestant view of the matter, had "worshipped stocks and stones." What is especially striking here is Milton's willingness to refer to the medieval Catholics as "our fathers" who had been engaged in this idol worship, for this sharpens the sense of the condemnation of the father by the son and underlines the revolutionary character of the Reformation attitude.

Is it not likely that the revolutionary ferment and hatred of tradition which is so widespread today, which leaves no tradition and no belief from the past untouched, may have had its origin in this revolt of Western Christendom against its medieval forefathers? For the spirit of revolution, then engendered in Western culture, and later more fully developed at the time of the French Revolution, has spread with the diffusion of Western ideas and technology, so that it is now worldwide. It affects the traditions handed down by the founding fathers of every world-religion culture. This development is often looked upon as a sign of progress, as a clearing of the ground for the erection of some new technological Utopia. But is it not likely that it destroys the basis for any continuing cultural effort?

In this connection, Christopher Dawson, citing St. Thomas Aquinas, has pointed out:

> For as St. Thomas shows, *Pietas*, which is the cult of parents and kinsfolk and native place as the principles of our being, by whom and in which we are born and nourished, has an essential relation to Religion which is the cult of God as our first principle. Hence piety in the classical sense of the word is not a matter of sentiment or social tradition, it is a moral principle that lies at the root of every culture and every religion, and the society that loses it has lost its primary moral basis and its hope of survival.[5]

William Cobbett and the Protestant Reformation in England

There was one English thinker and social critic, a little later than Edmund Burke and the latter's praise of the monasteries, who was a man of the people and largely self-educated. William Cobbett saw that what

---

[5]Christopher Dawson, *Tradition and Inheritance* (Wanderer Press, 1970). A reprint of this article from a British magazine, *The Wind and the Rain, 1949*), p. 9. Also reprinted in part in *The Dawson Newsletter*, VIII, No. 1, Section 2.

had happened in the sixteenth century Reformation was quite pertinent to the situation in which England found herself in the early nineteenth century. Cobbett, the writer of a simple and direct prose, was an immediate witness to the effect upon the English farming population of the enclosures of the commons which had been carried out by the landed nobility during the eighteenth century. He saw the ruin and impoverishment of the small farmer and agricultural worker which was the outcome of this naked act of class exploitation. In his book, *Rural Rides,* giving accounts of his travels around a great part of England during the 1820's, and in his paper, *The Political Register*, Cobbett raised his voice in vigorous denunciation of what had happened; he was the chief spokesman for the small farmer in the latter's fight against the plutocracy.

But, in his assessment of the situation which had led to the enclosures of the eighteenth century, Cobbett went back to the origins, as he saw it, in the earlier economic exploitation of the poor brought on by Henry VIII's destruction of the monasteries. This meant the distribution of monastery lands to the Crown and to the rich, especially the latter. Cobbett saw in this the beginning of the train of abuses which led to the enclosures of the eighteenth century. The seizure of the monasteries was the destruction of the barrier which had served to protect the poor against the greed of the wealthy during the Middle Ages. And then, at a later time, when the results of foreign commerce had further enriched the upper classes, the eighteenth century plutocracy had overrun the protective barrier of the common lands, without which the peasant could not survive. Thus Cobbett was led back to an examination of what was the social situation in the Middle Ages. And, drawing his evidence from what he saw around him in the countryside of what still survived of medieval buildings and churches, he reached the startling conclusion, quite at variance with the Whig interpretation of history, that the Middle Ages had a superior social structure to what now existed in England.

His conclusions were that the English countryside in the Middle Ages was much more heavily populated than it was in the first quarter of the nineteenth century, and that it possessed a great degree of wealth and prosperity, widely distributed among the small farmers and the peasants who cultivated the land. He drew very unfavorable comparisons between the size of the present rural population which he saw in his rides around the countryside and the population which he estimated was necessary in order to build the cathedrals and parish churches which were in such profusion in the areas through which he rode, and which still survived as witnesses to a vanished era of the prosperity of England in the Middle Ages.

But it was in his treatment of the English Reformation, and the effect that the Reformation had upon the economic and social life of the country through the destruction of the monasteries, that Cobbett was so strong in rejection of the Protestant interpretation of history. Remember that his *Political Register*, in which his *History of the Protestant Reformation* first appeared during the years 1824-27, dealt with the problems of the social situation of that day, in which his readers were deeply involved. Thus his ideas gained the widest currency and were related to the revolutionary ferment which led to the Reform Bill of 1832, which was to provide for a new organization of Parliament, a Parliament, in fact, to which Cobbett himself was elected.

Consequently what he said about the Reformation was not simply the production of a scholar whose researches might have little immediate impact, but was instead a kind of tocsin to the people, linking up the present difficulties of the Country with what had been done to its social structure three hundred years before by the seizure of the monasteries. It is true that Cobbett had for his chief authority on the monasteries the careful work of the Catholic scholar Lingard, but he also drew upon Protestant sources in making his case; and what is most important from the viewpoint of influence upon the social consciousness of a country, he diffused his conclusions abroad, so that they reached all classes of society. As the *Oxford History of English Literature* points out concerning the fact that Cobbett's writing had a far wider influence than any merely literary production could have:

> If the importance of a writer were to be gauged by his demonstrable influence upon his contemporaries, Cobbett would have no rival in our period except Jeremy Bentham. To us as we look back he seems less a man than a phenomenon. It is impossible to think of the development of England at the beginning of the nineteenth century without thinking of Cobbett.[6]

As we keep this fact in mind, here is Cobbett's view of the

---

[6]Ian Jack, *English Literature, 1815-1832* (Oxford Univ. Press).

Protestant interpretation of English history which he and his readers had received:

> I have shown you how grossly we have been deceived, even from our very infancy. I have shown you not only the injustice, but the absurdity of the abuse heaped by our interested deluders on the religion of their and our fathers. I have shown you enough to convince you that there was no obviously just cause for an alteration in the religion of our country.... But observe, my chief object is to show that this alteration made the main body of the people poor and miserable compared with what they were before; that it impoverished and degraded them.[7]

And this is Cobbett's description of the character of Henry VIII, and the effects of his revolution upon the life and liberties of the English people:

> Thus, then, all law and justice were laid prostrate at the feet of a single man, and that man a man with whom law was mockery, on whom the name of justice was a libel, and to whom mercy was wholly unknown. It is easy to imagine that no man's property or life could have security with power like this in the hands of such a man. Magna Carta had been trampled under foot from the moment that the Pope's supremacy was assailed.... Numerous things were made high treason which were never before thought criminal at all. The trials were for a long time a mere mockery, and at last they were altogether, in many cases, laid aside and the accused were condemned to death, not only without being arraigned and heard in their defense, but in numerous cases without being appraised of the crimes or pretended crimes for which they were executed. We have heard of Deys of Algiers and Beys of Tunis, but never have heard of them, even in the most exaggerated accounts, any deeds to be, in point of injustice and cruelty, compared with those of this man, whom Burnet calls "the first-born son of the English Reformation".[8]

After mentioning the numerous monasteries in England, how well they were laid out, and how much they contributed to the benefit of the people, Cobbett speaks of how they excited the cupidity of the nobility and the Protestant reformers:

---

[7]William Cobbett, *A History of the Protestant Reformation* (Tan Books, 1988; a reprint of the Benziger Bros. edition of 1896, with introduction by Cardinal Gasquet), p. 20.

[8]*Ibid.*, p. 78.

Here was enough, indeed, to make robbers on a grand scale cry out against "monkish ignorance and superstition!" No wonder that the bowels of Cranmer, Knox and all the rest, yearned so piteously as they did, when they cast their pious eyes on all the farms and manors, and on all the silver and gold ornaments belonging to these communities![9]

After speaking of the fact that the seizure of the monasteries by the rich "despoiled the working classes of their patrimony," Cobbett points out that the system of poor relief introduced as a substitute for the help given to the poor by the monasteries, is "calculated to make the poor and rich hate each other instead of binding them together as the Catholic mode did, by the bonds of Christian charity."[10]

But what especially arouses Cobbett's indignation is the manner in which highly regarded Protestant historians like David Hume, a Scotsman who wrote in the eighteenth century, have found it necessary to impugn the credit of the monasteries in order to justify the Reformation. Cobbett therefore quotes quite extensively from a Protestant scholar and bishop on whom Hume heavily relied as a source for his history, and shows that this same scholar was most laudatory of the contribution of the monasteries to English society and culture—an aspect of this scholar's work which Hume completely ignores when making his case against the monasteries. Here is Cobbett's point-by-point refutation of Hume.

Now, then, malignant Hume, come up and face this Protestant bishop, whose work you have quoted more than two hundred times, and who here gives the lie direct to all and to every part of your description. Instead of your "supine idleness," we have industry of the most patient and persevering; instead of your "profound ignorance," we have in every convent a school for teaching, *gratis*, all useful sciences; instead of your want of all "manly and elegant knowledge," we have the study, the teaching, the transcribing, the preserving of the classics; instead of your "selfishness," and your pious "frauds" to get money from the people, we have hospitals for the sick, doctors and nurses to attend them, and the most disinterested, the most kind, the most noble hospitality; instead of that "slavery" which, in fifty parts of your history, you assert to have

---

[9]*Ibid.*, p. 34.
[10]*Ibid.*, p. 93.

been taught by the monks, we have the freeing of people from the
forest laws, and the preservation of the Great Charter of English
liberty; and you know as well as I, that when this Charter was
renewed by King John, the renewal was in fact the work of
Archbishop Langton, who roused the barons to demand it, he
having, as Tanner observes, found the Charter deposited in an
abbey![11]

With this powerful and eloquent critique of the errors and
prejudices found in the usual Protestant interpretation of English
history, and being supported by the more careful scholarship of John
Lingard and his seven-volume *History of England*, the way was made
open for the Oxford Movement's attempt to emphasize the Catholic
elements remaining in the Church of England.   And it especially
prepared the way for the conversion to Catholicism of many participants
in the Oxford Movement, including its chief leader, John Henry
Newman.

"The Inns of God Where No Man Paid"

In our previous section we discussed William Cobbett's view of the
effects of the Protestant Reformation upon the welfare of the English
people. Because Cobbett had a diametrically opposite view to the usual
Protestant interpretation of English history, it is significant that he
himself remained a Protestant. It was, if one may put it that way, an
attempt on the part of one Protestant to do justice to the achievements
of the Catholic Church in the Middle Ages, and to dissociate himself
from the greed and exploitation which had wrecked those achievements
at the time of the Reformation. While it was no longer possible to
restore the monastic properties, it was possible to restore the good name
of the Catholic Church and the good name of that institution, the
monastic life, which had been one of the chief means by which the
Church carried on its work in the Middle Ages.

And that is what William Cobbett did, not only for himself but for
a considerable portion of the reading public in England. Thereafter, the
older Protestant practice of blackening the name of the Middle Ages

---

[11]*Ibid.,* pp. 100-101.

through strident denunciation of the monasteries, could not really be reestablished. Later advocates of Protestantism might try to modify Cobbett's thesis here and there, and show that it contained some elements of exaggeration and overstatement, but never again could the English Protestant rest secure in the self-righteousness of his forebears in justifying what had been done to the Catholic Church at the time of the Reformation. Whatever new justifications might be sought for the revolt of English Protestantism against the Catholic Church, this older form of rationalization for the robbery had been given the death blow. Protestantism would now have to be praised because it led to greater religious freedom or political freedom or economic development (none of which was the goal of early Protestantism, only incidental to the main thrust and purpose of the Protestant revolution); but the black-and-white contrast of the Middle Ages and the Reformation was no longer really believable. Even a man like John Addington Symonds, whom we have mentioned earlier as representing the liberal condemnation of the Middle Ages, based his rejection of the period on the fact that it was not worldly enough, that it was too much occupied with thoughts of the next life and not enough with the present one. This is, indeed, quite a turnabout from the denunciation of the Middle Ages by earlier Protestant controversialists, condemning the worldliness of the Church, its ignoring of the spiritual message of the Gospel and the early Church.

As to the influence of Cobbett on other English writers of the nineteenth century, Raymond Williams makes the following observation:

> The other aspect of Cobbett's work is his surprising share of responsibility for that idealization of the Middle Ages which is so characteristic of nineteenth century social criticism. As a literary movement, medievalism had been growing since the middle of the eighteenth century. Its most important aspect, for Cobbett, was its use of the monasteries as a standard for social institutions: the image of the working of a communal society as a working alternative to the claims of individualism. Burke made the point, in the Reflections; later, Pugin, Carlyle, Ruskin and Morris were all to make it, explicitly and influentially.... Yet not only did Cobbett make the point, he was responsible for a large measure of its popularization. He read Lingard's *History of England*, the work of a Catholic scholar, and used it, with characteristic license, as the basis of his *History of the Protestant Reformation*. This book had, by contemporary standards, a huge circulation, and there must for some time have been many thousands of readers who came to these

ideas through Cobbett rather than through contact with any of the more reliable sources.[12]

At this point I should like to examine the influence of Cobbett's ideas concerning monasticism and the English Reformation as these are reflected in the work of two Catholic writers of the past century. One of these was the nineteenth century leader of the Oxford Movement, John Henry Newman, and the other was possibly the foremost defender of Catholicism in the twentieth century, G. K. Chesterton. I choose these, not because the importance of monasticism has not received a great deal of attention from men like Philip Hughes and Dom David Knowles and other historians in our own century, but because Newman and Chesterton were, like Cobbett, writers who reached a large part of the reading public of England.

Here, for example, is Newman writing about the significance of the monasteries in the development of culture during the Middle Ages, showing how the monastery provided for renewal of cultural life despite the constant invasions which were visited upon early medieval Europe. One wonders if a passage like this would have been written if it had not been for the new appreciation of medieval monasticism, to which Cobbett is so striking a witness.

> The new world which he [i.e. St. Benedict] helped to create was a growth rather than a structure. Silent men were observed about the country, or discovered in the forest, digging, clearing, and building; and other silent men, not seen, were sitting in the cold cloister, tiring their eyes, and keeping their attention on the stretch, while they painfully deciphered and copied and recopied the manuscripts which they had saved . . .
>
> And then, when they had in the course of many years gained their peaceful victories, perhaps some new invader came, and with fire and sword undid their slow and persevering toil in an hour. The Hun succeeded to the Goth, the Lombard to the Hun, the Tartar to the Lombard; the Saxon was reclaimed only that the Dane might take his place. Down in the dust lay the labor and civilization of centuries—Churches, Colleges, Cloisters, Libraries—and nothing was left to them but to begin all over again; but this they did without grudging, so promptly, cheerfully, and tranquilly, as if it were by some law of nature that the restoration came, and they were like the

---

[12]Raymond Williams, *Culture and Society, 1780-1950* (Doubleday Anchor ed., 1960), pp. 20-21.

flowers and shrubs and fruit trees which they reared, and which, when ill-treated, do not take vengeance, or remember evil, but give forth fresh branches, leaves or blossoms, perhaps in greater profusion, and with richer quality, for the very reason that the old were rudely broken off . . .

, To the monk heaven was next door; he formed no plans, he had no cares; the ravens of his father Benedict were ever at his side. He "went forth" in his youth "to his work and to his labor" until the evening of life; if he lived a day longer, he did a day's work more; whether he lived many days or few, he labored on to the end of them.[13]

We note that, in this passage, the other-worldliness which is supposed to lead to the neglect of this world and to social stagnation, is seen by Newman as the very reason for the monks' resiliency in the face of adversity; since they had not set their hearts on the achievement of any temporal goal, they were not set back by discouragement when the work of their hands was destroyed.

Thus we have Newman on one aspect of the Cobbett thesis, of the social contributions of medieval monasticism; here is G. K. Chesterton presenting the other element of the Cobbett view of English history: how the Reformation was motivated by the desire of the Crown and the nobility for plunder of the monasteries. This selection is from *The Secret People*, written before 1915; the English people are the secret people, who never have spoken yet, but have had the decisions concerning their destiny reached for them by their rulers. (It must be admitted that the Pilgrimage of Grace and other popular outbreaks at the time of the Reformation, against the seizure of the monasteries, indicate that the people did indeed try to speak out, but were punished for it.) Here, then, is Chesterton on the seizure of the monasteries:

The blood ran red to Bosworth, and the high French lords went down;
There was naught but a naked people under a naked crown.
And the eyes of the King's Servants turned terribly every way,
And the gold of the King's Servants rose higher every day.
They burnt the homes of the shaven men, that had been quaint and kind.
Till there was no bed in a monk's house, nor food that man could

---

[13]John Henry Newman, *Historical Sketches*, Vol. II (Christian Classics, 1970), pp. 410-411; 426.

find.
The inns of God where no man paid, that were the wall of the weak,
The King's Servants at them all. And still we did not speak.

Chesterton saw the Reformation as weakening the power of the English monarchy. Not only did the new religion of Puritanism resist the Catholic tendencies of the Stuarts in the following century, but the theft of the monastic lands increased the power and wealth of the *nouveaux-riche* aristocracy. As a result, just one hundred years after the death of Henry VIII, Charles I lies in prison, awaiting a decision on his fate by the Parliament, which will eventually lead to his beheading.

And the face of the King's Servants grew greater than the King:
He tricked them, and they trapped him, and stood round him in a ring.
The new grave lords closed round him, that had eaten the abbey's fruits,
And the men of the new religion, with their Bibles in their boots;
We saw their shoulders moving, to menace or discuss,
And some were pure and some were vile; but none took heed of us.
We saw the King as they killed him, and his face was proud and pale;
And a few men talked of freedom, while England talked of ale.[14]

---

[14]G.K. Chesterton, *Poems*, 1915 (Republished in *Collected Poems*, 1932), p. 164.

6

Voltaire and the Enlightenment View of History

The Enlightenment Conception of God

Non-Christian and anti-Christian views of the meaning of history take their rise from the eighteenth century Enlightenment worldview. Although often borrowing key elements for their new ideas about history from Christianity and Judaism, they have transposed these elements so as to have them serve a quite different purpose. The general result is to set up a philosophy of history in which the City of Man becomes the center of the philosopher's attention, and the City of God is either rejected as a fantasy of the ages of Faith, or else is identified with the aspirations of the City of Man in one or another of its different forms. We will be concerned especially with the Enlightenment view of God and of man, for it is upon this view that its interpretation of history depends.

Lying behind the idea of history held by the Enlightenment was the conception of a God who did not interfere with the laws of nature once He had established these for the smooth and proper running of the universe. These laws were supreme; and any suspension of their operation in order to permit of miracles or of answer to prayers would show that God's original provisions for the universe were lacking in foresight and wisdom. Thus although many of the *philosophes* of the Enlightenment admitted the existence of a God, they made Him remote from the ordinary human being. They closed Him off from being willing to listen to prayer or able to grant its requests. In fact, they made Him a prisoner of the universe which He had created and had set in motion; the laws of the universe now stood between God and humanity.

Voltaire expressed this view of God in a passage from his *Miscellanies*; at the same time he unwittingly exposes the implicit anthropomorphism, and subjection to human limitations, which the Deist idea of God involves:

A metaphysician says to a young and pious nun: "My Sister, there is nothing so good as *Ave Marias*, especially when a girl recites them in Latin in a suburb of Paris; but I do not believe that God concerns Himself much with your sparrow, however pretty it may be; consider, I beg of you, how much other business He has. He must continually direct the courses of sixteen planets and the ring of Saturn, in the center of which He has put the sun, which is as big as a million of our globes. He has billions and billions of other suns, planets, and comets to govern. His unchangeable laws and His eternal concurrence keep entire nature in motion; everything is bound to His throne by an infinite chain, of which no link can ever be out of place. If *Ave Marias* had made your sparrow live an instant longer than it was to live, these *Ave Marias* would have violated all the laws established through all eternity by the Great Being; you would have deranged the universe; you would have necessitated a new world, a new God, and a new order of things."[1]

The bland optimism in which this conception often resulted, justifying the course of nature on the basis that everything was arranged for the best, is expressed in this passage from a poem by Alexander Pope, written a generation and more before the above Voltaire argument against miracles.

> Cease, then, nor Order imperfection name....
> All Nature is but art unknown to thee;
> All chance, direction, which thou canst not see;
> All discord, harmony not understood;
> All partial evil, universal good;
> And spite of Pride, in erring Reason's spite,
> One truth is clear, Whatever is, is right.

And developing the same argument which Voltaire used to show that miracles were impossible, Pope adds:

> And if each system in gradation roll,
> Alike essential to the amazing Whole.
> The least confusion but in one, not all
> That system only, but the Whole must fall.
> Let Earth unbalanced from her orbit fly,
> Planets and stars run lawless through the sky.

---

[1]Voltaire, *Miscellenies* in *Les Philosophes* ed. by Norman L Torrey (Capricorn Books, 1961), p. 273.

And then, turning to the person whose prayers request some change in what is bound to happen, the poet denounces him. "All this dread order break—for whom? for thee? Vile worm—O madness! pride! impiety!"[2]

Alexander Pope, it should be recalled, was a Catholic; but the influence of Newtonian physics was so strong upon him, or that particular interpretation given it by the eighteenth century, that the teachings of the Gospel came out a poor second by comparison. What the Deism of the eighteenth century could not see was that the omnipotence of God could just as easily suspend the operation of the laws of Nature in particular cases as it was able to establish these laws in the first place.

Chesterton has remarked on the contrast between the Christian and the scientific and Deist view of God and man, to show that many of those who claim to be fighting for the rights of humanity, are in fact quite inhumane in their basic conception of the universe:

> Exactly in proportion as you turn monotheism into monism you turn it into despotism. It is precisely the unknown God of the scientist, with His impenetrable purpose and His inevitable and unalterable law, that reminds us of a Prussian autocrat making rigid plans in a remote tent and moving mankind like machinery. It is precisely the God of miracles and of answered prayers who reminds us of a liberal and popular prince, receiving petitions, listening to parliaments and considering the cases of a whole people.[3]

Karl Adam has pointed out how the view of Jesus on the relationship between God and man is unequivocal and direct. It does not operate through intermediary and secondary causes of the laws of nature, which indeed, when seen in the manner of Deism, are an idolatry of the works of man's own mind.

> Jesus does not, like them, contemplate intermediate causes through which the creative God calls all Becoming and Being into existence. Still less do these intermediate causes combine for him into a constant self-sufficient order of Nature looming up between Creator and creature as a rival cosmos of created causal sequences. Such a belief in a rigid order of Nature Jesus never shared. Indeed

---

[2]Alexander Pope, *Essay on Man*, Epistle I, lines 247-258; 289-294.
[3]G.K. Chesterton, *The Everlasting Man* (Dodd, Mead & Co., 1925), p. 301.

it would have seemed to Him an idolatry of purely human conceptions and systems. For in the last resort, it is man himself who has contrived and gone on contriving such laws and systems, in the hope to master for the moment, the colossal, unfathomable, inexhaustible mystery of reality, and to repose therein for a little space.... Jesus sees things not where they have already been rigidified for human thought into a fixed significance and being, but where they proceed from the hand of the Creator, He sees them in their inner God-related dynamic, in the living flux of creation, in the creative process of their beginning in God. Hence these things are fundamentally at every moment subject to the Divine call. They cannot take refuge from God behind the armor plates of any kind of order of Nature. Naked and bare they lie in the hand of the creating God, and they have no other surety of existence but that of His almighty will.[4]

Voltaire considered the greatest enemy of this creed of Deism to be a French religious thinker, Blaise Pascal (1623-1662), who had died almost a century before the Enlightenment reached the height of its influence. Of Voltaire's attack on Pascal, and why Voltaire regarded it as necessary if he were to clear the ground of the teachings of the Christian religion, and replace that Faith with the few clear ideas of the Deist creed, Gustave Lanson has written:

The adversary, was well chosen. Blaise Pascal, that man "whom little minds hardly dare to examine," was the only apologist for revealed religion who really mattered in French letters and who was respected by the public at large. He was the only one who could prove, not the God common to Christians and Deists alike, through a reasoning that was both philosophical and commonplace, but specifically Jesus Christ and Christian mysteries, which were incomprehensible by any single method of argumentation. By virtue of his genius he had made people believe in the success of his "demonstration." By attacking him, no matter what precautions Voltaire might take in the choice of quotations, Voltaire was coming to grips with religion itself.[5]

Already in the seventeenth century in which Pascal did his brilliant work as a mathematician and scientist and religious thinker, a Deist conception of the universe had been making progress and

---

[4]Karl Adam, *The Son of God* (Image Books, 1960), pp. 113-14.
[5]Gustave Lanson, *Voltaire* (New York: Wiley, 1966), p. 46.

subverting the foundations of Christian belief. Here is an example of Pascal's reply to it:

> Though a man should be convinced that numerical proportions are immaterial truths, eternal and dependent on a first truth, in which they subsist, and which is called God, I should not think him far advanced towards his own salvation.
>
> The God of the Christians is not a God who is simply the author of mathematical truths, or of the order of the elements; that is the view of heathens and Epicureans. He is not merely a God who exercises His providence over the life and fortunes of men, to bestow on those who worship Him a long and happy life. That was the portion of the Jews. But the God of Abraham, the God of Isaac, the God of Jacob, the God of Christians, is a God of love and comfort, a God who fills the soul and heart of those whom He possesses, a God who makes them conscious of their inward wretchedness, and His infinite mercy, who unites Himself to their inmost soul, who fills it with humility and joy, with confidence and love, who renders them incapable of any other end than Himself.
>
> All who seek God without Jesus Christ, and who rest in nature, either find no light to satisfy them, or come to form for themselves a means of knowing God and serving Him without a mediator. Thereby they fall either into atheism, or into Deism. . . .[6]

Such a conception would impinge sharply upon the self-sufficiency with which Voltaire and the other *philosophes* regarded themselves. It would bring them back to an *accountability* to God for their actions which the God of Deism was unlikely to demand of them.

The Enlightenment and "The Dark Ages"

In earlier parts of this book, we have noted that the depreciation of the Middle Ages so characteristic of the Liberal conception of history, had its origin with the Renaissance and the Reformation. But it reached a new development with the rationalist Enlightenment of the eighteenth century. This proposed to sweep away all the social institutions from the past in order to construct a new system based on the principles of abstract reason. As a deputy to the French National Assembly expressed it, "Let us destroy everything, yes, everything, for everything has to be

---

[6]Pascal, *Pensées*, selec. 555.

remade" (quoted in Pieter Geyl, *The Use and Abuse of History*).

What had contributed to this wide-ranging rejection of the past? What had made men feel that they could remake everything so as to create an order that would be vastly superior to what had been achieved before? One important factor was the increasing prestige of science and technology. Here man's reason had been brilliantly successful in discovering the laws of nature and in applying them to mastery over the environment. The achievement of the seventeenth century from Kepler to Newton, which Whitehead has called the century of genius, had given men a knowledge of the laws governing astronomy and physics, with parallel developments in biology and chemistry. This made men feel that a new world could be created if only the same kind of scientific reason were applied to the problems of the social order. And since society was largely the result of social traditions, this meant that the whole foundation of society had to be radically rethought.

Moreover, if one were to rely essentially upon the analytic reason, then anything which was mysterious, anything which embodied truths which man could not readily comprehend, was simply a product of obscurantism. Man's mind must be supreme and everything must answer before the bar of reason; God Himself must be only the author of Nature, the Being Whom man could reason to as necessary for the existence of the universe. Dawson points out the influence of Newtonian science on this new world view:

> There was now substituted a conception of the world as a vast machine, consisting of material bodies situated in absolute space and moved by mechanical, physical laws. The ultimate realities were no longer spiritual substances and quantities, but Space, Matter, and Time.
>
> Thus, at the same time that spiritual forces were being excluded from society and from human experience by the new philosophy of Hobbes and Locke, their control of the world of nature was also being denied by the new science. God was no longer seen as the heavenly King and Father, Who ruled His world by the unceasing interposition of His all-seeing Providence, nor even as the Renaissance philosopher saw Him, as the immanent spiritual principle of nature. He was the Architect of the Universe, a sublime mechanic Who had constructed the cosmic machine and left it to follow its own laws.
>
> Hence the new science was as hostile to supernaturalism and to the miraculous element in Christianity as was the new philosophy,

and proved one of the chief factors in the secularization of European thought.[7]

What effect did this have on the conception of history? The term "Enlightenment" is suggestive of the historical viewpoint which was involved. Most preceding ages and peoples had lived in the darkness of superstition and ignorance and irrationality; but the *philosophes* of the present generation were the disciples of a new dawn in which man's reason would clear away error and clerical obscurantism like clouds vanishing before the sun. As Condorcet expressed it in his *Progress of the Human Mind,* "Everything tells us we are approaching the era of one of the grand revolutions of the human race."

> Will not every nation one day arrive at the state of civilization attained by those people who are most enlightened, most free, most exempt from prejudices, as the French, for instance, and the Anglo-Americans? ... Is there upon the face of the globe a single spot the inhabitants of which are condemned by nature never to enjoy liberty, never to exercise their reason?

Nevertheless, if one looked closely enough, the *philosophes* believed, there were certain ages in the past, in which the achievements of great literature and art showed that men had not always and everywhere been lost in darkness, but rather that the rational mind had already made its appearance and achieved certain triumphs. For though such ages were rare, they nevertheless were a testimony to the capacities of the human mind when led by the right principles. Voltaire identified four such ages in history before his own time: the Golden Age of Greece, from Pericles to Alexander; the age of Caesar and Augustus in Latin literature and culture; the period of the Italian Renaissance; and the age of Louis XIV, in the latter years of which Voltaire himself had been born.

Although Voltaire did not identify a fifth age, his respect for Confucius as the Chinese sage who had arrived at the basis for a just and harmonious social order, purely through reason, would suggest that for Voltaire ancient China also had one of those great ages in which mankind was able to rise above the superstition in which it was usually plunged. (Voltaire conveniently forgot the strongly traditional element

---

[7]Christopher Dawson, *The Gods of Revolution* (New York U.P.), p. 20.

in the thought of Confucius: "I am faithful to the men of old and love them." Or, again, "The Master said, I am not one who was born with knowledge. I am one who loves the past and earnestly seeks to know it.")

If these were the great ages of humanity, there was one age to which one could look as the opposite of all such greatness in human achievement, and that age was Europe during the Middle Ages. In this matter Voltaire's view of the medieval centuries is typical of the Enlightenment, for as Professor Ferguson points out: "No other historian so nearly personified the spirit of the Age of Reason. All its leading ideas and prejudices are to be found in his work, and one need not read between the lines to read them. His general view of the past may be accepted as the norm for rationalist historical thought." Professor Ferguson summarizes Voltaire's conception of the Middle Ages in these words:

> "It is necessary," said Voltaire, "to know the history of that age only in order to scorn it." As Voltaire presented it, medieval history was philosophy teaching by horrible examples. One had only to report the facts, he felt, to make the Middle Ages and all that sprang from them detestable—not that he could resist the temptation to editorial comment. His diatribes against medieval religion and scholastic philosophy were as bitter as any that emanated from the Protestant controversialists, if based on different grounds. Viewed *en philosophe,* Antichrist became *l'Infame. . . .*
>
> The whole of the Essay [i.e., *Essay on the Manners and the Spirit of Nations*] shows that he considered the destruction of Christian "superstition" the first necessary step in the progress of reason.[8]

Or as Carl Becker speaks of the purpose of this same work of Voltaire:

> [I]t was a general history from the earliest known times written to point a moral: to show that the history of great events in the world is scarcely more than a history of crimes; that the Dark Ages of human experience were precisely those when men were most dominated by the Christian church; and that almost the only times of light and learning, of progress in the arts and sciences, were the four heroic ages when the evils of priestcraft were somewhat abated and the

---

[8]Ferguson, *The Renaissance in Historical Thought,* pp. 89, 93.

minds of men were in consequence somewhat free to follow reason.[9]

Another outstanding historian of the eighteenth century Enlightenment was the Englishman, Edward Gibbon, author of the six-volume history on *The Decline and Fall of the Roman Empire*. A great part of his work dealt with the Middle Ages, in the Byzantine world and in the Islamic Near East and in Western Europe. And in his presentation he continually uses the acid of irony and skepticism to eat away at Christian beliefs. Byron spoke of this effect of his work as "sapping a solemn creed with solemn sneer." Here is Carl Becker's portrayal of the significance of Gibbon's work in relation to the Middle Ages:

> [I]t was Gibbon after all who sought out the enemy in his stronghold and made the direct frontal attack on the Christian centuries.... Gibbon is commemorating the death of ancient civilization; he has described, for the "instruction of future ages, the triumph of barbarism and religion."
>
> The triumph of barbarism and religion! The words fittingly call up the past as imagined by the philosophical century. It was as if mankind, betrayed by barbarism and religion, had been expelled from nature's Garden of Eden. The Christian Middle Ages were the unhappy times after the fall and expulsion, the unfruitful, probationary centuries when mankind, corrupted and degraded by error, wandered blindly under the yoke of oppression. But, mankind has at last emerged, or is emerging, from the dark wilderness of the past into the bright, ordered world of the eighteenth century.[10]

The revolutionary spirit which was implicit in the Enlightenment rejection of the past, and the attack upon the Catholic Church as the infamous thing, carried the movement of reform far beyond what most of the *philosophes* had envisioned. They thought of their blueprint for a new society as being realized by an enlightened despot like Frederick the Great of Prussia or Catherine the Great of Russia, for with the exception of Rousseau, they distrusted and feared the common people. They even held that something of religion should be maintained in order to keep the populace in good order, so that they would not menace the rights of property. The Marxist characterization of religion which was made a

---

[9]Carl Becker, *The Heavenly City of the Eighteenth-Century Philosophers* (Yale Univ. Press, 1932), p. 111.

[10]*Ibid.,* pp. 116-118.

century later—"Religion is the opiate of the people"—is an apt description of the way that Voltaire and his associates looked upon religion in relation to the social order. As Voltaire expressed this aspect of the goals of the Enlightenment, "We have never pretended to enlighten shoemakers and servant girls, that is the portion of the apostles." And again, "I doubt that the populace has either the time or the capacity for education. They would die of hunger before they became philosophers.... It is not the worker we must instruct, it is the *bon bourgeois* of the townsman."[11]

But once launched, the revolt against the Christian religion in France could not be checked; and the French Revolution eventually witnessed the outlawing of the Catholic Faith. Christopher Dawson describes the course of the development:

> At first the Revolution attempted to combine the new faith with the old religion by the creation of a "Constitutional Church" separated from Rome and inseparably bound up with the new State. But the victory of the Jacobins involved the abandonment of this compromise and the institution of the religion of Nature and the Supreme Being as the official faith of the republic. The feasts of the Church were abolished in favor of the new civic festivals, Sunday made way for the *Decadi,* and the churches were secularized or devoted to the new cult. Thus the democratic community became a counter-church of which Robespierre was at once the high priest and the grand inquisitor, while Catholicism and atheism alike were ruthlessly proscribed.[12]

Voltaire and the Religion of China

One of the most striking aspects of the Enlightenment revolt against Christianity was the way in which the *philosophes* of that age idealized the non-Christian cultures and set them off against Christian Europe in order to show the former's manifest superiority. The condition which allowed for this approach was the fact that Europe had been brought into contact with many new peoples and cultures in its age of exploration and discovery. In fact, the age of discovery still continued

---

[11]Dawson, *The Gods of Revolution,* p. 29, cites these passages from letters of Voltaire to his friends.

[12]Christopher Dawson, *Beyond Politics* (Sheed & Ward, 1939), p. 73.

throughout the eighteenth century, for it was only in the latter part of this century that Hawaii, Australia, Tahiti, and other islands of the South Seas were being discovered and made known to Europe.

Thus there was a keen awareness by Europeans of many different ways of life, ranging from the more primitive societies of the North American Indians to the highly sophisticated and scholarly culture of the Chinese. And that raised the question of how to relate these to Christianity, and to the idea that Europe's possession of the Christian faith made her especially favored among all the peoples of the earth.

The answer of the *philosophes* was that Europe was not, in fact, so favored. Instead, she labored under the burden of a corrupting and outworn superstition; and she must be prepared to learn from the Chinese, and even from the primitive peoples she had conquered, the elements of genuine religion. In order to drive home this message, the *philosophes* insisted upon the rationality and order which characterized, for example, the Chinese way of life. They pointed out how the scholars of China had simply followed reason and the law of nature to come to a knowledge of God and man's right relationship to Him. Everything that lay beyond the circle of religious ideas which could be discovered by man's unaided reason was so much excess baggage that weighed man down and prevented him from achieving the social progress which God had intended him to achieve.

The Enlightenment thinker who did most to popularize the supposed achievement of China was Voltaire, who thought of Confucius as a Chinese sage sharing the same general ideas as Voltaire himself. Here is one description by Voltaire of an idealized Chinese religion:

> Their religion was simple, wise, august, free from all superstition and barbarity... The Chinese emperors themselves offered to the God of the Universe, ... to the principle of all things, the first fruits of their harvest twice a year.... This custom was kept up for upwards of forty centuries, in the midst of revolutions, and even the most horrid calamities.
>
> Never was the religion of the emperors and of the tribunals dishonored with impostures; never was it troubled with quarrels between the priests and the empire; never was it burdened with absurd innovations.... Here the Chinese are particularly superior to all the nations of the universe.
>
> Their Confucius framed neither new opinions nor new rites. He neither intended to be an inspired man, nor a prophet. He was a magistrate, who taught the ancient laws. We sometimes say, very

improperly, "the religion of Confucius"; he had no other than that of all the emperors and all the tribunals; no other than that of the first sages; he recommends nothing but virtue, preaches no mysteries.[13]

Some comments are in order on this picture which Voltaire gives us. First, note his ideal that there should be no change in matters of religion; this seems to be in contrast to his desire to bring about considerable change in the social order of the *ancien regime*, and in the religion closely linked with that regime. But we must remember that he wished this change to be brought about by enlightened despots, acting on behalf of the ideas he had set forth, so as to create a settled bourgeois society.

Second, he seems unaware of how strong the conflict was at times between the Emperors of China and the Confucian *literati;* the first emperor of a united China was so incensed at the scholars that he ordered a wholesale burning of their books. And there was always a certain tension between the empire and the scholars, so long as the Confucianists did not become merely a willing instrument of government policy. Confucius himself never held political office for long, so he was definitely an outsider in his own lifetime, in contrast to the picture which Voltaire gives of him. Later on, some five hundred years after his death, when he was revered by the government, even if his principles often received only lip service, he was elevated to the status of a god and was worshipped as part of the Chinese pantheon. So Voltaire's picture of his place in Chinese culture is not very accurate.

Next we have a statement of Voltaire setting forth in more aggressive terms the contrast between Confucianism and Christianity. "Worship God and practice justice—this is the sole religion of the Chinese *literati.* . . . O Thomas Aquinas, Scotus, Bonaventure, Francis, Dominic, Luther, Calvin, canons of Westminster, have you anything better? For four thousand years this religion, so simple and so noble, has endured in absolute integrity; and it is probable that it is much more ancient." (from *God and Mankind*, 1769).

Confucius lived about 2300 years before Voltaire, so the latter is obviously inflating the period of Confucian dominance of Chinese culture. Moreover, for several hundred years after Confucius, there were intense conflicts between Chinese sages belonging to different

---

[13]Voltaire, *The Philosophy of History* (Philosophical Library, 1965), pp. 85-86.

schools of thought; Legalists, Moists, and Taoists, to mention only the most prominent. The object of each of them was to influence or determine the policies which the imperial government should follow. The Taoists, who were much more mystical in their worldview than the Confucianists, were often bitter in their denunciation of the latter. Christopher Dawson speaks of "their criticism of the artificial character of Confucian ethics, their hostility to the niceties of ceremonial etiquette and their ridicule of the Confucian cult of the precedents of antiquity."

> They compared the efforts of the disciples of Confucius to restore the ancient usages to an attempt to dress up a monkey in the robes of one of the princes of antiquity. The monkey remains a monkey, and the fine robes only accentuate its absurdity. Above all they condemned the futile optimism of the pedants who attempted to restore the golden age by external means.
> Chaung Tzu, one of the greatest of the early Taoists, writes "The wise men have squared up the empire with the ax and the saw. They have applied the hammer and the chisel to men's morals." And what is the result? "Today we see the corpses of the condemned piled up in heaps, those who carry the cangue pass in long files, everywhere one sees men condemned to different punishments. And amidst all these atrocities, among the handcuffs, the shackles and the instruments of torture, the disciples of Confucius and Mo Tzu stand on their toes to look important, and turn up their sleeves complacently in admiration for their work."[14]

This contemporary critic of early Confucian China provides quite a different picture from the one which Voltaire gives us. Moreover, the disagreement between different theological schools in Christendom to which Voltaire makes reference, including the conflicts between Catholics and Protestants, has its parallel in the ideological conflict between different schools of Chinese philosophy.

Where religion as such is concerned, Buddhism, from the third to the ninth centuries A.D., had a much more powerful influence than Confucianism on Chinese society, and this often included influence on the poets and *literati* as well. And when Confucianism was gradually restored to a position of preeminence, it was no longer the original philosophy of Confucius, but incorporated large   elements from Buddhism and Taoism. Of the resulting Neo-Confucian philosophy,

---

[14]Christopher Dawson, *Religion and Culture* (Sheed & Ward 1948), p. 168.

created by Chu Hsi (1130-1200), René Grousset, French historian of Chinese culture, points out:

> The whole synthesis has been so well thought out by a powerful intellect that the completed chain unrolls with an impressive scientific rigor.... The material, which in fact comes from varied sources, has been so efficiently cemented together by Chu Hsi that the final edifice shows no sign of crack or fissure.
>
> It was, however, something of a prison, from which the Chinese intellect was able only with difficulty to escape.... His doctrine, which eventually became a sort of official positivism, barred the way to further speculation, plunged the mandarinate into materialism and routine, and was largely responsible for the ossification of Chinese philosophy between the thirteenth and twentieth centuries.[15]

Now, if this is the later history of Confucianism in Chinese culture, how did it come about that Voltaire and the other *philosophes* were so easily able to base their case upon such a distortion of the reality of China? For the answer to that question, we must look to the French Catholics themselves, and especially to the reports sent back by the Jesuit missionaries working in China in the seventeenth and the early eighteenth centuries. The Jesuits had portrayed the Chinese scholars as possessed of a wisdom based on natural law, and had seen Christianity as coming to China to perfect the products of natural reason by adding to it the fruits of supernatural revelation. But the Jesuits had drawn too optimistic a picture of the actual Chinese condition, and had not given enough attention to the power of evil, error, and superstition in Chinese society. Moreover, they had tended to ignore the effects of Buddhism and Taoism, which exercised so powerful an influence on the religious consciousness of the Chinese people. Of the importance of the Jesuits for the Enlightenment view of China, John K. Fairbanks writes:

> The favorable picture of Cathay so brilliantly sketched by the Jesuit letters of the seventeenth century from Peking, tended to show that virtuous conduct, in many ways adequate to Christian standards, could be achieved without revealed religion. This afforded a basis for the separation of morality and religion as sought

---

[15]René Grousset, *The Rise and Splendour of the Chinese Empire* (Univ. of California Press, 1958), pp. 220-1.

by the Enlightenment. The translation of the Confucian classics into Latin at Paris in 1687 provided textual evidence.[16]

Consequently the *philosophes*, who had fixed their vision only on this world and paid little attention to the life to come, were able to say that if the Chinese had created such an ideal civilization based on nature and reason, who needs anything more? For the *philosophes*, the teachings of Christian Revelation were not necessary for either intellectual achievement or social concord, as the example of China so clearly showed. Hence, let us adopt the same religion of a simplified Deism which the Chinese *literati* also believed in, and forget all the unnecessary complexities of Christian theology. This was essentially, however, a utilitarian view of religion, a bourgeois reduction of its transcendent character in order to serve social purposes. In consequence, eighteenth century Deism was an artificial construction which had no spiritual life of its own and could offer no real inspiration through its teachings.

As European scholars gained a more exact knowledge of Chinese society and culture, the idealized picture which Voltaire draws for us became more and more untenable. It was now recognized that the elements in Chinese history which we have noted above, based on the work of recent scholars, are essential to a true understanding of China and of her place in world history. It is significant that René Grousset, great French scholar, whose work we have quoted from above, gives us the results of a more profound examination of Chinese thought and culture than the partisanship of Voltaire ever allowed him to achieve. Even as Voltaire idealized China, his portrayal of her history was quite superficial and was notably lacking in spiritual penetration. In contrast to this, the spiritual elements in Chinese culture are brought to the fore in the volume by Christopher Dawson, entitled *Religion and Culture*, from which we have quoted above.

---

[16]John K. Fairbank, *The United States and China* (Harvard Univ. Press, 1958), p. 114.

7

Edmund Burke Versus Jean Jacques Rousseau on the Social Contract in History

Forcing Men To Be Free

In our preceding chapter we presented the typical Enlightenment view of the Middle Ages, especially as expressed in the thought of Voltaire; and we identified certain basic features of the Enlightenment conception of history. But we have not yet mentioned the thinker whose ideas found realization in the later and more radical phases of the French Revolution: Jean Jacques Rousseau. It was he and his ideas which gave a dynamic force to the Revolution; it is said that Robespierre, for example, always had a copy of the Social Contract by his bedside; and his attitude to Rousseau, from the age of fifteen onward, was one of near idolatry. If Voltaire cleared the ground by means of his damaging criticism of existing social institutions, Rousseau provided the blueprint by means of which a new social edifice was to be constructed.

What, then, were some of Rousseau's key ideas which related to a concept of history? First, we might note his agreement with the Enlightenment view of the Middle Ages:

> ... [T]he inhabitants of that part of the world [i.e., Europe], which now makes so great a figure in knowledge, were plunged, some centuries ago, into a state which was worse than utter ignorance. A certain school jargon, more despicable than ignorance itself, had usurped the name of knowledge, and opposed an almost invincible obstacle to its restoration; a revolution became necessary to lead people back into common sense.[1]

As other features of his view of history, we should note Rousseau's belief in mankind's freedom from social bonds in a hypothetical state of

---

[1] Jean Jacques Rousseau, *A Discourse on the Arts and Sciences*, Part I.

nature before the rise of society. He felt that social institutions had enslaved men—"Man is born free, and everywhere he is in chains"; and he offered a hope for the restoration of the individual's freedom in a society based upon his politics of "the social contract." Yet this social contract was a formula for the complete sovereignty of the State over the citizens, and thus provided a theoretical justification for totalitarianism. It involved the idea of "forcing men to be free" by subordinating them wholly to the community. One observes here the kind of liberal justification for illiberal measures which is so much a feature of modern politics, both in democratic and in Marxist countries. Here is Rousseau's statement of the case for imposing "freedom":

> These clauses, rightly understood, are reducible to one only, viz., *the total alienation to the whole community of each associate with all his rights.* This is because in the first place, since each gives himself up entirely, the conditions are equal for all; and, the conditions being equal for all, no one has any interest in making them burdensome to others. (Emphasis added.)
>
> Further, the alienation being made without reserve, the union is as perfect as it can be, and an individual associate can no longer claim anything. . . .
>
> In order, then, that the social pact may not be a vain formulary, it tacitly includes this engagement, which can alone give force to the others, that whoever refuses to obey the general will shall be constrained to do so by the whole body; which means nothing else than that he shall be forced to be free; for such is the condition which, uniting every citizen to his native land, guarantees him from all personal dependence, a condition that insures the control and working of the political machine.[2]

Rousseau also traced back the ills which at present afflict human society, to the time when man, breaking out of the state of nature, first instituted private property; and he saw the State as merely the means by which the rich can protect themselves in the possession of the property they had thus gained.

> The first person who, having enclosed a piece of ground, bethought himself of saying, "This is mine," and found people simple enough to believe him, was the real founder of civil society.

---

[2]*The Social Contract* Book I, Chapters 6 and 7 in *Ideal Empires and Republics*, (1901). Emphasis added.

> From how many crimes, battles and murders, from how many
> horrors and misfortunes would not that man have saved mankind,
> who should have pulled up the stakes, or filled up the ditch, crying
> out to his fellows, "Beware of listening to this impostor; you are
> undone if you once forget that the fruits of the Earth belong to us
> all, and that the Earth itself belongs to nobody. . . ."
>   Such was, or may well have been, the origin of society and law,
> which bound new fetters on the poor, and gave new powers to the
> rich.[3]

After describing how the rich persuaded the poor to join in a
common association of force for the protection of property (this is
Rousseau's view of government), which must necessarily be to the poor's
disadvantage, Rousseau concludes with words which are in fact
prophetic of the result of his own ideology, and that of Marxism, when
these have been used to establish revolutionary governments which
promise the poor freedom and plenty: "All ran headlong to their chains,
in hopes of securing their liberty"[4]

In his view of human nature, Rousseau held that man is naturally
good, and consequently, that all the evils men practice today are simply
the result of the corrupting influence of social institutions upon the
human heart. Here is Rousseau's idea of the effects of society upon
mankind: "We may admire human society as much as we please; it will
be none the less true that it necessarily leads men to hate each other in
proportion as their interests clash, and to do one another apparent
services, while they are really doing every imaginable mischief."[5] Here,
and in his account of the origin of private property and its effects on
society, we have the essentials of society as class struggle, set forth
almost a century before Marx.

Rousseau believes that a kind of rational Deism should be the civil
religion, to serve as the cement which holds the society together and
gives sanction to social obligations. He makes the following explanation
of what it is to consist of and how it should be maintained:

> The dogmas of civil religion ought to be simple, few in number,
> stated with precision, and without explanations or commentaries.
> The existence of the Deity, powerful, wise, beneficent, prescient,

---

[3]Jean Jacques Rousseau, *Discourse on Inequality.*
[4]*Ibid.*
[5]*Ibid.*

and bountiful, the life to come, the happiness of the just, the punishment of the wicked, the sanctity of the social contract and of the laws; these are the positive dogmas. As for the negative dogmas, I limit them to one only, that is, intolerance; it belongs to the creeds which we have excluded.

Yet in the paragraph immediately preceding this one in *The Social Contract,* Rousseau has said:

Without having power to compel any one to believe them, the sovereign may banish from the State whoever does not believe them; it may banish him *not as impious, but as unsociable, as incapable of sincerely loving law and justice* and of sacrificing at need his life to his duty. *But if any one, after publicly acknowledging these dogmas, behaves like an unbeliever in them, he should be punished with death; he has committed the greatest of crimes, he has lied before the laws.*[6]

One assumes that this is merely part of the State's forcing the individual to be free, but without the use of any such negative dogma as intolerance, of course. That indeed is "part of the cults we have rejected."

One further point might be noted about Rousseau's civil religion, which links it with the general Enlightenment view of religion as a means to social order. In Rousseau's civil religion, mankind is not subordinated to God, as in authentic religion, but rather the belief in God becomes a mere social convenience, a means of keeping society running properly. This utilitarian attitude concerning belief in God cuts at the very root of any genuine religious feeling.

The most important contemporary response to Rousseau's view of the political order is to be found in Edmund Burke's *Reflections on the French Revolution,* published in 1790, twelve years after Rousseau's death. Burke's response to Rousseau is not so much a refutation of particular points as it is the presentation of an entirely different view of man and society, and thus of the function and purposes of government. Burke is thoroughly in disagreement with any form of thinking based on utopian premises. He remarks on the way in which the future can always be drawn upon as a blank check, in order to justify any kind of

---

[6]*The Social Contract,* Book IV, Chap. 8 in *Ideal Empires and Republics,* (1901), p. 124. Emphasis added.

irresponsible destruction in the present:

> Rage and frenzy will pull down more in half an hour than prudence, deliberation, and foresight can build up in a hundred years. The errors and defects of old establishments are visible and palpable. It calls for little ability to point them out; and where absolute power is given, it requires but a word wholly to abolish the vice and the establishment together. . . . To make everything the reverse of what they have been is quite as easy as to destroy. No difficulties occur in what has never been tried. Criticism is almost baffled in discovering the defects of what has not existed; and eager enthusiasm and cheating hope have all the wide field of imagination in which they may expatiate with little or no opposition.[7]

Writing in 1790—one year after the French Revolution began, Burke already sees that revolution as having the nature of a religious war against the common beliefs of Christendom:

> We cannot, if we would, delude ourselves about the true state of this dreadful contest. *It is a religious war.* It includes in its object, undoubtedly, every other interest of society as well as this; but this is the principal and leading feature. It is through this destruction of religion that our enemies propose the accomplishment of all their other views. . . . This religious war is not a controversy between sect and sect, as formerly, but a war against all sects and all religions.[8]

In connection with what he sees as the goal toward which the French Revolution is ultimately tending, Burke develops an analysis of the psychology of atheism:

> They who do not love religion hate it. The rebels to God perfectly abhor the Author of their being. They hate Him "with all their heart, with all their mind, with all their soul, and with all their strength." He never presents Himself to their thoughts but to menace and alarm them. They cannot strike the sun out of Heaven, but they are able to raise a smoldering smoke that obscures Him from their own eyes. Not being able to revenge themselves on God,

---

[7]Edmund Burke, *Reflections on the Revolution in France* (Reprinted in *Burke's Politics* ed. by Ross J. Hoffman and Paul Levack, Alfred Knoff, 1949), p. 348.

[8]*Ibid., p.* 448.

they have a delight in vicariously defacing, degrading, torturing, and tearing in pieces His image in man.[9]

Edmund Burke and Jean-Jacques Rousseau

In our previous section we discussed some of Jean-Jacques Rousseau's ideas as representative of the ideology of the French Revolution in its later, more radical development; and we noted a few of the ideas which Edmund Burke had voiced about that same Revolution. We should now like to present Burke's view of the character of Rousseau, and the key importance of Rousseau's influence on the objectives pursued by the leaders of the Revolution. More than any other Enlightenment thinker, Rousseau, in Burke's view, was the source of what was happening in France during the revolutionary period. Here is a passage from Burke in which he speaks of the open admiration for Rousseau among the leaders of the revolutionary National Assembly:

> Everyone knows that there is a great dispute amongst their leaders which of them is the best representative of Rousseau. In truth, they all resemble him. His blood they transfuse into their minds and into their manners. Him they study; him they meditate; him they turn over in all the time they can spare from the laborious mischief of the day or the debauches of the night. Rousseau is their canon of holy writ; in his life he is their canon of Polycletus; he is their standard picture of perfection. To this man and this writer, as a pattern to authors and to Frenchmen, the foundries of Paris are now running for statues, with the kettles of their poor and the bells of their churches.[10]

Since Rousseau visited England for a certain period in the 1760's, Burke had had the chance to make a personal estimate of his character. Here is his view of the man:

> As I had good opportunities of knowing his proceedings almost from day to day, he left no doubt on my mind that he entertained no principle, either to influence his heart or to guide his understanding, but *vanity*. With this vice he was possessed in a degree little short of madness [Rousseau went mad at the end of his

---

[9]*Ibid.,* p. 467.
[10]*Ibid.,* p. 385.

life some seven or eight years after his visit to England]. It is from the same deranged, eccentric vanity that this, the insane Socrates of the National Assembly, was impelled to publish a mad confession of his mad faults, and to attempt a new sort of glory from bringing, hardly to light the obscure and vulgar vices which we know may sometimes be blended with eminent talents.[11]

Burke then remarks on the incongruity of the admiration offered by the National Assembly to a man who took each of his five children to a foundling asylum as soon as they were born—even though he continued to live, out of wedlock, with the woman who had borne them. And Burke makes ironical comment on the literary moralist whose work overflowed with pious sentiments about universal love, while, in his personal life, he would not show a common parental affection toward his own children.

> He melts with tenderness for those only who touch him by the remotest relation, and then, without one natural pang, casts away . . . and sends his children to the hospital of foundlings. The bear loves, licks, and forms her young: but bears are not philosophers. Vanity, however, finds its account in reversing the train of our natural feelings. Thousands admire the sentimental writer; the affectionate father is hardly known in his parish. . . .
>
> As the relation between parents and children is the first among the elements of vulgar [i.e., of the people, ordinary], natural morality, they erect statues to a wild, ferocious, low-minded, hard-hearted father, of fine general feelings—a lover of his kind, but a hater of his kindred. Your masters reject the duties of this vulgar relation, as contrary to liberty, as not founded in the social compact, and not binding according to the rights of men; because the relation is not, of course, the result of *free election*—never so on the side of the children, not always on the part of the parents.[12]

It is significant, I think, that Burke finds one of the key issues which distinguish the French revolutionaries from the rest of mankind, precisely in this matter of the relationship between parents and children. For having seen in French Jacobinism the extreme development to which the original revolt against the medieval founding fathers of Western civilization could go, he realized the need to reassert tradition through

---

[11]*Ibid.*, p. 386.
[12]*Ibid.*, pp. 387-388.

the values of *pietas* binding together the generations. He points out the danger to which society is subject when respect for the past is ignored or denied:

> But one of the first and most leading principles on which the commonwealth and the laws are consecrated is lest the temporary possessors and life-renters in it, unmindful of what they have received from their ancestors, or of what is due to their posterity, should act as if they were the entire masters; ... by destroying at their pleasure the whole original fabric of their society: hazarding to leave to those who come after them a ruin instead of a habitation, and teaching these successors as little to respect their contrivances as they had themselves respected the institutions of their forefathers ... [T]he whole chain and continuity of the commonwealth would be broken; no one generation could link with the other; men would become little better than flies of a Summer.[13]

We have already seen Rousseau's prescription for his ideal of a totalitarian society, to be achieved by means of his social contract. There is, however, in Rousseau an atomistic conception of the relation of the individual to the community which leads him to hold that society and the state are not something native to man, but can be made and unmade at the will of the individual. This is probably the reason for the rigidity with which he proposes to maintain the terms of the social contract, once it has been brought into being.

Speaking, for example, of the legislator's relationship to the people, Rousseau says:

> He who dares undertake to give institutions to a nation ought to feel himself capable, as it were, of changing human nature; of transforming every individual, who in himself is a complete and independent whole, into part of a greater whole, from which he receives in some manner his life and his being; of altering man's constitution in order to strengthen it; of substituting a social and moral existence for the independent and physical existence which we have all received from nature. In a word, it is necessary to deprive man of his native powers in order to endow him with some which are alien to him, and of which he cannot make use without the aid of other people. The more thoroughly those natural powers are deadened and destroyed, the greater and more durable are the

---

[13]*Ibid.*, p. 316.

acquired powers, the more solid and perfect also are the institutions.[14]

The whole of this passage by Rousseau gives justification to governments to make over human nature into whatever form they wish it to take. To such governments, men and women have no definite enduring nature of their own which sets limits to the power and authority which may be exercised over them. By this charter for radically changing human nature, an idealogy can readily justify the mass starvation of peasants in the Ukraine by the forced collectivization program, the extermination of six million Jews in order to achieve a pure Aryan population, the massacres in Cambodia and in parts of Africa, or the American government's attempt at Cairo to use American financial power to impose a program of wholesale killing of unborn babies on every nation throughout the world.

Burke, on the other hand, sees society and the State as natural to man, as things which derive from the very nature of man's relationship to God and to his fellowmen. Society is not something artificial, not something alien to man which must be slipped over on him by an appeal to individual self-interest which binds fetters where only freedom existed before; it grows out of the very character of man as a social being; and man needs it in order to fulfill himself as a human person. Moreover, his basic social obligations are not arbitrary and self-chosen, but result from the very fact of his participation in society.

> The awful Author of our being is the Author of our place in the order of existence; and . . . having disposed and marshaled us by a Divine tactic, not according to our will, but according to His, He has in and by that disposition virtually subjected us to act the part which belongs to the place assigned us. We have obligations to mankind at large which are not in consequence of any special voluntary pact. They arise from the relation of man to man, and the relation of man to God, which relations are not matters of choice. On the contrary, the force of all the pacts which we enter into with any particular person or number of persons amongst mankind depends upon those prior obligations.[15]

---

[14]*The Social Contract*, Book II, chap. 7, in *Ideal Empires and Republics* (1901), pp. 343.

[15]*Burke's Politics*, pp. 318; 394.

Finally, we might note that Burke adopts a more sympathetic attitude toward Catholicism and the Middle Ages than we would expect from one who admired so greatly the achievements of the "Glorious Revolution" of 1688, which drove the Catholic King James II from the throne, and put in his place his Protestant daughter and her husband. Undoubtedly the threat to all religion posed by the French Revolution had something to do with this; but, on the other hand, Burke was not a representative Protestant. His mother and sister were Catholics, and although he himself had been reared as a Church of England adherent in Ireland, he remained sympathetic throughout his life to the cause of political emancipation of Irish Catholics, and used his influence in Parliament to try to achieve that goal.

With regard to the assumptions on which the Protestant view of English history was based, it is interesting to see Burke denouncing Henry VIII and comparing his spoliation of the English monasteries to the seizure of ecclesiastical properties in France by the revolutionaries. Burke observes:

> The tyrant Harry the Eighth of England, as he ... had not studied in your new schools [i.e., the ideas of the *philosophes*] did not know what an effectual instrument of despotism was to be found in that grand-magazine of offensive weapons, the rights of men ... Had fate reserved him to our times, four technical terms would have done his business and saved him all this trouble [i.e., of trumping up charges against the monasteries and bribing Parliament to accept them]; he needed nothing more than one short form of incantation —*Philosophy, Light, Liberality, the Rights of Men.*[16]

Most striking of all is Burke's defense of the monasteries of France whose property had been seized by the Revolution; for his discussion of their merits takes on a universal character which justifies monasticism as an institution. Burke thus departs from one of the most oft-repeated Protestant charges against the Middle Ages: that the monasteries were refuges for religious hypocrites who wished to hoodwink the people and avoid work. Here is the way Burke speaks of the social importance of the monasteries:

> In the monastic institutions, in my opinion, was found a great

---

[16]*Ibid.*, pp. 326-327.

power for the mechanism of politic benevolence. There were revenues with a public direction; there were men wholly set apart and dedicated to public purposes, without any other than public ties and public principles; men without the possibility of converting the estate of the community into a private fortune; men denied to self-interests, whose avarice is for some community; men to whom personal poverty is honor, and implicit obedience stands in the place of freedom. In vain shall a man look to the possibility of making such things [i.e., monastic institutions] when he wants them. The winds blow as they list. These institutions are the products of enthusiasm; they are the instruments of wisdom.[17]

Because of the immense influence which Burke had upon the development of English political thought and political parties after his death, his abandonment of the older Protestant viewpoint of mingled hostility and contempt for Catholicism must have had an important effect on English attitudes during the nineteenth century. Moreover, Burke's influence was not confined to England, but was widespread on the Continent of Europe during the period of the struggle against Napoleon, and for some time thereafter; and Burke's appeal to the importance of an organic relationship to the national past undoubtedly helped to open up the Middle Ages to more sympathetic attention by Romantic thinkers in both Germany and France.

Edmund Burke and Eighteenth Century England

After two earlier sections in which we presented Edmund Burke's ideas of the need of every society for strong roots in a social tradition, we now have to examine the issue of Burke's view of eighteenth century England. If he was justified in his defense of tradition as necessary for the life of society, was he also justified in looking upon England in the eighteenth century as an outstanding example of the value and achievements of the English political tradition?

Let us approach this question indirectly, by looking first in another direction—to that country in which Burke himself had been born and educated, and of whose social and political ills he was acutely aware—that is, of course, Ireland. He expended himself most generously

---

[17]*Ibid.*, p. 341.

for the cause of Irish Catholic emancipation, for he saw the defects of a political and social arrangement which made the great majority of Irishmen disenfranchised citizens in their own land; and throughout his life he strove to get Parliament and English government officials to correct these abuses. But when it came to England, the country of his adoption, where the results of the "Glorious Revolution" of 1688 had fixed on the English people an economic structure which was strongly oppressive and unjust, Burke was unable to see the realities of the situation he faced.

Because of this, Burke idealized the "Glorious Revolution" and identified it with the basic values of the English political tradition. He was therefore unable to see the great gap which existed between the structure of class oligarchy in eighteenth century England and the protection of the rights of the people at which the genuine English tradition had aimed. There is a contradiction here which threatens to discredit Burke's whole view of tradition—because of the oppression and injustice which prevailed in that society which Burke deemed traditional. It renders his arguments vulnerable to counterattack, and suggests that arguments about tradition are only a concealment for class interest. It is therefore important to disentangle the Burkean argument in favor of tradition from the political and social facts which he used to support it.

It seems to me that Burke speaks too much from the side of Parliament, and assumes that if the power of the king is checked or reduced, the result is a gain for the rights of the people and an increase in governmental responsibility. Whereas it is quite likely that the destruction of the power of the monarch can lead to the dominance of an aristocracy, and the irresponsible use of parliamentary power to maintain class interests. In other words, oligarchy instead of monarchy. And as Chesterton notes, there is no government more selfish than an oligarchy.

We here in the United States are apt to overlook this possibility because, from the beginning, we have had a strong monarchical office in the form of the chef executive—that is, one whose power in government is quite considerable and is indeed modeled in part on what had been the powers of the king in England. It is true, of course, that the American president is limited by the fact of election, and by the checks and balances between the president and other branches of government which have been built into the American system; but the existence of strong presidential power is a very real factor in American history, and its potentialities can be expanded if the president is popular with the people. In other words, there is a focus within the government where popular leadership can be exercised, with the people giving support to the limited monarch for which the Constitution provides. This was lacking in eighteenth century England; and instead a corrupt and self-serving Parliament was the seat of power.

And when George III, in 1760 and thereafter, tried to recover power for the monarchy, he followed the same procedure of buying votes which his parliamentary opponents had done. Whether this was the only way in which he could achieve his aim, the result was to make him largely a manipulator of an oligarchical class system embodied in Parliament. And the loss of the American colonies, due in great part to the policies he had followed, led to the collapse of his attempt to restore the power of the king.

Under any circumstances, the view which modern Catholic writers have had of eighteenth century England, and the "Glorious Revolution" of 1688 which produced it, has not been favorable to the Whig interpretation of history. The latter saw 1688 as the triumph of representative and responsible government over the power of an arbitrary monarchy. This is the view which Burke, as a member of the Whig Party—the party opposed to the power of the king—himself holds. But the Catholic view has almost invariably been Tory—finding in the power of the king a protection for the people against a selfish plutocracy, which latter gained the ascendancy in government by means of the Revolution of 1688. And it sees in the history of eighteenth century England the triumph of mercantilism and the bourgeoisie, in alliance with the nobility who had founded their fortunes on the seizure of the monastery lands two centuries earlier.

G. K. Chesterton even has a conception of English eighteenth century literature which sees some of the greatest figures in that literature as defeated Tories, who were in protest against the rapacity and greed of the new parliamentary masters, now clothed often enough in the robes of aristocracy, but possessed of no real sense of social responsibility. In an article called "Milton and Merry England," Chesterton speaks of the eighteenth century as a time when "the last of the Tories drank wine with Bolingbroke or tea with Johnson." Among the eighteenth century writers whom he identifies as belonging to this group he includes Swift (Chesterton has a most original interpretation of the Yahoos in *Gulliver's Travels* as being a satirical representation of the English plutocracy), Samuel Johnson himself, and Oliver Goldsmith. Following are passages from the Chesterton article in which he refers to the Tory protest in English literature of the eighteenth century:

> For Macaulay and Thackeray and the average of Victorian liberality the Revolution of 1688 was simply an emancipation, the defeat of the Stuarts was simply a downfall of tyranny and superstition; the politics of the eighteenth century were simply a progress leading up to the pure and happy politics of the nineteenth century; freedom slowly broadening down, etc., etc. This makes the attitude of the Tory rebels entirely meaningless; so that the critics in question have been forced to represent some of the greatest Englishmen who ever lived as a mere procession of lunatics and ludicrous eccentrics. But these rebels, right or wrong, can only be understood in relation to the real power against which they were rebelling; ... That power was a positive thing; it was anything but a mere negative emancipation of everybody. It was as definite as the monarchy which it had replaced; for it was an aristocracy which had replaced it. It was the oligarchy of the great Whig families, a very close corporation indeed, having wealth for its essential substance.... And the whole position of these men of letters is that they were denying, and denouncing something which was growing every day in prestige and had, not only the present, but the future on its side. The only thing it had not got on its side was the ancient tradition of the English populace. That populace was being more and more harried by evictions and enclosures, that its old common lands and yeoman freeholds might be added to the enormous estates of the all-powerful aristocracy. One of the Tory rebels has himself made that infamy immortal in the great line of the *Deserted Village*.[18]

Chesterton then refers to the fact that the author of a study of Hilaire Belloc's work in a London magazine had:

> ... used the phrase that Mr. Belloc had been anticipated by Disraeli in his view of England as having evolved into a Venetian oligarchy. The truth is that Disraeli was anticipated by Bolingbroke and the many highly intelligent men who agreed with him, and not least by Goldsmith. The whole view, including the very parallel with Venice, can be found stated with luminous logic and cogency in the Vicar of Wakefield. And Goldsmith attacked the problem entirely from the

---

[18]G.K. Chesterton, *Fancies versus Fads* (Dodd, Mead & Co., 1923), pp. 265-6.

popular side. Nobody can mistake his Toryism for a snobbish submission to a privilege or title: Princes and lords may flourish or may fade—/ A breath can make them, as a breath has made/ But a bold peasantry, their country's pride,/ When once destroyed can never be supplied.

I hope he was wrong; but I sometimes have a horrible feeling that he may have been right.[19]

There is, therefore, a great difference between Burke's view of the "Glorious Revolution" of 1688, and the view of Chesterton and those eighteenth century writers whom he calls upon as his witnesses as to what really happened after that Revolution.

---

[19]*Ibid.*, pp. 272-273.

8

Karl Marx and Christopher Dawson on Capitalism, Christianity, and Communism

A great deal in the modern conservative movement, the libertarian conception of conservatism, is quite incompatible with Catholic thought. This is shown, in one way, by the strong hostility with which a part of the conservative movement regards any criticism of capitalism. It is no doubt a temptation for conservatives, in revulsion against the prostitution of Catholic teaching by so-called Christian Marxists, to adhere strictly to the capitalist system as a defense against the atheism of Communism and its wholesale violation of human rights. Nevertheless the Catholic position, as repeatedly expressed in Papal encyclicals—not only those of recent Popes, but all the way back to Leo XIII—differs sharply from both of these systems; and the fact that Marxism is so thoroughly atheistic and materialist in its worldview, should not lead us blindly to embrace the capitalist ideology as a means for the defense of Christian principles and social justice. We must be prepared to make clear distinctions between Christian principles and the principles which have been a part of the capitalist ethic from its very beginning, and which still prevail when this system has not been subject to restraint by outside forces.

So far as Marx was concerned, Christianity and Catholicism had little importance for the future. They were outmoded survivals from the past, fated to perish with the earlier social order which had given them birth and which had provided the basis for their existence and their influence. Their teachings therefore could be dismissed as irrelevant to the social issues confronting mankind in the great progressive era of the nineteenth century. Dawson describes the attitude of Marx in these terms:

> Catholicism was something quite outside the orbit of Marx's thought. He seems to have regarded it, not as a dangerous rival, but as a dying force which belonged essentially to the past. In his

historical theory Catholicism is bound up with feudalism: it is the ideological reflection of feudal society, and consequently it had little significance for the modern world, save in a few backward regions where the social structure was that of a past age. The real enemy in Marx's eyes was not Catholicism or Christianity, but the power that had, so Marx believed, already dethroned God and set up a purely secular culture and new secular standards of value—the power of Capitalism.[1]

This real enemy, which had to be overcome in order that the economic determinism of Marx's theory of history could usher in the classless society of the Communist future, is spoken of with a great deal of admiration by Marx. As Marx saw the picture, the historical achievements of the bourgeoisie had swept away much from the past with its social traditions, and had now rendered these of little importance. So Marx felt that Capitalism, or bourgeois civilization, as he terms it, was engaged in a common work with Marxism, the former opening the world revolution which Marxism was destined to bring to full completion. In a striking passage from the *Communist Manifesto* of 1848, Marx pays this tribute to the class which was responsible for the growth and development of *laissez-faire* capitalism:

> The bourgeoisie, historically, has played a most revolutionary part. The bourgeoisie has disclosed how it came to pass that the brutal display of vigor in the Middle Ages, which reactionaries so much admire, found its fitting complement in the most slothful indolence. It has been the first to show what man's activity can bring about.   It has accomplished wonders far surpassing Egyptian pyramids, Roman aqueducts, and Gothic cathedrals; it has conducted expeditions that put in the shade all former exoduses of nations and crusades.
>
> The bourgeoisie has subjected the country to the rule of the towns. It has created enormous cities, has greatly increased the urban population as compared with the rural, and has thus rescued a considerable part of the population from the idiocy of rural life. Just as it has made the country dependent on the towns, so it has made barbarian and semi-barbarian countries dependent on the civilized ones, nations of peasants on nations of bourgeois, the East on the West.
>
> The bourgeoisie, during its rule of scarce one hundred years, has created more massive and more colossal productive forces than

---

[1]*Religion and the Modern State* (1935), p. 59.

have all preceding generations together. Subjection of nature's forces to man, machinery, application of chemistry to industry and agriculture, steam-navigation, railways, electric telegraphs, clearing of whole continents for cultivation, canalization of rivers, whole populations conjured out of the ground—what earlier century had even a presentiment that such productive forces slumbered in the lap of social labor?[2]

Dawson himself had never looked upon the capitalist ideology with favor, for he saw it as the fruit of an abandonment of the Christian principles which were accepted as the moral basis for both society and economics when Europe was still professedly Christian. The revolt against Christianity which took place at the time of the European Enlightenment of the eighteenth century was not restricted simply to the realm of philosophy and religion; it was at the same time a revolt against Christian teaching governing the economic order. The right of a man to be his own master in the sphere of religion, leading either to atheism, or to a Deism in which man rather than God decided what the tenets of religion should be, and which therefore did not depend upon a Revelation guarded and explained by the Church, was at the same time the right of the man of property to do whatever he wanted with his money. He was not to be restrained or restricted in its use by principles derived from the moral order. Economics became a self-governing area of life and could set up its own laws, as with the famous Iron Law of Wages postulated by David Ricardo in the early nineteenth century. This law claimed that, if you paid the worker above a subsistence wage, you were only preparing for the starvation of future generations of workingmen. For the worker would use this amount over and above subsistence to beget more children, and the resulting surplus of labor on the market, when those children came of working age (which was usually 9 or 10) would lead to unemployment and hence starvation for those not able to find work. So, no matter how much you as a Christian or as a humanitarian felt sympathy for the wretched plight of the worker, you must not allow that sympathy to lead you to interfere with the inescapable laws of economics. For you would only bring the worker to a worse condition than the one in which he now existed.

We too easily forget that such economic beliefs were central to the ideology of early capitalism. We therefore assume that capitalism is a

---

[2]Karl Marx, *The Communist Manifesto*, (1848), quoted in *Ibid.*, pp. 61-62.

kind of morally neutral system for producing goods, that has no ideology attached to it. In fact, of course, no system of economics or politics, or of any other sphere of human endeavor, can be morally neutral. It is governed by certain basic ideas and values, since man is a value-bearing animal. And those ideas and values either recognize the supremacy of the moral order and hence the subordination of economics and politics, or any other area, to that order or else they assert their independence of morality and religion. In the latter case, they try to push religious and moral principles off into some corner where they will apply only to a limited part of man's life and not to the forum or the market place or to society in general.

Let us first consider Dawson's distinction of the different meanings of the word capitalism:

> The fact is the word Capitalism is commonly used to cover two entirely different things and consequently is responsible for an endless series of misunderstandings and confusions of thought. In the strict sense it means the use of private wealth for the purpose of economic production, whether by the individual as in early times, or cooperatively, as in the joint-stock company which is the characteristic form of capitalism in modern times.
>
> Both these forms of capitalism are accepted by Catholic social theory as lawful and just, and in this sense alone it can be said that the Church approves of capitalism. In the current use of the word, however, Capitalism stands for much more than this. Indeed it stands for so much that it is almost impossible to give an exact definition of it. Broadly speaking it may be described as the economic aspect of that philosophy of liberal individualism which was the religion of the nineteenth century and which found its political expression in parliamentary democracy.
>
> Now this creed—and the social and economic order which arose from it—is entirely inconsistent with Catholic principles and was in fact the most dangerous enemy and rival that the Catholic Church had to meet in modern times. It is a philosophy of separation and irresponsibility which breaks up the moral organism of society into a chaos of competitive individualism. It denies the sovereignty of the moral law in the economic world, the principle of authority in politics, and the existence of an objective divine truth in religion. It makes self-interest the supreme law in economics, the will of the majority the sovereign power in the State, and private opinion the only arbiter in religious matters.[3]

---

[3]Dawson, *op. cit.*, pp. 132-133.

Moreover, Dawson sees a strong cause-and-effect sequence between the assertion of the supremacy of economic factors in society in *laissez-faire* capitalism and the more thorough economic determinism of Karl Marx's theory of society. Marxism brought to a more complete realization the implicit but unorganized materialism of economic Liberalism. In addition, early capitalism provided the social basis for the growth of Marxism by the wretchedness and misery which capitalists inflicted on the working class, while telling them that unalterable economic laws prevented them from ever improving their condition. This was a counsel of despair, and under these circumstances it is understandable that Marx and Engels found in the condition of the working classes in England the basis for their theory of social revolution. That revolution was thought to be coming in the near future, with the overthrow of capitalism by a working class which, as Marx put it in *The Communist Manifesto* of 1848, "had nothing to lose but its chains."

So what the Catholic Church found herself faced with by the latter part of the nineteenth century was not one, but two different enemies to Christian morality and Christian principles of society. On the one hand, there was the predominant capitalist system with its rugged individualism and its atomization of society into social particles, each seeking to maximize his own profit at the expense of everyone else, with the capitalist succeeding at this far better than the worker because of his greater degree of initiative and enterprise—as the capitalist ideology gave the reason for the stark contrast between rich and poor. And, on the other hand, there were the doctrines of Marxian socialism, gaining ever-increasing influence, not only among the workers, but also among the bourgeois intellectuals. These teachings replaced the war of individuals against each other in the competitive ideology of capitalism by the war of the classes against each other in the historical determinism of Marxism. Individualism was to be replaced by class solidarity, but the domination of society by economic motives and economic warfare was retained in Marxism, and in fact intensified.

Thus Marx writes concerning the meaning of history and the principles which govern it, and relates this to what he believes to be the unique character of the present epoch:

The history of all hitherto existing society is the history of class struggles, Freeman and slave, patrician and plebeian, lord and serf, guildmaster and journeyman, in a word, oppressor and oppressed, stood in constant opposition to one another, carried on uninterrupted, now hidden, now open fight, a fight that each time ended, either in a revolutionary re-constitution of society at large, or in the common ruin of the contending classes....

The modern bourgeois society that has sprouted from the ruins of feudal society, has not done away with class antagonisms. It has but established new classes, new conditions of oppression, new forms of struggle in place of the old ones.

Our epoch, the epoch of the bourgeoisie, possesses, however, this distinctive feature: it has simplified the class antagonisms. Society as a whole is more and more splitting up into two great hostile camps . . . : bourgeoisie and proletariat.[4]

When Leo XIII wrote his famous encyclical, *Rerum Novarum,* in 1891, he was thus forced to fight a war on two fronts, even as we must still do today. On the one hand, he must correct the errors and speak out against the evils of *laissez-faire* capitalism and its worship of economic success. And on the other front, he must expose the errors to be found in the more recent ideology of Socialism, which was being presented as the answer to all the ills and injustices of the capitalist system.

By the time that Pius XI wrote his encyclical *Quadregesimo Anno* in 1931, the 40th anniversary of the publication of *Rerum Novarum,* Marxism had become established as the reigning theory and practice of government in the largest of the European States—Soviet Russia—and was seeking to export its idea of world revolution. At the same time the claims of *laissez-faire* capitalism to produce economic abundance had suffered a grievous setback through the worldwide economic depression, which began with the collapse of the stock market in the United States in October 1929. The claims of Marxist Communism were thus being given much more attention in capitalist countries than had been true when capitalism was flourishing. Now that it seemed possible that capitalism had received a mortal blow, many thinkers and intellectuals were turning to Communism to provide society and economic life with the kind of principles they needed.

When Dawson wrote the chapters in *Religion and the Modern State* some three to four years after *Quadregesimo Anno,* the capitalist

---

[4]*The Communist Manifesto* (1848).

economy had still not recovered from the depression. Moreover, National Socialism had taken over Germany in 1933 and claimed to be a working alternative to Communism, while Fascism in Italy was trying to organize society on the basis of corporative bodies which should be completely subordinate to the State.

First, let us note Dawson's idea of what the Catholic attitude should be when confronted with the two ideologies of *laissez-faire* capitalism and Marxian Communism, neither of them in accord with Christian principles for the social order:

> Actually the Church regards the organized materialism of the Socialist State as a more formidable enemy than the unorganized materialism of Capitalist society, since the former is more exclusive and more intolerant of spiritual independence. Nevertheless this does not mean that she is prepared to accept the Capitalist ideal as legitimate or as morally defensible. Catholicism condemns the Capitalist principle of competitive individualism as well as the Socialist principle of class war. Society is not a mere collection of irresponsible individuals, nor is it a machine for the production of wealth; it is a spiritual organism in which each individual and every class and profession has its own function to fulfill and its own rights and duties in relation to the whole.[5]

Or again, with a stronger emphasis on the menace of Marxism to Christian society:

> Today the social revolution is no longer merely an ideal, it is a fact that rules the lives of millions of men and women. Over a considerable part of the globe from the Baltic to the Pacific it has established a new order, an order that denies God and the human soul not in theory but in grim reality.
>
> Now whatever system of government Catholics may favor it must be one that will protect society from any revolutionary movement that would lead to the establishment of this anti-Christian order. For even a dictatorship which would deprive us of our political liberty would be preferable to an order which denies those fundamental spiritual rights without which human life loses its *raison d'être*.[6]

Is it any wonder that conservatives with a strong sense of the

---

[5]Dawson, *op cit.*, pp. 133-134.
[6]*Ibid.*, pp. 131-132.

reality of what Marxist Communism means for the extinction of human liberty and an assault upon Divine truth, are tempted to fall back upon a wholehearted defense of capitalism? Nevertheless, as the Popes have consistently taught, this is not the way to the establishment of a society which is morally justifiable in the eyes of God. We must continue to work for the Christian reconstruction of the social order, and not allow the rival systems of Marxism and *laissez-faire* capitalism to become substitutes for that.

As a means to recognizing the dangers inherent in the ideology which gave birth to economic Liberalism, let us see Dawson's account of the origins of modern capitalism:

> Rousseau was profoundly hostile to the apologists of luxury, like Mandeville and Voltaire, and to the representatives of economic liberalism such as Turgot and Adam Smith. Here he was on the side not only of conservative critics of the Enlightenment . . but still more of the champions of orthodoxy like the Abbe Prigent and Pere Hyacinthe Gasquet, who maintained the traditional Catholic doctrine with regard to usury and the rights of the poor. As Groethuysen has shown with copious illustrations from Eighteenth- century preachers and theologians [i.e., in *The Bourgeois*, subtitled "Catholicism vs. Capitalism in Eighteenth Century France"], the Church down to the eve of the Revolution maintained a stiff opposition to the capitalist philosophy and the economic view of life which were already triumphant in Protestant England and Holland. For behind the open battle of the Enlightenment which was being fought out on the ground of philosophy and freedom of thought, there was a deeper and more obscure struggle being waged by the bourgeois spirit, not only against the traditional order, which limited the freedom of commerce and bound industry within the narrow frontiers of the Corporation or Guild, but also against the religious tradition which idealized poverty and condemned the acquisitive and competitive spirit which was inseparable from the new commercial society.[7]

Dawson does not deny that there was an element of humanitarian idealism in this Liberal ideology which had helped to free business from social restraints and advanced the cause of *laissez-faire* capitalism. But he sees that ideal element, to which he refers several times in the course of his various works, as essentially an inheritance from the Christian

---

[7]*The Gods of Revolution*, p. 137.

culture of the past, from which indeed Liberalism took it over without acknowledging its debt. And these ideals are essentially transitional, for they cannot survive the passing of Christian culture, any more than the flower can survive when cut off from its root. As an illustration of that, in our own time, in latter twentieth century America, in a society founded upon the ideals of the Liberal Enlightenment, we see the political acceptance of the killing of the unborn child, the putting to death of the elderly, the degradation of the human person by means of commercially presented violence and the spread of pornography. All these are now considered part of the American way of life. But central to all of this anti-human movement is the loss of a sense of the transcendent, of the idea of an overarching spiritual order which governs man's actions and to which his social life must conform, if society is not to run blind and plunge mankind into the abyss.

In *Religion and the Modern State*, Dawson notes that it was the element of Liberal idealism which Marx condemned in his analysis of bourgeois culture because he regarded it as essentially hypocritical, seeing it as a facade to conceal the reality of exploitation which lay behind it. For Christians on the other hand, Dawson points out, "We may look on the faith of the nineteenth century in liberal ideals, in freedom and justice and humanity and progress, as a redeeming trait in the harsh and unlovely features of bourgeois civilization," even while we "condemn the ruthless subordination of human life to economic ends and the wholesale secularization of culture."[8]

In one of the most striking passages in his writing, Dawson shows how the historical development from the Enlightenment to twentieth century capitalist society has meant the triumph of hedonism at the expense of the moral ideals which originally inspired the movement of Liberal thought. It is noteworthy that, in this passage of sixty years ago Dawson anticipates the ideas of the ecologists and the environmentalists of our own time, and also sees capitalism as becoming essentially a consumer culture—a theme to which John Paul II has referred in several of his addresses.

> ... [T]oday its ideals [i.e., of the Enlightenment] are being swallowed up by the subversive forces which it has itself liberated. The idealism of the great Liberal thinkers ended in the materialism

---

[8]*Religion and the Modern State*, p. 64.

of the acquisitive capitalist society against which the conscience of the modern world is in revolt. What we are suffering from is the morbid growth of a selfish civilization which has no end beyond itself—a monstrous cancer that destroys the face of nature and eats into the heart of humanity. As in the days of ancient Rome, but on a far larger scale, men have made themselves the masters of this world, and find themselves left with nothing but their own sterile lusts. For this "leisure civilization" in which the people sit down to eat and to drink and rise up to play is the dark world which has turned its face from God and from which God's face is hidden. It is terrible not only on account of its emptiness but because there is a positive power of evil waiting to fill the void, like the unclean spirit in the parable that came out of the waste places into the empty soul.[9]

After referring to the slavery of lust which overcame the leisure civilization of the ancient Roman Empire, Dawson adds:

At the present day we feel this slavery in its economic rather than in its sensual aspect. Nevertheless the Kingdom of Mammon and the Kingdom of Belial are one, and it matters little which of them is the nominal master, so long as the world is theirs.
It is the horror of this empty and sterile world far more than any economic hardship or political injustice that is driving men to revolutionary action. Nevertheless, the materialism of the Communist state is but the same thing in another form. It may relieve the tension on the individual by merging his consciousness in that of the mass, but at the same time it shuts out all hope of escape and thus completes his imprisonment.[10]

Now let us take a more extended look at Dawson's conception of Marxism. Before discussing his critique of the Marxist theory, let us first give his description of what Marxist practice was like, in the Soviet Russia of the early to mid-1930's. This was the time of the forced collectivization of agriculture, especially in the Ukraine, which Stalin later told Churchill resulted in ten million deaths among the *kulaks,* the so-called rich peasants. In Stalinist terms, this meant anyone who owned a farm and did not want to hand it over to the Soviet collective and become a hired hand on the State-run farm. Of this period Dawson writes, "In Russia, however, there is no such contradiction between the

---

[9]*Ibid.*, p. 143.
[10]*Ibid.*, p. 144.

State and the Communist party . . . The State has become nothing more than the instrument of the party, and the power of the party is shown by the Assyrian ruthlessness with which it has in the last few years destroyed the independent life of the Russian peasantry at the cost of an incalculable amount of human suffering."[11]

Then, noting the way in which at this very time of wholesale killing of the peasants by Stalin, the leaders of Liberal thought in the West were promoting the cause of Communism and seeing in it the ideal society of the future, Dawson declares:

> . . . [T]hey rally to Communism, because in spite of its cruelties and intolerances, it seems modern and progressive and anti-religious. As Mr. Malcolm Muggeridge has pointed out with such biting emphasis in his Winter in Moscow, all those Platonic admirers of Communism from the West find in Russia something that they can understand—a State run on advanced lines by advanced people; whereas the victims of the Soviet system, the wretched peasants and underprivileged workers and priests, are people of the underworld with whom they have nothing in common, and whose sufferings seem distant and unreal.[12]

With regard to the Marxist ideology, Dawson's first criticism of it has as its target the economic determinism on which Marx's theory is founded:

> He [i.e. Marx] condemned the whole humanistic morality and culture as bourgeois, and accepted the machine, not only as the basis for economic activity, but as the explanation of the mystery of life itself. The mechanical processes of economic life are the ultimate realities of history and human life. All other things—religion, art, philosophy, spiritual life—stand on a lower plane of reality; they are a dream world of shadows cast on the sleeping mind by the physical processes of the real world of matter and mechanism. Hence Marxism may be seen as the culminating point of the modern tendency to explain that which is specifically human in terms of something else. For the Marxian interpretation of history is in fact nothing but an explaining away of history. It professes to guide us to the heart of the problem, and it merely unveils a void.[13]

---

[11]*Ibid.*, p. 66.

[12]*Ibid.*, pp. 67-68.

[13]Christopher Dawson, *Christianity and the New Age* (Sophia Institute Press, 1985), pp. 12-13.

But if indeed Marxist theory has at its heart this metaphysical emptiness, why has it had such an attraction for so many people in the West, including especially the intellectuals? For it is the latter, far more than the proletariat, who have been responsible for the rise and spread of Communism, as we see in the case of Marx and Engels, Lenin and Trotsky, and numerous other advocates and disciples of Marx among the intelligentsia of the West. What element in Marxism recommends itself to them, if they are not motivated by a nihilistic rejection of life itself? While not ignoring the influence of nihilism—the turning against society in a blind impulse of destruction, because social life has lost all ultimate meaning with its loss of its spiritual dimension—Dawson believes that another reason for the appeal of Communism is that it links together economic determinism with an apocalyptic element of moral denunciation. This latter element is incompatible with the economic interpretation of history. For if all other elements in society are ultimately reducible to economic factors and have no real existence independent of the economic determinism of which they are but the reflection, then this moral indignation against injustice and exploitation has no more validity that the bourgeois ideals of freedom and humanity which the Marxists so bitterly denounce. According to Dawson, Marx himself inserted this moral element into his economic interpretation of history, however much it contradicted it, because his ultimate inspiration was Messianic, and he transposed into secular terms the Jewish Prophetic conception of history. Dawson speaks of the historical environment which had kept alive the strength of apocalyptic expectations in the Jewish communities of Germany and Eastern Europe in the centuries prior to the emancipation of the Jews:

> The Messianic hope, the belief in the coming destruction of the Gentile power and the deliverance of Israel were to the Jew not mere echoes of Biblical tradition; they were burnt into the very fiber of his being by centuries of thwarted social impulse in the squalid Ghettos of Germany and Poland. And in the same way the social dualism between the people of God and the Gentile world power, was a fact of bitter personal experience of which even the most insensitive was made conscious in the hundred petty annoyances of Ghetto life.[14]

---

[14]*Religion and the Modern State*, pp. 86-87.

After the emancipation took place, Marx's father became a Christian convert and served as a minor official under the Prussian government, and Karl Marx himself was able to attend German universities and gain an intimate acquaintance with German philosophic thought of that period. Dawson writes of him:

> He had lost his membership of the Jewish community, for he was the son of a Christian convert, but he could not deny his Jewish heredity and his Jewish spirit and become the obedient servant of the Gentile civilization as his father had done. His whole soul revolted against the standards and ideals of the petty bourgeois society in which he had been brought up; yet he had tasted the forbidden fruit of the new knowledge and he could not go back to the Talmud any more than he could return to the Ghetto. The only way of escape that remained open to him was by the revolutionary tradition, which was then at the height of its prestige and popularity. In this he found satisfaction at once for his conscious hostility to bourgeois civilization and for the deeper revolt of his repressed religious instincts.... For Karl Marx was of the seed of the prophets, in spite of his contempt for anything that savored of mysticism or religious idealism.[15]

Thus there is in Communism a strong spiritual element which has no basis in the governing principles of Marx's philosophy and in his interpretation of history in purely economic terms. As Dawson has observed:

> This strange paradox of a godless religion and a materialist spirituality has its basis in the internal contradictions of the revolutionary tradition of which Communism is the final product. For that tradition unconsciously drew its dynamic force from religious sources, though it denied and rejected them in its rationalized consciousness. In the same way the Marxian theory of history, for all its materialism, is dependent to a degree that Marx himself never suspected, on the antecedent religious view of history which had been formed by the Jewish and Christian traditions.[16]

Consequently, for Western intellectuals who hold to the idea that religion is merely the opiate of the masses, and who believe that a

---

[15]*Ibid.*, p. 86.
[16]*Ibid.*, pp. 70-71.

secularist worldview is the only intelligent explanation of reality, the appeal of Marxism comes with peculiar force. For it allows them to appease their spiritual hunger while still denying the fact of its existence, and to reject any transcendent spiritual reality which could satisfy it. Dawson points out how Communism serves to fulfill this religious need:

> Nevertheless it is impossible to deny that Russian Communism does resemble a religion in many respects. Its attitude to the Marxian doctrines is not the attitude of an economist or an historian towards a scientific theory, it is the attitude of a believer toward the gospel of salvation; Lenin is far more than a political hero, he is the canonized saint of communism with a highly developed cultus of his own; and the Communist ethic is religious in its absoluteness and its unlimited claims to the spiritual allegiance of its followers.
>
> Thus Communism is not simply a form of political organization; it is an economy, a philosophy, and a creed. And its hostility to Christianity is due not to its political form, but to the philosophy that lies behind it. Communism, in fact, challenges Christianity on its own ground by offering mankind a rival way of salvation. In the words of a Communist poster, "Jesus promised the people Paradise after death, but Lenin offers them Paradise on earth."[17]

Dawson makes another criticism of the Marxist philosophy, based on the fact that Marx's economic determinism cannot explain the machine order which is the element required to bring Marx's dialectic of history to its culmination in the classless society. For that order would never have come into existence if economic factors alone were determinative, and there had been no antecedent inventive ideas. Dawson first speaks of the fact that Marx's own motivation for constructing his theory was essentially a Messianic one, not the consequence of economic pressures; and he adds:

> Thus Communism, like every other living power in the world of men, owes its existence to spiritual forces. If it were possible to eliminate these, as the Communist theory demands, and to reduce human life to a purely economic activity, mankind would sink back into barbarism and animality. For the creative element in human nature is spiritual, and it triumphs only by mortifying and conquering the natural conservatism of man's animal instincts. This is true above all of science, for the path of the scientist leads him farther

---

[17]*Ibid.,* p. 58.

from the animal than the rest of men. He lives not in the concrete reality of sensible experience, like the animal or the savage, but in a rarefied atmosphere of mathematical abstraction in which the ordinary man cannot breathe. If the materialist interpretation of history were true, the scientific intellectualization of nature could no more have arisen than could the metaphysical intuition of reality, and without science there could be no machine order. The true Marxian Communism is not that of a machine order which is the work of the creative scientific spirit, but rather that of the Eskimo, which is the direct product of economic necessity. For the machine is a proof not of the subordination of mind to matter, but of the subordination of matter to mind.[18]

Since Marx was so very much concerned with the dialectic between different classes as providing the dynamics for historical development, and since he especially stresses its dependence on economic structures, I find particularly valuable Dawson's critique of the Marxian view of the origins of the revolutionary movement. Going back to the eighteenth century, the time when the revolutionary movement in ideas first became widespread, and which, within a relatively short time, led to political and social revolution—the French Revolution in all of its phases—Dawson notes certain facts about the classes which promoted and led this twofold revolution in ideas and political structures. In fact, contrary to Marx's analysis:

> In Germany and throughout Eastern Europe, as well as in Italy and Spain, the agents of change were not the new capitalist *bourgeoisie* but the old professional middle class, the men of letters and the professors, the lawyers and the government officials. Even in France, where economic conditions were more advanced, the capitalists who played a part in the Enlightenment were not the industrial capitalists, but chiefly the "Farmers General" and the government contractors who represented a tradition as ancient as the *publicani* of the Roman Empire.
> As in Russia so in Europe generally it was the intelligentsia, the class to which Marx himself belonged, and not the capitalists or the proletariat, who were the real agents of change and the source of the revolutionary tradition.[19]

Dawson then points out that this class had close relationships with

---

[18]*Christianity and the New Age*, pp. 97-98.
[19]*Christianity in East and West* (1981), pp. 85-86.

the eighteenth century State, the so-called enlightened depotisms which represented the tradition of a strong centralized government, along the lines which had first been developed in France in the century of Richelieu and Louis XIV. These traditions were then allied with the movement of Enlightened thought in the eighteenth century. The power of the absolute monarch was to be used to transform society in accordance with the new ideas, and to make government an effective agent for change.

Thus we find that the situation in Soviet Russia was not the result of some new and unique development in history which revolutionary economic factors had brought into being. Instead it was the perpetuation of a pattern which was already characteristic of the bureaucratic government of enlightened depotism in the eighteenth century. The governing class in Marxist states occupies the same position as before; what has changed is the increased power over the working class and over all of society which the progress of technology has allowed the government to assume. The development of the new technological order, instead of being a force for the liberation of the workers, as Marx predicted, has become the means for the creation of depotisms more absolute than any ever before known in the history of the world.

Consequently, Marx's conception of class relationships in the dialectic of history is quite different from the actual historical development. As we have seen, rather than industrial capitalism having produced the situation which led to social revolution, the revolutionary ideas were powerful before the industrialization of Europe occurred, and they were promoted by a class having the least connection with industrial development. Moreover, the later economic development of capitalism did not fulfill Marx's expectation of ever increasing misery and poverty for the workers, but developed in the opposite direction—to a greater participation by the working class in capitalist prosperity. In Western industrialized nations, through the influence of both Christian and humanitarian idealists, the power of government was employed to give greater protection to the workers and to legalize labor unions, by which the workers might move towards equality in bargaining with their employers. Hence, as Dawson has noted, ours has become a thoroughly bourgeois society. The most important causes for social revolution lie not in the economic condition of the workers, but in the spiritual emptiness which the hedonism of modern industrial society carries with it. What has been the Achilles heel of capitalist or bourgeois society is its moral relativism, and its implicit belief that advances in material well-being are all that are needed in order to make men happy and contented. The mistake of capitalist ideology in this regard is apt to be its undoing, for its basic worldview is so set upon making money and making products that it has no time or energy left for considering the ultimate significance of the society it is creating. It wishes to ignore the basic question of whether a material cornucopia can compensate for a spiritual vacuum in the heart of a society.

So far as Marxism is concerned, it is obvious that the dynamic on which Marx relied for the movement of history has been checkmated by the absolute despotisms created by the Communist governments. Marx's own materialism, instead of providing an ongoing dialectic of social progress, has destroyed the spiritual freedom needed for creative new developments. It would be well, therefore, to look again to the Christian Faith which has not only been the source of Western man's hope for a city set in the Heavens, but has also served as the inspiration for Western culture's transformation of the earthly city, first in Europe, and then, in recent times, throughout the rest of the world as well. It was not the material advances upon which Marx fixed his gaze which were the important factor in the development of world history, but the sense of dynamic spiritual purpose which Christianity has imparted to Western culture.

9

Friedrich Nietzsche
and G.K. Chesterton on the Meaning
of Christianity

Christianity: Anti-Life or Praise of God's Creation?

It seems appropriate, in a conference on "Chesterton and Human Dignity," that one should speak of Chesterton's Christian response to Nietzsche. For it was by the dialectic of challenge and response to anti-Christian ideas that Chesterton developed some of his most striking testimony to the dignity of the ordinary human being. If Nietzsche is the philosopher of elitist aristocracy, Chesterton is the philosopher of Christian democracy. As Chesterton wrote in *Heretics* in comment upon the democratic idea of man:

> It is a certain instinctive attitude which feels the things on which all men agree to be unspeakably important, and all the things in which they differ (such as mere brains) to be almost unspeakably unimportant. The nearest approach to it in our ordinary life would be the promptitude with which we should consider mere humanity in any circumstances of shock or death. We should say, after a somewhat disturbing discovery, "There is a dead man under the sofa." We should not be likely to say, "There is a dead man of considerable personal refinement under the sofa".... Nobody would say, "There are the remains of a clear thinker in your back garden." Nobody would say, "Unless you hurry up and stop him, a man with a very fine ear for music will have jumped off that cliff."[1]

Now Friedrich Nietzsche had his own idea of human dignity, and there is no doubt that his emphasis on aristocracy was in considerable part a response to the leveling results of the growth of capitalism, which submerged the individual in the crowd and demanded a kind of herdlike response. Nietzsche was also reacting against the stifling materialism of the nineteenth century, which reduced everything to rational calculation,

---

[1] G.K. Chesterton, *Heretics* (London: John Lane, 1905), pp. 272-273.

to a simple arithmetic of buying in the cheapest market and selling in the dearest, and in public policy to an automatic weighing of the amount of pains and pleasures which would result from this or that course of action. Quantity, not quality, was the criterion, and against this Nietzsche wished to reassert the qualitative elements in life and human society. Chesterton remarks on this element in Nietzsche in a passage from his book on George Bernard Shaw:

> All that was true in his teaching was simply this: that ... the mere achievement of dignity, beauty, or triumph is strictly to be called a good thing ... [I]t seems to me that all that is creditable or sound in Nietzsche could be stated in the derivation of one word, the word "valor." Valor means valeur; it means a value; courage is itself a solid good; it is an ultimate virtue; valor is itself valid. ... Nietzsche imagined he was rebelling against ancient morality; as a matter of fact he was only rebelling against recent morality, against the half-baked impudence of the utilitarians and the materialists. He thought he was rebelling against Christianity; curiously enough he was rebelling against the special enemies of Christianity. ... Historic Christianity has always believed in the valor of St. Michael riding in front of the Church Militant; and in an ultimate and absolute pleasure, not indirect or utilitarian, the intoxication of the spirit, the wine of the Blood of God.[2]

Now, let us consider certain basic facts about Nietzsche and his attack on the Christian worldview. Nietzsche was born in 1844 and became insane in January, 1889, so he was less than 45 years old when his writing career came to an end. He published a number of important works on history, aesthetics, and philosophy, with special emphasis on Greek culture, in the 1870s, but it was not until the 1880s that his anti-Christian ideas reached their full development. His first reference to the death of God is found in *The Joyful Wisdom* of 1882; and in *Thus Spake Zarathustra*, written a year or so later, he presents his idea of the development of the Superman as a replacement for God, and his idea of eternal recurrence of the universe as a replacement for immortality. As the decade progressed, Nietzsche's work became more and more stridently anti-Christian, culminating in *The Antichrist* of 1888, which is one long diatribe against Christianity.

Gilbert K. Chesterton was born in 1874, a generation or so after

---

[2]G.K. Chesterton, *George Bernard Shaw* (John Lane, 1909), pp. 197-198.

Nietzsche, and his first work was published in 1900. The books in which he especially deals with Nietzsche's ideas are *Heretics*, published in 1905, consisting of a number of essays on leading writers of his day and of the preceding generation, and *Orthodoxy*, appearing in 1908. This is a book of Christian apologetics which shows how Christianity fulfills the psychological needs of human nature. *Orthodoxy* is probably Chesterton's most brilliant book, and *Heretics* is not far behind. In addition, Chesterton deals briefly with Nietzsche in his book on Shaw in 1909, and again, a quarter of a century after *Orthodoxy*, in *St. Thomas Aquinas*, published in 1932. .

It is my belief that some of Chesterton's most effective writing was devoted to refutation of one or another key idea of Nietzsche. Even in passages where Nietzsche is not mentioned, it is often his ideas that are Chesterton's target. The fact that George Bernard Shaw, with whom Chesterton was so often in friendly controversy, had taken up ideas of Nietzsche, like that of the Superman and the worship of the life force, made Chesterton especially aware of Nietzsche's worldview.

What was the nature of Nietzsche's attack on Christianity? Nietzsche's charge against the Christian Faith is that it is anti-human and anti-life. He reiterates this charge through a large number of denunciations of particular Christian positions. Thus Christianity, by teaching mankind of Almighty God and His power and wisdom and control of the universe, diminishes the importance of man and makes him unable to control his own destiny; Christianity, by its absolute moral principles, cripples man and prohibits him from realizing the proper development of his powers. Christianity, by its negative attitude toward sexuality and creative violence, makes man psychologically sick and distrustful of life. Christianity, by teaching of a life beyond the present one where alone true happiness is to be found, leads man to despise the present life and turn away from it. Christianity, by teaching of the equality of all men before God, wars against all noble instincts and all that is heroic in life, and leads to social leveling and spiritual mediocrity. Christianity, by exalting the poor and the lowly, inculcates envy and resentment against the upper classes and all natural nobility. (Notice that this is the opposite of the charge leveled against Christianity by Karl Marx—that Christianity is the opiate of the people and leads them to accept willingly and submissively the exploitation of an upper class.)

Here are two examples, among many, of Nietzsche's oft-repeated denunciations of Christianity and Christian belief:

> The Christian concept of God—God as the deity of the sick, God as spirit—is one of the most corrupt concepts of God that has ever been attained on earth. . . .—God degenerated into the contradiction of life, instead of being its transformation and eternal Yea! With God, war is declared on life, nature and the will to life! God is the formula for every calumny of this world and for every lie concerning a beyond![3]

Or again:

> From the very first Christianity was essentially and thoroughly, the nausea and surfeit of Life for Life, which only disguised, concealed, and decked itself out under the belief in "another" or "better" life. The hatred of the "world," the curse on the affections, the fear of beauty and sensuality, another world, invented for the purpose of slandering this world the more, at bottom a longing for Nothingness, for the end, for rest, for the "Sabbath of Sabbaths"—all this, as also the unconditional will of Christianity to recognize only moral values, has always appeared to me as the most dangerous and ominous of all possible forms of a "will to perish"; at the least, as the symptom of a most fatal disease, of profoundest weariness, despondency, exhaustion, impoverishment of life—for before the tribunal of morality (especially Christian, that is, unconditional morality) life must constantly and inevitably be the loser, because life is something essentially unmoral.[4]

　　　Now over and above the specific replies which Chesterton makes to Nietzsche concerning Christianity, it is the whole of Chesterton's life and work which is a standing refutation of Nietzsche's charge that Christianity is anti-human and anti-life. This great Christian apologist, the "defender of the Faith," as Pope Pius XI called him in a telegram to the people of England upon Chesterton's death, shows that it is an exultant joy and gratitude for life which are fundamental to the Christian worldview. Chesterton also demonstrates that Christianity fulfills the deepest needs of human nature, in contrast to the disappointment and

---

[3]Friedrich Nietzsche, *The Antichrist* (Oscar Levy trans, pub. in German in 1889), sec. 18, vol. 16, p. 146.

[4]Friedrich Nietzsche, *Preface to the Birth of Tragedy,* a work originally published in 1874. (*In the Philosophy of Nietzsche* ed. by Geoffrey Clive, New American Library), p. 147.

frustration which result from a merely naturalistic view of life.   In *Orthodoxy* he pointed out the basic difference between Christianity and all those philosophies which confine man to this life alone. He might well have had in mind Nietzsche's declaration when speaking of the Superman:

> I conjure you, my brethren, remain true to the earth, and believe not those who speak unto you of superearthly hopes! Poisoners are they, whether they know it or not.
>
> Despisers of life are they, decaying ones and poisoned ones themselves, of whom the earth is weary: so away with them!
>
> Once blasphemy against God was the greatest blasphemy, but God died, and therewith also those blasphemers. To blaspheme the earth is now the dreadfulest sin.[5]

Here is Chesterton's response to this Nietzschean idea:

> But all the optimism of the age had been false and disheartening for this reason, that it had always been trying to prove that we fit in to the world. The Christian optimism is based on the fact that we do not fit in to the world. I had tried to be happy by telling myself that man is an animal, like any other which sought its meat from God. But now I was really happy, for I had learnt that man is a monstrosity. I had been right in feeling all things as odd, for I myself was at once worse and better than all things. . . . The modern philosopher had told me again and again that I was in the right place, and I had still felt depressed, even in acquiescence. But I had heard that I was in the wrong place, and my soul sang for joy, like a bird in spring.[6]

The vision of reality which inspires all of Chesterton's work and thought, which he tells us he arrived at before he became a Christian, but which he found pre-eminently expressed in Christianity, is given in the following passage from Chesterton's book on Chaucer.

> There is at the back of all our lives an abyss of light, more blinding and unfathomable than any abyss of darkness; and it is the abyss of actuality, of existence, of the fact that things truly are, and that we ourselves are incredibly and sometimes almost incredulously

---

[5]*Thus Spake Zarathustra, Zarathustra's Prologue*, sec. 3., Clive volume above, p. 432.

[6]G.K. Chesterton, *Orthodoxy* (John Lane, 1908), pp. 146-7.

real. It is the fundamental fact of being, as against not being; . . .
Chaucer was the immediate heir of something like what Catholics
call the Primitive Revelation; that glimpse that was given of the
world when God saw that it was good; and so long as the artist gives
us glimpses of that, it matters nothing that they are fragmentary or
even trivial. . . . Creation was the greatest of all revolutions. It was
for that, as the ancient poet said, that the morning stars sang
together; and the most modern poets, like the medieval poets, may
descend very far from that height of realization and stray and
stumble and seem distraught; but we shall know them for the sons of
God, when they are still shouting for joy. This is something much
more mystical and absolute than any modern thing that is called
optimism; for it is only rarely that we realize, like a vision of the
heavens filled with a chorus of giants, the primeval duty of praise.[7]

And it is upon this primeval duty of praise for the wonder of
existence that Chesterton's critique of Nietzsche is largely based. This,
of course, reverses the charge that Christianity is anti-life and implies
that it is really Nietzsche who is stricken by that disease. Let us consider,
for example, Nietzsche's conception of the Superman, or the
Ubermensch, more properly translated as the Overman. Here is
Nietzsche's expression of this idea as given in *Thus Spake Zarathustra:*

I teach you the Superman. Man is something that is to be
surpassed. What have ye done to surpass man?
All beings hitherto have created something beyond
themselves: and ye want to be the ebb of that great tide, and would
rather go back to the beast than surpass man?
What is the ape to man? A laughingstock, a thing of shame.
And just the same shall man be to the Superman; a laughingstock, a
thing of shame.
Ye have made your way from the worm to man, and much
within you is still worm. Once were ye apes, and even yet man is
more of an ape than any of the apes.
Even the wisest among you is only a disharmony and hybrid of
plant and phantom. But do I bid you become phantoms or plants?
Lo! I teach you the Superman!
The Superman is the meaning of the earth. Let your will say:
The Superman shall be the meaning of the earth![8]

Now Chesterton's response to this has several different

---

[7]G.K. Chesterton, *Chaucer* (Sheed & Ward: New York, 1956), pp. 26-27.
[8]*Thus Spake Zarathustra, Zarathustra's prologue,* sec. 3.

approaches. One of these is to point out that Nietzsche substitutes metaphor for moral reality: "So, when he describes his hero, he does not dare to say 'the purer man,' or 'the happier man,' or 'the sadder man,' for all these are ideas; and ideas are alarming. He says; 'the upper man,' or 'over man,' a physical metaphor from acrobats or alpine climbers. Nietzsche is truly a very timid thinker."[9]

A second approach is to note that Nietzsche's calling upon men to labor to produce the Superman and strive to "create something beyond themselves," is really unnecessary if the Superman or Overman is to be the inevitable product of evolution anyway. And if men are to be the agents for his coming, instead of the forces of nature, then what are the criteria by which men are to know toward what model they are to direct their efforts? Chesterton puts this question:

> If the Superman will come by human selection, what sort of Superman are we to select? If he is simply to be more just, more brave, or more merciful, then Zarathustra sinks into a Sunday-school teacher; the only way we can work for it is to be more just, more brave, or more merciful; sensible advice, but hardly startling. If he is to be anything else than this, why should we desire him, or what else are we to desire? These questions have been many times asked of the Nietzscheites, and none of the Nietzscheites have even attempted to answer them.[10]

But Chesterton's more fundamental answer to Nietzsche and the Superman, and to Nietzsche's scorning ordinary human beings as "a laughing stock and a painful embarrassment," is to emphasize the wonder and the miracle of what man as such really is. In a passage in *Heretics* in which Chesterton is responding to Shaw's promotion of this idea of the Superman, Chesterton writes:

> But the sensation connected with Mr. Shaw in recent years has been his sudden development of the religion of the Superman. He who had to all appearance mocked at the faiths in the forgotten past discovered a new god in the unimaginable future. He who had laid all the blame on ideals set up the most impossible of all ideals, the ideal of a new creature. . . .
> For the truth is that Mr. Shaw has never seen things as they really are. If he had he would have fallen on his knees before

---

[9]*Orthodoxy*, pp. 192-3.
[10]*George Bernard Shaw*, pp. 199-200.

them. . . . It is not seeing things as they are to think first of a Briareus with a hundred hands, and then call every man a cripple for having only two . . . And it is not seeing things as they are to imagine a demi-god of infinite mental clarity, who may or may not appear in the latter days of the earth, and then to see all men as idiots. And this is what Mr. Shaw has always in some degree done. When we really see men as they are, we do not criticize, but worship; and very rightly. For a monster with mysterious eyes and miraculous thumbs, with strange dreams in his skull, and a queer tenderness for this place or that baby, is truly a wonderful and unnerving matter. It is only the quite arbitrary and priggish habit of comparison with something else which makes it possible to be at our ease in front of him. A sentiment of superiority keeps us cool and practical; the mere facts would make our knees knock under with religious fear. It is the fact that every instant of conscious life is an unimaginable prodigy. It is the fact that every face in the street has the incredible unexpectedness of a fairy-tale.[11]

On the Death of God and on the Oriental Religions

A second striking challenge to the Christian worldview is Nietzsche's proclamation of the death of God, first set forth in *The Joyful Wisdom* of 1882. The death of God implies, of course, that God has never really existed, but is simply a creation of man's imagination, so that when man stops believing in this subjective fantasy, God ceases to exist. But since the individual's experience of God as a living reality may differ from that of Nietzsche or that of the secularized world which Nietzsche saw coming into being, why should a person accept the view that God is dead? Nietzsche, although he pretends to be appealing to the insight of the prophetic individual, is instead appealing to the sociological process of secularization. Man becomes enslaved to society rather than being able to transcend it in true individuality. Here is Nietzsche's proclamation of the death of God:

> The Madman.—Have you ever heard of the madman who on a bright morning lighted a lantern and ran to the market-place calling out unceasingly: "I seek God! I seek God!"—As there were many people standing about who did not believe in God, he caused a great deal of amusement. The insane man jumped into their midst and

---

[11]*Heretics,* pp. 63-64.

transfixed them with his glances. "Where is God gone?" he called out. "I mean to tell you! We have killed him, —you and I! We are all his murderers! But how have we done it? How were we able to drink up the sea? Who gave us the sponge to wipe away the whole horizon? What did we do when we loosened this earth from its sun? God is dead! God remains dead! And we have killed him! How shall we console ourselves, the most murderous of all murderers? The holiest and the mightiest that the world has hitherto possessed, has bled to death under our knife,—who will wipe the blood from us? Is not the magnitude of this deed too great for us? Shall we not ourselves have to become Gods, merely to seem worthy of it? There never was a greater event,—and on account of it, all who are born after us belong to a higher history than any history hitherto!"[12]

Four years later, in 1886, in an addition to the same volume, Nietzsche wrote:

Are we still, perhaps, too much under the immediate effects of the event—and are these effects, especially as regards ourselves, perhaps the reverse of what was to be expected—not at all sad and depressing, but rather like a new and indescribable variety of light, happiness, relief, enlivenment, encouragement, and dawning day? ... In fact, we philosophers and "free spirits" feel ourselves irradiated as by a new dawn by the report that the "old God is dead"; our hearts overflow with gratitude, astonishment, presentiment and expectation. At last the horizon seems open once more, granting even that it is not bright; our ships can at last put out to sea in face of every danger; every hazard is again permitted to the discerner; the sea, our sea, again lies open before us; perhaps never before did such an "open sea" exist.[13]

Chesterton's response to this, I believe, is to be found in the chapter in *Orthodoxy* called "The Maniac." Although the subject deals with a number of different matters which involve the rejection of God, it seems that it is especially meant as a response to Nietzsche's idea that the death of God opened up the way for "philosophers and 'free spirits' " to become gods themselves. Notice that in Nietzsche's account the tidings are brought to mankind by a madman, although Nietzsche sees the madman as possessed of a perception which ordinary humanity does

---

[12]Friedrich Nietzsche, *The Joyful Wisdom* (1882), sec. 125 (In Clive volume, p. 388).
[13]*Ibid.* (1886 addition), pp. 389-390.

not yet have. Chesterton's chapter, "The Maniac," appears to be a definite takeoff from this image. But where Nietzsche proclaims the superiority of the madman's insight, Chesterton contrasts his narrow and concentrated reasoning with the healthy sanity of ordinary mankind. Nietzsche implies that the madman is the only one who sees things clearly; Chesterton says that that kind of clarity can only be achieved by forgetting a large part of what constitutes reality.

It is this ignoring of reality which leads on to that state of mind in which the individual thinks he has become God and has created everything else. Chesterton points out there is no reasoning with such a position, that the only hope is to jar it out of the insane groove in which it has become fixed. The response which Chesterton gives to the madman applies also to Nietzsche and his idea that he and a few other free spirits—Nietzsche later confessed that the others never really measured up to his own standard—will "become gods" now that God is dead. Here is Chesterton's reply to the madman who called himself Christ (remember that Nietzsche signed himself "the Crucified One" a month or so before he went mad):

> If we said what we felt, we should say, "So you are the Creator and Redeemer of the world; but what a small world it must be! What a little Heaven you must inhabit with angels no bigger than butterflies! How sad it must be to be God; and an inadequate God! Is there really no life fuller and no love more marvelous than yours; and is it really in your small and painful pity that all flesh must put its faith? How much happier you would be, how much more of you there would be, if the hammer of a higher God could smash your small cosmos, scattering the stars like spangles, and leave you in the open, free like other men to look up as well as down!"

Notice the direct contrast between Nietzsche's seeing the death of God as leading men to an open sea, a sea that has never been so open before, and Chesterton's portrayal of the man who thinks himself God as imprisoned within a very narrow universe. In fact, later on Chesterton compares this narrowing of reality to a madman's cell: "The stars will be only dots in the blackness of his own brain; his mother's face will be only a sketch from his own insane pencil on the walls of his cell. But over his cell shall be written, with dreadful truth, 'He believes in himself'."[14]

---

[14]*Orthodoxy*, pp. 35-36; 46.

Another challenge which Nietzsche flings at Christianity is made through comparative religion. As an element of this strategy, Nietzsche attacks Christianity from the vantage-point of the Oriental world religions. Thus he has some good words to say for the Hindu Laws of Manu, which set forth the basis of the caste system. Nietzsche writes of these caste regulations:

> The unholiness of Christian means is caught in flagranti, if only the end aspired to by Christianity be compared with that of the Law-Book of Manu; if only these two utterly opposed aims be put under a strong light. The critic of Christianity simply cannot avoid making Christianity contemptible.—A Law-Book like that of Manu comes into being like every good law-book: it epitomizes the experience, the precautionary measures, and the experimental morality of long ages, it settles things definitely.
> To draw up a law-book like Manu's, is tantamount to granting a people mastership for the future, perfection for the future,—the right to aspire to the highest Art of Life. To that end it must be made unconscious; this is the object of every holy lie.—The order of castes, the highest, the dominating law, is only the sanction of a natural order, of a natural legislation of the first rank, over which no arbitrary innovation, no "modern idea" has any power.
> It is Nature, not Manu, that separates from the rest, those individuals preponderating in intellectual power, those excelling in muscular strength and temperament, and the third class which is distinguished neither in one way nor the other, the mediocre,—the latter as the greatest number, the former as the élite. The superior caste—I call them the fewest,—has, as the perfect caste, the privileges of the fewest; it devolves upon them to represent happiness, beauty and goodness on earth.[15]

It would seem that the reply by Chesterton best suited to emphasize the fundamental cleavage between his conception of mankind and that of Nietzsche is given in certain observations he made about the significance of America. Here he speaks of the American idea of human equality—an idea utterly in contrast with the Hindu caste system which Nietzsche so greatly admired. Chesterton wrote:

> [Human equality] is an absolute of morals by which all men have a value invariable and indestructible and a dignity as intangible as death. In truth it is inequality that is the illusion. The extreme

---

[15]*The Antichrist*, sec. 57, Oscar Levy trans., vol. 16, p. 219.

disproportion between men, that we seem to see in life, is a thing of
changing lights and lengthening shadows, a twilight full of fancies
and distortions. We find a man famous and cannot live long enough
to find him forgotten; we see a race dominant and cannot linger to
see it decay. It is the experience of men that always returns to the
equality of men; it is the average that ultimately justifies the average
man. It is when men have seen and suffered much and come at the
end of more elaborate experiments, that they see men under an
equal light of death and daily laughter; and none the less mysterious
for being many. Nor is it in vain that these Western democrats have
sought the blazonary of their flag in that great multitude of immortal
lights that endure behind the fires we see, and gathered them into
the corner of Old Glory whose ground is like the glittering night.
For veritably, in the spirit as well as in the symbol, suns and moons
and meteors pass and fill our skies with a fleeting and almost
theatrical conflagration; and whenever the old shadow stoops upon
the earth, the stars return.[16]

Also relevant is the passage from *Heretics* quoted earlier, in which
Chesterton is responding to Shaw's promotion of the idea of the
Superman.

However, Nietzsche's preferred adversary to Christianity among
the religions of the Orient is Buddhism. Although Nietzsche is opposed
to all religions that involve asceticism and that do not find their center of
gravity in the worship of the forces of natural vitality, he manages to
develop quite a defense of Buddhism when comparing it to Christianity.
Most of all he likes the fact that Buddhism rejects the idea of a personal
God and thus makes its efforts center on man's own ability to escape
from pain and sorrow in life.

He also manages to misrepresent Buddhism as not involving
asceticism, when in fact its primary procedure for avoiding pain is
through withdrawal from sexual pleasure, since it sees this as the means
by which pain is perpetuated through the life of future generations, and
also through man's attachment to the offspring he has thus brought
forth.

In addition, Nietzsche seems unaware that the spread of
Buddhism in India under the emperor Asoka, who became converted to
the Buddhist religion, was by means of Asoka's wielding fire and sword
in order to propagate it. So Nietzsche draws a picture of Buddhism

---

[16]G.K. Chesterton, *What I Saw in America*, pp. 17-18.

which suits his own fancy, rather than being tied down to the inconvenience of historical fact. Nietzsche's praise of Buddhism runs as follows:

> With my condemnation of Christianity I should not like to have done an injustice to a religion which is related to it and the number of whose followers is even greater; I refer to Buddhism. Buddhism is a hundred times more realistic than Christianity—it is part of its constitutional heritage to be able to face problems objectively and coolly, it is the outcome of centuries of lasting philosophical activity. The concept "God" was already exploded when it appeared. Buddhism is the only really positive religion to be found in history, even in its epistemology (which is strict phenomenalism)—it no longer speaks of the "struggle with sin," but fully recognizing the true nature of reality it speaks of the "struggle with pain." It already has—and this distinguishes it fundamentally from Christianity,—the self-deception of moral concepts beneath it,—to use my own phraseology, it stands Beyond Good and Evil. [Buddha] understands goodness—being good—as promoting health. Prayer is out of the question, as is also asceticism; there is neither a Categorical Imperative nor any discipline whatsoever, even within the walls of a monastery (—it is always possible to leave it if one wants to). All these things would have been only a means of accentuating the excessive irritability already referred to. Precisely on this account he does not exhort his followers to wage war upon those who do not share their views; nothing is more abhorred in his doctrine than the feeling of revenge, of aversion, and of resentment (—"not through hostility doth hostility end": the touching refrain of the whole of Buddhism). . . . In Buddha's doctrine egoism is a duty: the thing which is above all necessary, i.e., "how canst thou be rid of suffering" regulates and defines the whole of the spiritual diet.
>
> The pre-requisites for Buddhism are a very mild climate, great gentleness and liberality in the customs of a people and no militarism. The movement must also originate among the higher and even learned classes. Cheerfulness, peace and absence of desire are the highest of inspirations, and they are realized. Buddhism is not a religion in which perfection is merely aspired to: perfection is the normal case.
>
> Buddhism, I repeat, is a hundred times colder, more truthful, more objective.[17]

Chesterton's response to all this unreal dogmatizing on the part of Nietzsche, and the perverted picture he draws of Christianity, is to be

---

[17]*The Antichrist,* secs. 20, 21, 23.

found in Chesterton's book on St. Thomas Aquinas. Speaking of St. Thomas, Chesterton declares:

> But we must look elsewhere for his real rivals; and the only real rivals of the Catholic theory. They are the heads of the great heathen systems; some of them very ancient, some very modern, like Buddha on the one hand or Nietzsche on the other. It is when we see his gigantic figure against this vast and cosmic background, that we realize: First, that he was the only optimist theologian; and second, that Catholicism is the only optimist theology. Something milder and more amiable may be made out of the deliquescence of theology, and the mixture of the creed with everything that contradicts it; but among consistent cosmic creeds, this is the only one that is entirely on the side of Life.[18]

Then, specifically dealing with Buddhism as an alternative to Christianity, and Nietzsche's involvement in promoting it, Chesterton makes these observations:

> The more we really appreciate the noble revulsion and renunciation of Buddha, the more we see that intellectually it was the converse and almost the contrary of the salvation of the world by Christ. The Christian would escape from the world into the universe; the Buddhist wishes to escape from the universe even more than from the world. One would uncreate himself; the other would return to his Creation [i.e. his having been created]; to his Creator. Indeed, it was so genuinely the converse of the idea of the Cross as the Tree of Life, that there is some excuse for setting up the two things side by side, as if they were of equal significance. They are in one sense parallel and equal; as a mound and a hollow, as a valley and a hill. There is a sense in which that sublime despair is the only alternative to that divine audacity. It is even true that the truly spiritual and intellectual man sees it as a sort of dilemma; a very hard and terrible choice. There is little else on earth that can compare with these for completeness. And he who will not climb the mountain of Christ does indeed fall into the abyss of Buddha.[19]

Chesterton notes the fact that Nietzsche's praise of Buddhism came just before he went mad, and that this may account for his lack of balanced judgment.

---

[18]G.K. Chesterton, *Saint Thomas Aquinas* (Image Books, 1956), pp. 113-114.
[19]*Ibid.*, pp. 114-115.

The same is true, in a less lucid and dignified fashion, of most other alternatives of heathen humanity; nearly all are sucked back into that whirlpool of recurrence which all the ancients knew. Nearly all return to the one idea of returning. That is, what Buddha described so darkly as the Sorrowful Wheel. It is true that the sort of recurrence which Buddha described as the Sorrowful Wheel, poor Nietzsche actually managed to describe as the Joyful Wisdom. I can only say that if bare repetition was his idea of Joyful Wisdom, I should be curious to know what was his idea of Sorrowful Wisdom. But as a fact, in the case of Nietzsche, this did not belong to the moment of his breaking out, but to the moment of his breaking down. It came at the end of his life, when he was near to mental collapse; and it is really quite contrary to his earlier and finer inspirations of wild freedom or fresh and creative innovation. Once at least he had tried to break out; but he also was only broken—on the wheel.[20]

Finally, in the context of the comparison of Catholic Christianity with the Oriental religions, Chesterton is much more generous in appreciation of these religions of the East than Nietzsche is in dealing with Christianity. Chesterton recognizes certain positive values in them which need to be brought to fulfillment and greater realization in the Christian Faith. Nietzsche, on the other hand, is never tired of denouncing Christianity as a religion of slaves who make use of their religion to express their suppressed resentment against being dominated by the noble class who rightly control the society in which the Christians live. This extreme lack of generosity on Nietzsche's part, which makes him incapable of seeing anything but a caricature of Christianity in the picture he gives us, leads one to suspect that he is projecting on to Christianity the resentment which he himself strongly feels. We must not forget that Nietzsche came of a line of Protestant pastors, and his own rebellion against that tradition, with consequent social isolation in a German society still dominated by Protestantism, was a fertile ground for feelings of resentment for not being accorded the importance which he attributed to himself and to the anti-Christian message he wished to spread.

Here is Chesterton's comparison of the Gospel story of the Infancy narratives with the teaching of the pre-Christian sages, among whom he included the founders of the Oriental philosophic religions:

---

[20]*Ibid.*, p. 115.

There came with them [the Magi] all that world of wisdom that had watched the stars in Chaldea and the sun in Persia; and we shall not be wrong if we see in them the same curiosity that moves all the sages. They would stand for the same human ideal if their names had really been Confucius or Pythagoras or Plato. They were those who sought not tales but the truth of things; and since their thirst for truth was itself a thirst for God, they also have had their reward. That reward was the completion of the incomplete.

Such learned men would doubtless have come, as these learned men did come, to find themselves confirmed in much that was true in their own traditions and right in their own reasoning. Confucius would have found a new foundation for the family in the very reversal of the Holy Family; Buddha would have looked upon a new renunciation, of stars rather than jewels and divinity than royalty. These learned men would still have the right to say, or rather a new right to say, that there was truth in their old teaching. But after all these learned men would have come to learn. They would have come to complete their conceptions with something they had not yet conceived; even to balance their imperfect universe with something they might once have contradicted. Buddha would have come from his impersonal paradise to worship a person. Confucius would have come from his temples of ancestor-worship to worship a child.

We must grasp from the first this character in the new cosmos; that it was larger than the old cosmos. In that sense Christendom is larger than creation; as creation had been before Christ.[21]

Nietzsche Versus the Gospels on the Person of Jesus

In our preceding section we examined Nietzsche's attempt to undermine Christianity by an appeal to comparative religion.

Another attack which Nietzsche made upon Christianity was through the use of a certain kind of biblical criticism. Here the extravagances of the higher critics in Germany in the half-century which preceded Nietzsche's *Antichrist*, made it possible for Nietzsche to be quite subjective in offering his own picture of Christ. Because of the higher critics' disregard of the Gospels as having historical value, they made use of their own philosophies, whether of rationalism or idealism, to determine which elements in the Gospel they would choose to regard

---

[21]*The Everlasting Man*, pp. 211-212.

as valid. One critic might differ widely from another in his conclusions, but they all agreed in rejecting the validity of the supernatural, and hence they found one means or another to explain away this element in the Gospel narrative.

It was in France, however, that the results of this subjective approach to the Gospels found its most popular presentation, with Ernest Renan's *Life of Jesus*, published in 1863 and going into eight printings in three months. By the time Nietzsche was writing *The Antichrist,* a quarter of a century later, Renan's book was known all over Europe, and represented the most appealing presentation of the life of Christ for those who no longer believed in the supernatural.

The basic defect with all such "historical" scholarship, including that of the German higher critics on which Renan's life was based, Chesterton has pointed out in a brief observation in *Orthodoxy*:

> [A] glance at it [Anatole France's life of *Joan of Arc*] was enough to remind me of Renan's *Vie de Jesus*. It has the same strange method of the reverent skeptic. It discredits supernatural stories that have some foundation, by telling natural stories that have no foundation. Because we cannot believe in what a saint did, we are to pretend that we know exactly what he felt.[22]

Now with this kind of groundwork laid by biblical criticism, Nietzsche felt free to develop whatever picture of Christ he wanted so as to suit his own preconceptions. It is a process of so-called scholarship which Arnold Lunn was later to call the "scissors-and-paste approach." If you don't like something which the Gospels record about Jesus, cut it out with your scissors, and paste in something which you do like.

What, then was the view which Nietzsche took of Jesus? It was, in fact, drawn largely from the liberal Protestant interpretation. That is, it was anti-miraculous, it emphasized Christ's pacifism and gentleness, and it saw Him as seeking only an inward Kingdom of God. Unlike Schweitzer of less than a generation later, Nietzsche did nothing to reverse this liberal view. Instead, he exaggerated it still further till it became a caricature. Hence Nietzsche's being able to say that "the last Christian died upon the cross," and his claim that Christ's Apostles completely misunderstood His message, His rejection of all rites and institutions, His complete otherworldliness.

---

[22]*Orthodoxy*, p. 77.

Possibly the best way to see the direction which Nietzsche wished to take in his portrayal of Jesus is to note the strength of his reaction against the picture of Jesus given us by Renan. For it cut straight across the conception which Nietzsche himself had formed. As a result, he deals with Renan with the splenetic rancor he usually reserves for Christians and Christianity. The following passage is from *The Antichrist*:

> M. Renan, that buffoon in *psychologicis*, has contributed the two most monstrous ideas imaginable to the explanation of the type of Jesus: the idea of the genius and the idea of the hero. But if there is anything thoroughly unevangelical surely it is the idea of the hero. It is precisely the reverse of all struggle, of all consciousness of taking part in the fight, that has become instinctive here: the inability to resist is here converted into a morality ("resist not evil," the profoundest sentence in the whole of the gospels, their key in a certain sense), the blessedness of peace, of gentleness, of not being able to be an enemy. What is the meaning of "glad tidings"?—True life, eternal life has been found—it is not promised, it is actually here, it is in you; it is life in love, in love free from all selection or exclusion, free from all distance. Everybody is the child of God—Jesus does not by any means claim anything for himself alone,—as the child of God everybody is equal to everybody else.[23]

To see how far Nietzsche's subjective fantasies depart from the figure of Jesus in the Gospels, consider the following passages in which the division between good and evil is so sharply etched. It would appear that Nietzsche cannot afford to come to grips with what the Gospel presents to us, and thus must conceal it from himself by whatever means he can dream up.

> You have heard that it was said to them of old: Thou shalt not commit adultery. But I say to you, that whosoever shall look on a woman to lust after her, hath already committed adultery with her in his heart.
> If thy right eye scandalize thee, pluck it out and cast it from thee. For it is expedient for thee that one of thy members should perish, rather than that thy whole body be cast into hell. And if thy right hand scandalize thee, cut it off and cast it from thee. For it is expedient for thee that one of thy members should perish, rather than that thy whole body go into hell.[24]

---

[23]*The Antichrist*, Sec. 29, Oscar Levy Trans., vol. 16, pp. 164-165.
[24]*Matt* 5:27-30.

Then there is this parable which gives an account of the growth of good and evil in the world, the cause for each, and the consequences which follow, so strikingly different in each case. As we read this, we need to remember the description of the message of Jesus given by Nietzsche: "It is life in love, in love free from all selection or exclusion, from all distance. Everybody is the child of God . . ."

Jesus tells his disciples:

> The Kingdom of heaven is like a man who sowed good seed in his field; but while men were asleep, the enemy came and sowed weeds among the wheat and went away. And when the blade sprang up and brought forth fruit, then the weeds appeared as well. And the servants of the householder came and said to him, "Sir, didst thou not sow good seed in thy field? How then does it have weeds?" He said to them, "An enemy has done this."[25]

Later Jesus explains this parable which makes clear that those who do evil are not the children of God. It is indeed striking how Nietzsche can completely disregard the records we have of the words of Jesus in order to fabricate some myth which better suits his own resentment of the Christian ethic and what it demands. Here is the account which Jesus gives of the meaning of the parable. When the disciples were again indoors with Jesus, they said to Him: "Expound to us the parable of the cockle of the field."

And Jesus said:

> He that soweth the good seed is the Son of Man. And the field is the world. And the good seed are the children of the Kingdom. And the cockle are the children of the wicked one. And the enemy that sowed them is the devil. But the harvest is the end of the world. And the reapers are the angels.
> Even as the cockle therefore is gathered up, and burnt with fire; so shall it be at the end of the world. The Son of Man shall send his angels, and they shall gather out of his kingdom all scandals, and them that work iniquity. And shall cast them into the furnace of fire: there shall be weeping and gnashing of teeth. Then shall the just shine as the sun, in the kingdom of their Father. He that hath ears to hear, let him hear.[26]

---

[25]*Matt* 13:24-28.
[26]*Matt* 13:36-43.

Nietzsche continues with his vitriolic denunciation of Ernst Renan's *Life of Christ*:

> Fancy making Jesus a hero!—And what a tremendous misunderstanding the word "genius" is! Our whole idea of "spirit," which is a civilized idea, could have had no meaning whatever in the world in which Jesus lived. In the strict terms of the physiologist, a very different word ought to be used here.... We know of a condition of morbid irritability of the sense of touch, which recoils shuddering from every kind of contact, and from every attempt at grasping a solid object. Any such physiological habitus reduced to its ultimate logical conclusion, becomes an instinctive hatred of all reality, a flight into the intangible, into the "incomprehensible"; a repugnance to all formulae, to every notion of time and space, to everything that is established such as customs, institutions, the church; a feeling at one's ease in a world in which no sign of reality is any longer visible, a merely "inner" world, a "true" world, an "eternal" world. . . . "The Kingdom of God is within you."[27]

Nietzsche could not afford to allow Christ to be either a hero or a genius, even on the natural level, so he poured scorn on Renan for proposing such a description of Jesus. If Christ were regarded as a hero by the first Christians, this would undermine Nietzsche's claim that Christianity was opposed to all that was noble and heroic and his charge that it represented merely a reaction of envy and resentment. Hence Christ must be portrayed as a completely otherworldly individual, who found all contact with reality distressing. Neither could Nietzsche allow Christ to be a genius, for that would mean that He possessed intellectual acumen and outstanding intellectual resources, and this would have given a different character to Christianity from what Nietzsche wished to give it. It would no longer be possible to portray the Christian religion as the vampire which had destroyed the intellectual heritage of the ancient world, as Nietzsche portrayed it in a later section of *The Antichrist*.

Here is a further statement by Nietzsche of the kind of figure of Christ he has devised from his "psychological" approach to the Gospels:

> He is totally incapable of denying anything. In the same way he shuns logic and does not believe that any faith or any "truth" can be provided by argument. His own proofs are "the light within". . . .

---

[27]*The Antichrist*, Sec. 29, Oscar Levy Trans., vol. 16, pp. 164-165.

People who hold such a doctrine cannot contradict anything. They do not even realize that other points of view exist, or can exist. They are absolutely incapable of imagining anything opposed to their own way of thinking.[28]

The following passage by Chesterton is a challenge to the liberal interpretation of Christ, but it is also, I think, a deliberate response to the "psychological" picture of Christ which Nietzsche had given:

Instead of looking at books and pictures about the New Testament, I looked at the New Testament. There I found an account, not in the least of a person with His hair parted in the middle or His hands clasped in appeal, but of an extraordinary being with lips of thunder and acts of lurid decision, flinging down tables, casting out devils, passing with the wild secrecy of the wind from mountain isolation to a sort of dreadful demagogy; a being who often acted like an angry god--and always like a god. Christ had even a literary style of His own, not to be found, I think, elsewhere; it consists of an almost furious use of the *a fortiori*. His "how much more" is piled one upon another like castle upon castle in the clouds. The diction used about Christ has been, and perhaps, wisely, sweet and submissive. But the diction used by Christ is quite curiously gigantesque; it is full of camels leaping through needles and mountains hurled into the sea. Morally it is equally terrific; He called Himself a sword of slaughter, and told men to buy swords if they sold their coats for them. That he used other even wilder words on the side of nonresistance greatly increases the mystery; but it also, if anything, rather increases the violence. We cannot even explain it by calling such a being insane; for insanity is usually along one consistent channel. The maniac is generally a monomaniac. Here we must remember the difficult definition of Christianity already given; Christianity is a superhuman paradox whereby two opposite passions may blaze beside each other. The one explanation of the Gospel language that does explain it, is that it is the survey of one who from some supernatural height beholds some more startling synthesis.[29]

Notice in this passage of Chesterton the statement that Christ "often acted like an angry god--and always like a god." There is a more psychological realism in that one sentence than in all of Nietzsche's carefully constructed figure of Christ, and the latter collapses like a

---

[28]*The Antichrist*, sec. 32, Oscar Levy Trans. vol. 16, pp. 168-170.
[29]*Orthodoxy*, pp. 271-2.

house of cards when subjected to its impact. And Chesterton's portrayal, of course, is a direct contradiction of Nietzsche's claim that the Christ of the Gospels is not a hero. Chesterton's noting the elements of decisive action and speaking ("lips of thunder and acts of lurid decision"), amounting even to violence in the effect produced on His hearers, shows us a being who cannot be reconciled with the milk-and-water categories into which both Nietzsche and the liberal Protestant critics had tried to fit Him.

Moreover, from the viewpoint of Nietzsche's attempt to portray Christ as a person who sought to escape from reality (such persons, Nietzsche tells us, "are absolutely incapable of imagining anything opposed to their own way of thinking"), Chesterton points out that Christ in His speech sharpens the contrast between different positions and makes them even more severe. And because the startling paradoxes are to be found not only on one side, but on either side of an issue as the occasion warranted, the key to the character of Christ is not a simplicity bordering on the infantile, as Nietzsche had claimed, but a high degree of intellectual complexity.

Finally, as to Nietzsche's statement that the Person presented to us in the Gospels "is totally incapable of denying anything," and does "not even realize that other points of view exist, or can exist," the following passage from the Catholic theologian, Karl Adam, supplies a needed corrective.

> It was a psychological necessity that this tremendously concentrated and disciplined will, this pent-up spiritual power should discharge itself in stern language and bold action when powers of evil arrayed themselves against Him. On such occasions Jesus could wax wroth and show His displeasure like any prophet of the Old Testament, an Osee or a Jeremias, or like Moses when he threw the tables of the law to the ground.... In Jesus there dwelt not only mighty powers held in restraint and a disciplined will, but the fire of a holy zeal... "Begone Satan," was how he frightened away the devil who came to tempt Him (Matt. 4:10). "Go behind me, Satan, thou art a scandal unto me," was how He rebuked Peter when the latter wished to break down His will to pursue the road which led to the Cross (Matt. 16:23). "I know not whence you are; depart from me, you that work iniquity," is what He will profess to those who have neglected to do good to His suffering brethren on earth (Luke 13:27; cf.. Matt. 7:23). It is not quiet, peaceful reserve of spirit that we have here, but deep emotion and passion. Not a

few of His parables breathe the same fiery spirit . . .

It is because He was so consistently true to His Father's will, because He was only "yea and nay," that He reacted with unequaled severity against anything that was ungodly or hateful to God, whether this found expression in perverse theological formularies or in the decree of a ruler. And the story of His life proves that in harmony with His uncompromising words He was ready to stake His own life for the truth and to die for it.[30]

Nietzsche's arbitrary selection and rearrangement of material from the Gospels in order to make it fit in with his own worldview is not essentially different from the practice of many Modernist biblical critics today. Not only Nietzsche, but also the Modernist critics, suffer from a fundamental *hubris*, the belief that they are entitled to sit in judgment on a Divine Person. If the nemesis which overtakes them is not the obvious madness to which Nietzsche succumbed, it is nevertheless equally crippling to the sanity of their judgments. As Chesterton has remarked concerning their treatment of the Christ of the Gospels:

There is a huge and heroic sanity of which moderns can only collect the fragments. There is a giant of whom we see only the lopped arms and legs walking about. They have torn the soul of Christ into silly strips, labeled egoism and altruism, and they are equally puzzled by His insane magnificence and His insane meekness. They have parted His garments among them, and for His vesture they have cast lots; though the coat was without seam woven from the top throughout.[31]

In a passage shortly before this reference to the critics' inability to understand Christ, Chesterton points out one of the major difficulties with Nietzsche's philosophy of life. It will be recalled that Nietzsche's view of Christ, so completely at odds with the Figure we see in the Gospels, is that Jesus has "an instinctive hatred of all reality, a flight into the intangible '. . . a world in which no sign of reality is any longer visible, a merely inner world'."[32]

Now, in his description of Nietzsche, Chesterton shows how the ideas of Nietzsche contradict the principles for any significant action, and thus cut off Nietzsche from the real world. Chesterton writes:

---

[30]*The Son of God,* pp. 99-101; 104-105.
[31]*Orthodoxy,* p. 80.
[32]*The Antichrist,* sec. 29.

All the will-worshippers, from Nietzsche to Mr. Davidson, are really quite empty of volition. They cannot will, they can hardly wish. And if any one wants a proof of this, it can be found quite easily. It can be found in this fact: that they always talk of will as something that expands and breaks out. But it is quite the opposite. Every act of will is an act of self-limitation. To desire action is to desire limitation. In that sense every act is an act of self-sacrifice.... It is the existence of this negative or limiting side of will that makes most of the talk of the anarchic will-worshippers little better than nonsense.... The moment you step into a world of facts, you step into a world of limits....

Nietzsche had some natural talent for sarcasm: he could sneer, though he could not laugh; but there is always something bodiless and without weight in his satire, simply because it has not any mass of common morality behind it. He is himself more preposterous than anything he denounces. But, indeed, Nietzsche will stand very well as the type of the whole of this failure of abstract violence....

Nietzsche scales staggering mountains, but he turns up ultimately in Tibet. He sits down beside Tolstoy in the land of nothing and Nirvana. They are both helpless—one because he must not grasp anything, and the other because he must not let go of anything. The Tolstoyan's will is frozen by a Buddhist instinct that all special actions are evil. But the Nietzscheite's will is quite equally frozen by his view that all special actions are good; for if all special actions are good, none of them are special. They stand at the cross-roads, and one hates all the roads and the other likes all the roads. The result is—well, some things are not hard to calculate. They stand at the cross-roads.[33]

In strong contrast to that paralysis of the will to which Nietzsche's principles led him, Chesterton notes the sense of clear direction and purpose shown in the life of Christ. This, of course, is the complete opposite of the picture which Nietzsche draws of Jesus. But then Chesterton's portrait is closely linked to the story we find in the Gospels, whereas Nietzsche's as we have seen, is a result of his own subjective desires.

After mentioning a number of philosophers of the ancient world, whose wanderings took them to many different places, Chesterton declares:

---

[33]*Orthodoxy*, pp. 70-71; 75-76.

Now compared to these wanderers, the life of Jesus went as swift and straight as a thunderbolt. It was above all things dramatic; it did above all things consist in doing something that had to be done. . . . It is a journey with a goal and an object, like Jason going to find the Golden Fleece, or Hercules the golden apples of the Hesperides. The gold that he was seeking was death. The primary thing that he was going to do was to die. . . .

Therefore the story of Christ is the story of a journey, almost in the sense of a military march; certainly in the manner of the quest of a hero moving to his achievement or his doom.[34]

It is of some interest to see the quite different manner in which Chesterton uses the mountain metaphor to give the opposite significance of Nietzsche and of Christ. "Nietzsche scales staggering mountains" only to end up "in the land of nothing and Nirvana." Christ, on the other hand, in accord with the clear awareness of purpose in his life, is seen as mounting toward his death in the mountain city of Jerusalem:

It is a story that begins in the paradise of Galilee, a pastoral and peaceful land having really some hint of Eden, and gradually climbs the rising country into the mountains that are nearer to the storm-clouds and the stars, as to a Mountain of Purgatory. He may be met as if straying in strange places, or stopped on the way for discussion or dispute, but his face is set towards the mountain city. That is the meaning of that great culmination when He crested the ridge and stood at the turning of the road and suddenly cried aloud, lamenting over Jerusalem. . . .

Every attempt to amplify that story has diminished it. . . . The grinding power of the plain words of the Gospel story is like the power of mill-stones; and those who can read them simply enough will feel as if rocks had been rolled upon them.[35]

---

[34]*The Everlasting Man,* pp. 253-254.
[35]*Ibid.,* pp. 254-256.

10

Sigmund Freud and Christopher Dawson on Civilization and its Discontents

In a comparison of the ideas of Christopher Dawson and Sigmund Freud, one needs certain facts in order to set each of them in his particular cultural environment. First, Freud was born in Moravia in 1856, lived most of his adult life in Vienna, and died in England in 1939, where he had arrived as a refugee from the Nazi seizure of Austria the year before. Dawson was born in England, near the border of Wales, in 1889 (his mother was Welsh, his father English), lived all his life in England, except for a four-year professorship at Harvard from 1958 to 1962, and died in Devon in southern England in 1970. A generation or more thus separated the two men, although Freud's most important work on religion and culture did not appear until 1928, the same year that Dawson's first book was published.

Second, Freud was of Jewish origin, and although agnostic in his religious views, retained a strong sense of Jewish identification throughout his life. Dawson was born and reared an Anglican, with a father who, although an army officer, was quite learned in both the Greek and Roman Classics and ancient and modern philosophy; he also had a great deal of liking for Catholic liturgical prayers and a great admiration for Dante. Dawson became a Catholic at age 24, in early 1914, and all of his writing was done after his conversion to the Catholic Church.

Third, Freud was basically a psychoanalyst whose later studies led him to become interested in religion and anthropology, while Dawson was essentially a cultural historian whose scholarship in that field led him to range widely in other disciplines as well.

Fourth, Freud was not greatly interested in history as such, for he considered that the answer to all important questions in the history of mankind was to be found by analysis of the human psyche. Although Freud was concerned with empirical facts and particular case studies when it came to psychoanalysis, for these provided the data he needed to draw conclusions about mental illness, he did not manifest a like empiricism in connection with history and anthropology. Dawson, on the other hand, had a historian's concern with particular historical events and with the developments in ideology and culture which gave those events their special significance. His study of ancillary disciplines to gain historical understanding led a reviewer in *The American Historical Review* to remark of a synthesis volume of his work: "It reveals Dawson as a writer ... well versed in anthropology, sociology, psychology, and the basic ideas which have dominated historical perspectives over the ages."[1]

Like Freud, Dawson had a particular conception of human nature, but he did not claim that this was derived from his study of history and anthropology, but from the teachings of Christian Revelation. No doubt Dawson believed that history and anthropology would give evidence in support of the Christian conception of man. But this is quite different from deriving one's basic view of man from empirical study, as Freud claimed to be doing by his analysis of the human psyche.

There is another point of contrast between these two thinkers. Freud sees existing social restraints as the cause for man's dissatisfaction with contemporary society, and the chief source for the creation of his neuroses. He observed, "It was found that men become neurotic because they cannot tolerate the degree of privation that society imposes on them in virtue of its cultural ideals."[2]

Dawson, on the other hand, sees the chief cause for man's present social discontent to lie in society's frenetic pursuit of the goals of the here-and-now and its disregard of the spiritual dimension in human life. He sees in modern revolutionary movements the revolt of the human spirit against the emptiness of secular civilization. "For the failure of our civilization to satisfy man's deeper needs has created a spiritual vacuum, a heat of darkness and chaos beneath the mechanical order and the scientific intelligence of the modern world."[3]

Therefore, although Dawson occasionally makes use of certain Freudian terms in his analysis of cultural phenomena, his view of culture

---

[1]*American Historical Review*, vol. 63, no. 1, Oct. 1957, p. 77, in review of the *Dynamics of World History*.

[2]Sigmund Freud, *Civilization and its Discontents* (Doubleday Anchor, n.d.), p. 30.

[3]Christopher Dawson, *The Judgment of the Nations* (Sheed & Ward, 1942), p. 132.

is based upon quite different premises from those of Freud. This is because Freud thinks of man as a biological organism motivated by his physical appetites and oppressed by social restraints, whereas Dawson looks upon man as not only biological, but also having a transcendent element which is ultimately the most powerful force in his desires and in his attitude toward reality.

The relationship which exists between Freud's view of the human psyche and his conception of culture is described by Will Herberg, who brings together what Freud has written on the subject in several of his major works. Herberg states:

> All of Freud's thinking in the field of human relations hinges on a two-fold dualism—the dualism of ego and id within the psyche, and the dualism of individual and society within the culture. The two dualisms are not unrelated.
>
> In his mature account of the structure and "topography" of the psyche, Freud repeatedly emphasizes that it is the id, the repository of the deep instinctual drives, which is the dynamic part of the self. It is the "oldest of mental provinces or agencies"; it is wholly unconscious and supplies the psychic energy for the functioning of the entire organism. Its law is to press for immediate gratification. . . .
>
> But the immediate gratification for which these instincts in the id press might well imperil the entire organism by bringing it into conflict with its environment, natural and social. Of this, the id knows and cares nothing, since it is governed entirely by the pleasure principle. The survival of the organism requires the functioning of another agency that will restrain and control the unregulated activity of the id. This agency is the ego, described by Freud as "a special organization which henceforward acts as an intermediary between the id and the external world." The ego is concerned with "keeping down the instinctual claims of the id," but also with "discovering the most favorable and least perilous method of obtaining satisfaction, taking the external world into account."[4]

So far, there is no reference to morality, but only to a dualism between the desire for pleasure by the id, and the ego's awareness that certain

---

[4]Will Herberg, "Freud, the Revisionists, and Social Reality," in *Freud and the 20th Century,* edited by Benjamin Nelson (New York: Meridian Books, 1957), pp. 146-147. The Freud books Herberg drew upon for this recapitulation of Freud's views on the psyche are: *An Outline of Psychoanalysis, New Introductory Lectures on Psychoanalysis: The Ego and the Id, Moses and Monotheism, Civilization and its Discontents.*

cautions and restraints must be observed if the impulses of the id are to find their best outlet. Reason, as Freud sees it embodied in the ego, has nothing whatever to do with morality, but only with expediency. That is, how it can arrange for the desires of the id to get their way with the least possible interference from the external world.

Thus there is a chasm which separates Freud's concept of reason from the Christian understanding of the term. For the Christian, reason is used to discover what is true, not merely what is expedient. And therefore, the reason is an instrument by which the conscience makes its moral judgments. For Freud, on the other hand, the conscience, which he calls the superego, is something irrational and is imposed by guilt feelings upon the clarity of the reason.

Herberg describes Freud's conception of the superego in these terms: "The picture becomes even more complicated as we recognize a third agency in the psychic life, the superego, the internalized 'successor and representation of the parents and educators,' which stands over the ego, out of which it has emerged, as an inward monitor, exercising the powers of 'observation, criticism, and prohibition'." Herberg then adds, linking up Freud's view of the psyche and his view of culture: "The conflict between the ego and the id takes place within the depths of the psyche, but it is a conflict writ large in the life of society."[5]

Thus Freud explains the superego as being derived from the stern moral prohibitions imposed on the child by his parents and educators. But that leaves us with a twofold question. First, does not this explanation merely push back to a preceding generation the problem of where this superego or conscience came from? To say that such a moral element in the child came from the parents is simply avoiding the issue—like the infinite regress argument.

Second, if the child himself were not possessed of some innate moral sense, which needs to be developed by being instructed and appealed to, and given a chance to be exercised, he would not recognize, let alone respond to, the moral injunctions of the superego. And if the superego becomes internalized, as Freud claims it does, then there must be some element in the nature of the child in which it can take root. Without a moral sense, the child could only operate in terms of the reality principle which Freud refers to—that such and such actions are

---

[5]*Ibid.*, pp. 147-148.

dangerous or likely to lead to the loss of rewards or to the incurring of punishments. The fact that such dangers and threats are translated into a moral language means that there must be an aptitude on the part of the child for receiving that translation. As C.S. Lewis has observed in this same connection, in a country where there were no eyes, dark would be a word without meaning. And in a society or culture where people had no sense of morality, things morally good and evil could not be recognized as such. The superego would simply never have come into existence.

Philip Rieff points out other factors which Freud ignored in his claim that the superego is simply a means for assuring submission to existing authority, and for acceptance of established beliefs and institutions. These factors include the fact that "conscience may be at odds with its social sources." The refusal of Freud to recognize this means that, in consequence, he "overestimates the degree of consistency in the ethical injunctions to which people are exposed.... He assumes that parents, as well as 'teachers, authorities, (or) self-chosen models and heroes venerated by society,' all preach the same line."[6]

As an example of Freud's failure to be realistic in this matter, due to the rigid structure he had imposed on reality, consider the conflict today between parents of orthodox Catholic belief and many of the Modernist Catholic teachers and priests to whom they may send their children for instruction. But even in Freud's time, a fair number of teachers and other authority figures must have been willing to promote the counsels of expediency and a surrender to the *Zeitgeist*, rather than insist on the strict moral injunctions which Freud claims to be characteristic of all those who are in positions of authority.

In contrast to the attitude of prohibition and threats which Freud ascribes to parents and to other people in authority as the cause for the formation of the superego, Freud reverses his field when he seeks an explanation for the origin of religion. Here it is the child's need for protection by the father, and the continuation of that sense of need over into adulthood, where Freud discovers the origins of religion. He states:

> Religious ideas ... are not the residue of experience or the
> final result of reflection; they are illusions, fulfillments of the oldest,
> strongest, and most insistent wishes of mankind; the secret of their

---

[6]Philip Rieff, *Freud: the Mind of the Moralist* (New York: Doubleday, Anchor edition, 1961), p. 299.

strength is the strength of those wishes. We know already that the terrifying effect of infantile helplessness aroused the need for protection—protection through love—which the father relieved, and that the discovery that this helplessness would continue through the whole of life made it necessary to cling to the existence of a father—but this time a more powerful one.[7]

As Rieff remarks about the nature of Freud's argument here, "The rhetoric of Freud's analysis depends almost entirely upon evocations of 'childishness'.... Religion is linked with the weakness of childhood and contrasted with the heroism of true maturity."[8]

We might note two other mistaken assumptions in Freud's analysis of religion. First, the fact that an idea satisfies certain psychological needs does not thereby prove it to be untrue. In fact, it could have the opposite significance, if one believes that the universe manifests purpose, and that the existence of a need points to the likelihood of the existence of that which can satisfy it. As Arnold Lunn has remarked about this kind of argument, the fact of hunger does not disprove the existence of food. What Freud does is to assume that religion corresponds to no objective reality, and then attempts to explain how such an illusion could have arisen. The psychoanalytic game as a substitute for rational examination is very easy to play, and it removes the necessity for having to think about issues which you would prefer to see decided without discussion or argument.

The same procedure could be used on Freud himself, to explain how he ever came to believe that religion is an illusion. Religious beliefs being based on objective reality, what was it that led Freud to come to his misconception of them? What special and peculiar set of circumstances in the relationship between Freud and his father led him to adopt the irrational but wish-fulfilling conclusion that God doesn't exist?

As against Freud's view of religion as an illusion and his claim that psychological maturity requires escape from the father and from the father-image found in God, Christopher Dawson gives a more balanced view of man's relationship to God. He notes the psychological soundness of establishing a principle of continuity between the earthly father whom

---

[7]Sigmund Freud, *The Future of an Illusion* (New York: Sheed and Ward, 1948), p. 29.

[8]Rieff, *Mind of the Moralist*, p. 291.

we have revered in childhood, and the Heavenly Father after whom all paternity in Heaven and earth is named. Dawson writes:

> For as St. Thomas shows, *Pietas*, which is the cult of parents and kinsfolk and native place as the principles of our being, by whom and in which we are born and nourished, has an essential relation to religion which is the cult of God as our first principle. Hence piety in the classical sense of the word is not a matter of sentiment or social tradition, it is a moral principle that lies at the root of every culture and every religion, and the society that loses it has lost its primary moral basis and its hope of survival.[9]

One of the most striking divergences of viewpoint between Dawson and Freud lies in their different conceptions of the nature of childhood. Where Freud finds this stage in human life to be the time of the unfettered domination of the id, Dawson sees it as the time when the human being has most awareness of the transcendent element in existence. The child, for Freud, is summed up as a self-centered and grasping little bundle of animal impulses. For Dawson, who is not without recognition of the influence of original sin upon the child's nature (Dawson has a definite affinity with St. Augustine in certain elements of his worldview), the more important fact about the child is his openness to the world of spiritual reality. In the first volume of his Gifford Lectures Dawson writes:

> This element of transcendence is a primordial element of human experience. Man is born into a world that he has not made, that he cannot understand, and on which his existence is dependent. In actual fact, social authority and the world of culture take hold of him from the cradle and thrust back the frontier of transcendence behind the authority and omniscience of parents and schoolmasters. It is only in the poetic imagination which is akin to that of the child and the mystic that we can still feel the pure sense of mystery and transcendence which is man's natural element.[10]

It is in connection with Freud's view about religion that we first find Dawson controverting Freud. Although Dawson makes a passing

---

[9]Christopher Dawson, *Tradition and Inheritance* (St. Paul, Minn: The Wanderer Press, 1970), p. 9.

[10]Christopher Dawson, *Religion and Culture* (New York: Sheed and Ward, 1948), p. 29.

reference to Freud in a volume of 1932 — "In physical science the dominant figure is Einstein, in psychology it is Freud . . . — and each of them has exerted an influence on the thought of the age that far transcends the limits of his particular subject,"[11] — it is not until 1942 that he mentions a particular idea of Freud and takes issue with it. He refers to Freud's belief that "the religions of mankind must be classified as mass delusions of this kind," and explains that for Freud they are, in Dawson's words, "delusional transformations of reality based on the desire to obtain assurance of happiness and protection from suffering."

Dawson points out that this view means that religion is a substitute for reality, and hence a source of weakness to society, "a kind of collective neurosis which perverts and saps social energy." As against that conception Dawson asserts that history gives us a quite different account of the influence of religious belief on social effort:

> But is it possible to reconcile such a view with the facts of history? For religion has undoubtedly been one of the greatest motive powers in human history. It seems to have increased collective energy rather than diminishing it, and whenever humanity has been on the move, religion has been like the pillar of fire and the cloud that went before the Israelites in their desert journeyings.
>
> It seems to me impossible to believe that the power of the spirit is nothing but a perversion and consequently a degradation of physical energy, yet this is the logical conclusion of the rationalist argument. It is as though one were to say that reason itself arises from the perversion of the irrational. It is a line of thought that leads to the blank wall of nihilism and nonsense.[12]

Thus there is a fundamental conflict between Dawson and Freud on the nature of religion and on the nature of its influence on society and culture. In fact, I think it may be said that Dawson's whole career as a sociologist and a historian has been devoted to demonstrating the exact opposite of what Freud held to be true concerning the influence of religion. And of Christianity in particular, which is really Freud's primary target, Dawson holds that it has been more dynamic than any other social force in world history. For Dawson, the dynamic motivation which Christianity imparted to Western man has been the source of the

---

[11]Christopher Dawson, *Christianity and the New Age* (London: Sheed and Ward, 1931), p. 19.

[12]Dawson, *Judgment of the Nations,* pp. 127-128.

world-transforming achievements of Western civilization.[13]

Let us now examine what is implied in the anthropologists' use of the concept of culture, for it is upon this concept that Freud and Dawson both rely in their analysis of human society. One standard textbook in anthropology speaks of the nature of culture in these terms:

> Culture is, therefore, wholly the result of social invention, and it may be thought of as the social heritage, for it is transmitted by precept to each new generation. . . . What is more, its continuity is safeguarded by punishment of those members of a society who refuse to follow the patterns for behavior that are laid down for them to follow.[14]

Now it is this last element in culture, the punishments by which the patterns of behavior are enforced, which is of special interest to Freud. For Freud regards culture as being oppressive to the individual and his desires, and therefore as having to be imposed externally on the individual and maintained by a system of rewards and punishments. For him, there is no inner link or responsiveness in human nature to culture; for in Freud's psychology the deeper levels of the individual are essentially antisocial, intent only upon individual satisfaction; and this satisfaction, society and its culture prevent him from having, or from having in the degree to which he wants it. This antagonistic view of culture, which was very popular in the 1960's with the younger generation of revolutionaries, and which still exists as a strong undercurrent of influence on our society today, is a result of Freud's conceiving the human being as a sexual anarch in his desires and motivations. This is a sexuality which, although it uses the term love, is basically grasping and self-centered.

Here is Sigmund Freud's conception of culture as given in *The Future of an Illusion,* a volume published in 1928 which presented his analysis of religion:

> Human culture includes on the one hand all the knowledge and power that men have acquired in order to master the forces of nature and win resources from her for the satisfaction of human

---

[13]See Christopher Dawson, *Religion and the Rise of Western Culture* (New York: Sheed and Ward, 1950), pp. 8-14.

[14]E. Adamson Hoebel, *"The Nature of Culture"* in *Man, Culture, and Society* edited by Harry L. Shapiro (New York: Oxford U.P., 1960), pp. 168-169.

needs; and on the other hand it includes the necessary arrangements whereby men's relations to each other, and in particular the distribution of the attainable riches, may be regulated. The two tendencies of culture are not independent of each other, first, because the mutual relations of men are profoundly influenced by the measure of instinctual satisfaction that the existing resources make possible ... and (also) because *every individual is virtually an enemy of culture,* which is nevertheless ostensibly an object of universal human concern. ... *Thus culture must be defended against the individual,* and its organization, its institutions, and its laws, are all directed to this; they aim not only at establishing a certain distribution of property, but also at maintaining it. (Emphasis added).

A further comment by Freud makes more explicit the similarity between Freud's view of society and culture and that of Karl Marx. Both of them conceive of society as a means for the exploitation of the weaker by the stronger. Thus Freud writes: "So one gets the impression that culture is something which was imposed on a resisting majority by a minority that understood how to possess itself of the means of power and coercion."[15]

Therefore while Freud admits the need for accepting the renunciations required by culture, he does so only reluctantly, and after having removed from culture any moral basis for its restrictions on the human being's desires. As a result, as he sees it, "At every period, as again now, many men have asked themselves whether this fragment that has been acquired by culture [i.e., what Freud has earlier called 'solid advances in the conquest of nature'] is indeed worth defending at all."[16]

This is, of course, the question asked by Jean-Jacques Rousseau in the mid-eighteenth century, and it is a heritage of the Enlightenment hostility toward established institutions.

From what we have said so far, it is clear that Freud's view of society is subversive of its continued existence. If Freud's view of the relation between the human being and culture were true, there would be no reason for a person's being willing to accept the restraints which society places upon him.

Freud's theory is essentially a part of the process of liquidation of the heritage of European and Christian culture upon which the

---

[15]Freud, *Future of an Illusion,* pp. 9-10.
[16]*Ibid.,* p. 10.

nineteenth century, and now the twentieth century, have been actively engaged. Freud himself was formed in a culture which still gave him reason to continue to live under the restraints imposed by society, accepting with stoic endurance what his theory of culture should have led him to reject. But a later generation, having lost contact with the Christian past and having been brought up on Freud's view of the primacy of the instinctual life, sees no reason to imitate Freud in his endurance. His own theory makes Freud himself a kind of late-nineteenth-century relic, who failed to grasp, or at least to take advantage of, the liberation from social control which Freudian ideas of human nature and of society's oppression actually afforded him.

That Freud's view of society is basically nihilistic and thus provides no good reason for an individual's accepting any social controls, is testified to by Philip Rieff in this passage:

> Yet if moral rules come only from cultures which legislate deviously for their own advantage, against the freedom of the individual, how can any part of conduct be taken for granted? If every limit can be seen as a limitation of personality, the question with which we may confront every opportunity is: after all, why not? ... And those who have interpreted Freud as advocating, for reasons of health, sexual freedom—promiscuity rather than the strain of fidelity, adultery rather than neuroses—have caught the hint, if not the intent, of his psychoanalysis.[17]

An even more striking testimony to the subversive element in Freud's thought is to be found in the essay of Lionel Trilling called *"The Teaching of Modern Literature,"* which is based on his own experience in teaching certain works in Columbia University's program in the humanities. Trilling is a strong admirer of Freud, and he believes that Freud is one of the chief intellectual pioneers whose thought finds expression in modern literature—or at least in those works which Trilling himself finds most valuable or most relevant.

It is quite possible, of course, that some of the books with which Trilling chooses to support his theses could be interpreted quite differently by someone having other than the Freudian perspective from which Trilling himself approaches them. But granted that particular reservation, the important point is that Trilling believes that modern

---

[17]Rieff, *Mind of the Moralist,* p. 359.

literature has as its goal the subversion of society. Consequently, when it is taught by a teacher sensitive to its inner meaning, he will communicate that message of subversion to his students. And this message is linked to Trilling's insight that Freud emancipated the individual from having to accept any intellectual basis for the restraints imposed by society. Trilling declares:

> For one thing, he [i.e., Freud] puts to us the question of whether or not we want to *accept* civilization. . . .
> But just here lies the matter of Freud's question that the world more and more believes Freud himself did not answer. The pain that civilization inflicts is that of the instinctual renunciation that civilization demands, and it would seem that fewer and fewer people wish to say with Freud that the loss of instinctual gratification, emotional freedom, or love, is compensated for either by the security of civilized life or by the stern pleasures of the moral masculine character.[18]

One might note that the linking in parallel form of "instinctual gratification, emotional freedom, or love, " implies a certain equivalence among them, which is contrary to Christian belief and also to human experience. In fact, an enslavement of the human person to lust comes from attempts at unrestrained instinctual gratification. Moreover, if love requires self-sacrifice for its happiness to be deep and lasting, then love will not be a means for escaping from renunciation, as Trilling implies it to be.

Here is Trilling's final view of the results of the Freudian conception of culture: here is what students are expected to gain as a result of their study of modern literature:

> The end is not merely freedom from the middle class but freedom from society itself. I venture to say that the idea of losing oneself up to the point of self-destruction, of surrendering oneself to experience without regard to self-interest or conventional morality, of escaping wholly from societal bonds is an "element" somewhere in the mind of every modern person. . . .
> But the teacher who undertakes to present modern literature to his students may not allow that idea to remain in the *somewhere*

---

[18]Lionel Trilling, "On the Modern Element in Modern Literature" in *The Idea of the Modern,* edited by Irving Howe (New York: Horizon Press, 1967), pp. 76-77. The Trilling article was first published in 1961.

of his mind; he must take it from the place where it exists habitual and unrealized and put it in the conscious forefront of his thought. And if he is committed to an admiration of modern literature, he must also be committed to this chief idea of modern literature.[19]

Lionel Trilling was a very sensitive and intelligent man, but here we have him undermining the ground by which he and his sensitivity were supported. Is it merely a coincidence that it was at Columbia University, some four years after Trilling committed this article to print, that Mark Rudd and his SDS started their campaign that clearly indicated what they thought of society, including especially the university and its reason for existence?

Notice that what is implicitly assumed in the choice about culture set before us by both Freud and Trilling is that there is no life beyond the present one. And that therefore it is merely a matter of calculation as to which option one wishes to take: that of hedonistic gratification of the instincts, or that of renunciation for the sake of society's continued existence. Thus the value of human life is seen to exist only on a natural level, and one's choice has to be made on that basis alone. No other culture, it seems to me, has ever thought it could justify the sacrifices demanded of men by obedience to the laws of society without seeing those laws as participating in a higher law which gave them value and sanction.

To naturalize the options for the choice of the individual, as both Freud and Trilling have done, is to invite the triumph of hedonism. For while experience may eventually show that unrestrained gratification and hedonism become but ashes in the mouth, by the time they do, most people have become so enslaved that it is unlikely they will ever escape from the toils in which they have been bound by their own previous self-indulgence.

The violence of the revolt against middle-class culture and eventually against society itself, which Trilling believes to be characteristic of modern literature, prompts the question, What is the relationship between modern rationalism and this discontent with society? Does it not seem likely that the very rationalism which Freud and Trilling represent, with its weighing of different options for conduct on a purely self-regarding basis—which of these promises the greatest

---

[19]*Ibid.*, pp. 81-82.

satisfaction and advantage for me?—is itself at the root of this discontent with modern civilization which they identify? Such discontent they hold to be the consequence of any social order whatever, and not simply the result of the spiritual emptiness in modern society which they themselves have helped to create.

Dawson has a quite different conception of the causes of the present condition of modern culture. He points out:

> Nevertheless, man cannot live by reason alone. His spiritual life, and even his physical instincts, are starved in the narrow and arid territory of purely rational consciousness. He is driven to take refuge in the non-rational, whether it be the irrational blend of spirituality and emotionalism which is termed romanticism, or, as is increasingly the case today, in the frankly subrational sphere of pure sensationalism and sexual impulse.[20]

In contrast to this, Dawson sets before us the Baroque culture of Catholic and parts of Protestant Europe which prevailed as the dominant form of Western culture from about 1550 to 1750, and even for some time after that in certain parts of Europe. (Johann Sebastian Bach, one of the great masters of Baroque music, died in 1751.) Dawson gives us this description of the spirit of the Baroque culture:

> It is not merely that it was an *uneconomic* culture which spent its capital lavishly, recklessly, and splendidly whether to the glory of God or for the adornment of human life. It was rather that the whole spirit of the culture was passionate and ecstatic, and finds its supreme expression in the art of music and in religious mysticism. . . . The bourgeois culture has the mechanical rhythm of a clock, the Baroque the musical rhythm of a fugue or a sonata.[21]

This Baroque culture spread with Spanish and Portuguese colonization to the Americas and to the Indies, and it also had considerable influence on England and on the Lutheran as well as the Catholic parts of Germany. Dawson believes that it was more sympathetically received by the peoples of the newly discovered lands than has been the exported culture of Western liberalism in the

---

[20]Dawson, *Christianity and the New Age,* pp. 49-50.
[21]Christopher Dawson, *Dynamics of World History* (New York: Sheed and Ward, 1957), p. 207.

nineteenth and twentieth centuries. He thus draws a contrast between the Baroque culture and the bourgeois culture of the last two centuries. This suggests that the revolt against the middle class in modern literature to which Trilling refers, may be seen as an instinctive groping after this more vital and spontaneous kind of society which characterized the Baroque period in Western history. Dawson states:

> For the expansion of the Baroque culture was not merely an ideological movement, like the Enlightenment in the eighteenth century or the diffusion of nineteenth-century liberalism. It appealed to the heart as well as the head and satisfied the emotional as well as the intellectual needs of human nature. And thus it was never merely the culture of an educated minority, since its religious ideals embodied in painting and architecture and music were the common heritage of the people as a whole and not the exclusive possession of a privileged class.
>
> Owing to this character, the Baroque culture possessed exceptional powers of diffusion even among peoples of alien traditions. On the whole, the modern expansion of European culture has been external and material. It has forced non-European peoples to recognize the superiority of Western techniques and Western scientific knowledge, but it has failed to bridge the spiritual gap between East and West. But within the sphere of the Baroque culture this was not so. Mexico and Peru and the Portuguese settlements in Asia assimilated the Baroque culture and produced their own local styles of Baroque art.[22]

What, then, is the basic difference between Dawson's conception of culture and that of Freud? First, there are certain similarities. Like Freud, Dawson recognizes three different dimensions of human life, each based on a different level in the human psyche. In a general way, Dawson's analysis corresponds to Freud's three levels of id, ego, and superego. But important distinctions must be noted, especially with regard to the third level. While Freud identifies the superego as negative and prohibiting, a source of criticism and rebuke, Dawson gives this third element in the human psyche a much wider range of meaning and a much more positive character. With Freud, it is the id which is the source of all that is positive and vital in the human being; as Herberg

---

[22]Christopher Dawson, *The Movement of World Revolution* (New York: Sheed and Ward, 1959), p.44.

observes, it "supplies the psychic energy for the functioning of the entire organism."[23]

In contrast to Freud, Dawson, since he does not limit the third level of human life to a merely negative function, finds on this level the source of man's deepest aspirations and of human society's greatest achievements. This particular dimension of human existence is the means by which man is most open to God, and it also serves to redirect the desires of the instinctual level so that they are able to serve a higher purpose. Thus Dawson's psychology of man, although it has some definite points of contact with Freud's, reverses the whole scale of values which we find in Freud's view of culture and in Freud's conception of the human psyche. Dawson writes:

> Human life—and especially the life of man in the higher cultures—involves three different psychological levels. There is first the subrational life of unconscious instinct and impulse which plays such a large part in human life, especially the life of the masses. Secondly there is the level of conscious voluntary effort and rational activity which is the sphere of culture, *par excellence*. And finally there is the super-rational level of spiritual experience, which is the sphere not only of religion but of the highest creative forces of cultural achievement—the intuitions of the artist, the poet and the philosopher—and also of certain forms of scientific intuition which seem to transcend the sphere of rational calculation and research . . .
>
> For the third psychological level which I have mentioned—the plane of spiritual experience and religious faith and intuitive vision—is also the center of unity for man and society. It is here that a culture finds its focus and its common spiritual ends; and here also is the source of the higher moral values which are accepted not merely as rules imposed by society for its own welfare, but as a sacred law which finds its tribunal in the human heart and the individual conscience.
>
> In the last resort every civilization depends not on its material resources and its methods of production, but on the spiritual vision of its greatest minds and on the way in which this experience is transmitted to the community by faith and tradition and education. Where unifying spiritual vision is lost—where it is no longer transmitted to the community as a whole—the civilization decays. "Where there is no vision, the people perish."[24]

---

[23]Herberg, *op. cit.,* p. 146.

[24]Christopher Dawson, *The Historic Reality of Christian Culture* (New York: Harper and Brothers, 1960), pp. 92-93.

11

Arnold Toynbee: From Christianity to Religious Syncretism

Arnold Toynbee's Philosophy of History

Arnold Toynbee (1889-1975) is probably the best-known philosopher of history of the twentieth century. He has set forth his ideas concerning the growth and decline of civilizations in the ten volumes of *A Study of History,* published over a period of 20 years—1934 to 1954. By comparing the life history of many different civilizations, he hoped to arrive at a definite conclusion as to the factors that either encourage or impede cultural growth and vitality. In the first six volumes of the *Study,* which were brought to completion in 1939, he arrived at a religious solution to his quest for meaning in history, by identifying Christ and Christianity as the answer he had sought.

By 1954, however, when he published the remaining four volumes of the *Study,* he had radically altered the direction of his course and its goal. Already in the seventh volume, completed in 1947, Toynbee had turned to Mahayana Buddhism as the most desirable form of religion he had encountered in his study of the different civilizations in world history. Nevertheless, he was not willing to put all his emphasis on Mahayana Buddhism alone, so he proposed a syncretism of the four major religions which he judged to be still living ones, that is, not existing in some fossilized condition. These four were Mahayana Buddhism, Hinduism, Islam, and Christianity. He urged the adherents of these four religions to submerge all of their theological and moral differences and to unite in one single body of what he called the Church Militant. (How he expected any militancy to be left in these religions, in the amalgam of them which he desired, after each had surrendered its own distinctive beliefs, Toynbee did not tell his readers.) The first fact to be noted about Arnold Toynbee is that his philosophy of history is apparently developed with a view to avoiding the errors of Oswald Spengler. Where Spengler emphasizes the predetermined outcome of the life cycle of cultures and the predominance of racial and biological factors in cultural growth and decline, Toynbee emphasizes the theoretical freedom of every culture to grow indefinitely—that is, so long as it continues to meet its challenges successfully. Moreover, the Toynbee dialectic of challenge and response by which a culture grows and achieves greater complexity, is conceived of as manifesting the moral freedom of the society in the kind of choices it makes. The choice thus made determines the kind of character which the civilization will have. Thus, for example, for Toynbee, Athens and Sparta made different responses to the problem of overpopulation and thus determined the kind of values and ideals that were to be predominant in their social life.

The second thing to note about Toynbee is how he solved the problem presented by the alleged freedom of societies, when in fact almost all of them, possessed of this freedom, are now, according to Toynbee, either dead or in the process of dissolution. The one exception is Western civilization, about which Toynbee in his earlier volumes is undecided. Indeed, for Toynbee, the problem of cultural fatalism is much greater than it would be for Spengler (if the latter believed in freedom), for Toynbee identifies between twenty-one and twenty-nine civilizations that have existed in the past, and yet all but one of these are now either gone or on their way out.

Toynbee's answer to this is to see a dialectic of cultural growth or decline in which a society is tempted to make the response of self idolatry, or infatuation with one's past achievements. Thus a culture which has met a previous challenge successfully is by that very fact in danger of not meeting a new challenge or problem creatively, but by a mere repetition of a previous response. But this is of no value in the changed circumstances of the new cultural situation which gave rise to the challenge.

The likelihood of the failure of a society to meet new challenges successfully is increased by the fact that, for Toynbee, societies are led by minority groups who won the leadership of the society by having succeeded in constructing a suitable response to an earlier challenge. This minority is likely to be wedded to its own past successes, to the actions that brought them to their present position of eminence, and thus to repeat those actions when they are no longer suitable. Thus, in addition to self idolatry by the whole society, there is also, and intimately responsible for this wider social attitude, self idolatry by an upper class or governing group. In this way Toynbee explains cultural growth and decline by something that parallels the Christian doctrine of Original Sin.

Although Toynbee sees the initial challenge to a society as consisting in some environmental problem to be overcome, he believes that as society grows or advances, its challenges become primarily moral rather than physical ones, and thus it is in the response made by the soul of the society that the real answer to growth or decline is to be found. It is for this reason that Toynbee is inclined to discount physical factors to a considerable degree when it comes to seeking the causes for the breakdown of the culture. And it is for this reason also that he puts the fall of classical culture much earlier than most historians: that is, in 431 B.C., the year of the outbreak of the long-drawn-out war between Athens and Sparta within the area of Hellenic culture. According to Toynbee, this initial breakdown was never recovered from. Consequently, all the history of Rome's subsequent growth and expansion (for Toynbee sees Rome as a constituent part of Hellenic culture) was rendered useless by the failure of the Greek city states to settle their social problems without recourse to militarism.

This is one of the chief weaknesses of Toynbee's view of history—that a society loses its power of cultural choice fairly early in its history and simply repeats unproductive responses thereafter, in trying to meet new challenges. Thus, while using the language of freedom for a society, Toynbee seems little different from the fatalism of Spengler, who sees every culture as required to go through a definitely ordained life cycle from birth to death. If anything, Spengler's view of a culture is more optimistic than Toynbee's, for he allows for outstanding cultural achievement in three out of the four stages of a culture. Only the last stage, the winter of a culture, to which he attaches the term civilization in a pejorative sense, is without any real cultural value.

It seems that there is another criticism which might be made of Toynbee's view of culture. In seeking to emphasize the priority of factors of will and moral choice and to depreciate environmental and other physical factors, Toynbee is detaching himself from the solid earth and trying to remove all problems to the stratosphere. For social breakdown is not only a matter of wrong choice, it may be a matter of obstacles too great to be overcome. What about the thriving medieval civilization of Russia centered in Kiev in Ukraine in the tenth to twelfth centuries which was overrun by the Mongol hordes and thereafter never recovered from the blow? What about the striking decline of Spain from the cultural pre-eminence it enjoyed from about 1500 to 1700? For the cause of this was the accident of not having a Hapsburg as heir, and so replacing the Spanish dynasty with a French one, which brought into Spain the destructive ideas of the eighteenth century Enlightenment. Spain never fully recovered from the damage that this inflicted on her earlier cultural tradition.

Consequently, Toynbee's immense erudition should not blind us to the fact that his ideas concerning culture are far too facile and superficial. They are based on a certain lack of realism in recognizing the factors which often do cause a nation's or a culture's decline. They posit a supremacy of the human will over difficulties that it encounters which does not correspond to either personal or social experience. Especially applicable to Toynbee is Christopher Dawson's reply to a writer who criticized his explanation of the causes of schism as showing a materialistic interpretation of history. Dawson responded:

> Nevertheless, the limitations imposed on the freedom of the individual by the limitations of his social environment and tradition are facts of experience which the Christian, no less than the secular historian, is bound to take account of, and we cannot escape them by shutting our eyes to their existence. For human freedom is not the freedom of a pure spirit, it is the difficult freedom of a creature bound to his body, his country, and his people, the member of a society unable to disembarrass himself of the inheritance of the past and the countless limitations that are inseparable from the conditions of material existence.
>
> No doubt it is difficult for the theologian or the metaphysician who moves in the free atmosphere of spiritual truth to realize the limitations and obscurity of the lower world of material and temporal existence in which men live and work.

Dawson added as a conclusion, and it seems especially to apply to Toynbee's invoking the power of moral choice as the chief reason for the rise or decline of civilizations: "Thus while spiritual freedom is of the very essence of human personality, its exercise is conditioned and limited by the countless circumstances of man's social and historical existence."[1]

---

[1]Christopher Dawson, *The Frontiers of Necessity: The Social Factor in Religious Belief* in *The Tablet* (London), May 28, 1938. Reprinted in *The Dawson Newsletter*, Vol. IV, No. 1, Spring 1985, p. 4.

In fact, it would seem that Toynbee's own analysis of the breakdown of Hellenic culture is an excellent example of the power of forces other than those of moral choice. Let us suppose that Toynbee is correct in seeing the war between Athens and Sparta as the beginning of the breakdown of Hellenic culture. Why is it that all future generations of Greeks and Romans could not reverse the wrong decision made at that time, so as to seek some other means than militarism as an answer to their problems? If it is simply a matter of choice alone, there is nothing to prevent later generations from taking a different course of action from their ancestors. Toynbee leads us to believe that once a wrong moral choice has been made by a society, nothing can be done in the future to reverse it. So while Toynbee preaches moral freedom, his analysis of history is based on the fatality of one wrong choice. And there is no way to explain that, if one does not take into account the limiting effects of particular circumstances and social traditions. Moreover, while militarism between states may be a source of a loss of power on the part of a civilization, this loss can also occur when a nation or a civilization is not capable of defending itself against external aggression.

There is also the fact that the great expansion of Greek culture in the Hellenistic age, which aided its internal development as well,—e.g., in science and mathematics—was only made possible by the successful militarism of Alexander the Great. Unless Toynbee wishes to write off the Hellenistic age as of no importance to Greek and world civilization, this development in Greek culture, which resulted from militarism, cannot be ignored.

Here is the way Christopher Dawson speaks of the nature of a culture, in response to the idealist view of R. G. Collingwood—and since Toynbee's emphasis on the all importance of moral choice manifests the same kind of idealist approach to culture as Collingwood—this statement applies equally well to Toynbee's views. Dawson writes:

> In reality a culture is neither a purely physical process nor an ideal construction. It is a living whole from its roots in the soil and in the simple instinctive life of the shepherd, the fisherman, and the husbandman, up to its flowering in the highest achievements of the artist and the philosopher; just as the individual combines in the substantial unity of his personality the animal life of nutrition and reproduction with the higher activities of reason and intellect. It is impossible to disregard the importance of a material and non-rational element in history. Every culture rests on a foundation of

geographical environment and racial inheritance, which conditions its highest activities.[2]

To return to Arnold Toynbee. Possibly because of his implicit realization that, in terms of his dialectic, societies were not going anywhere except to breakdown and dissolution, Toynbee turned to the world religions as providing the real meaning of mankind's strenuous toil up the cliff wall of historical development. (The metaphor, by the way, is Toynbee's.) By the end of his first six volumes published in 1934 and 1939, Toynbee seemed to have reached a position of accepting Christianity, and even Catholic Christianity, as embodying the fullest truth realizable in human history. In a famous passage comparing the figure of Christ with the figures of the various dying gods of Greek and Near Eastern mythology, Toynbee portrays the experience of Jesus recorded in the Gospels as something unique in the religious history of humanity. Making effective use of English poetry and Biblical quotation, Toynbee concludes his survey of the various saviors of society with these words:

> In what spirit does the dying god go to his death? If, with this question on our lips, we address ourselves once more to our array of tragic masks, we shall see the perfect separating itself from the imperfect sacrifice. Even in Calliope's lovely lamentation for the death of Orpheus there is a jarring note of bitterness which strikes, and shocks, a Christian ear.
> "Why do we mortals make lament over the deaths of our sons, seeing that the gods themselves have not the power to keep Death from laying his hand upon their children."
> What a moral to read into the dying god's story! So the goddess who was Orpheus' mother would never have let Orpheus die if she could have helped it.... But Antipater's poem is answered in another and greater masterpiece:
> "For God so loved the world that He gave His only begotten Son, that whosoever believeth in Him should not perish but have everlasting life."
> When the Gospel thus answers the elegy, it delivers an oracle: "The One remains, the many change and pass" (Shelley, *Adonais,* liii). And this is in truth the final result of our survey of saviors. At the final ordeal of death, few, even of these would-be savior gods, have dared to put their title to the test by plunging into the icy river. And now, as we stand and gaze with our eyes fixed upon the farther

---

[2]*Progress and Religion*, p. 45.

shore, a single figure rises from the flood and straightway fills the whole horizon. There is the Savior; "and the pleasure of the Lord shall prosper in his hand; he shall see of the travail of his soul and be satisfied" (*Isa.* 53:10-11).[3]

And in a lecture delivered at Oxford University in May 1940, when the Nazi armies were overrunning Belgium and France, Toynbee again centered attention on the importance of Christianity. He interpreted the unification of the modern world brought about by the West as the Providential means by which Christianity would spread to the rest of the world—even as the Pax Romana of the Roman Empire had given Christianity a similar opportunity in the ancient world. Toynbee writes:

> At its first appearance, Christianity was provided with a universal state, in the shape of the Roman Empire with its policed roads and shipping routes, as an aid to the spread of Christianity round the shores of the Mediterranean. Our modern Western civilization in its turn may serve its historical purpose by providing Christianity with a completely worldwide repetition of the Roman Empire to spread over.... The unification of our present world has long since opened the way for St. Paul, who once traveled from the Orontes to the Tiber under the aegis of the Pax Romana, to travel on from the Tiber to the Mississippi and from the Mississippi to the Yangtze; while Clement's and Origen's work of infusing Greek philosophy into Christianity at Alexandria might be emulated in some city of the Far East by the infusion of Chinese philosophy into Christianity.[4]

There is a hint in the above passage of a certain syncretism in which Christianity is mixed with other religions and philosophies without any definite principle for discriminating truth from error; and this attitude is even more marked in a passage which follows the above quotation. Such syncretism is what Toynbee eventually ended up with, so that he turned away from the Catholic Christianity he had reached at the end of his sixth volume, in order to pursue his search for religious fulfillment among the religions of the East.

For in his last four volumes of *A Study of History* published in 1954, which had been in process of preparation since 1946, Toynbee's view of

---

[3]*A Study of History,* Somervell Abridgement of first six volumes, (Oxford Univ. Press, 1947), p. 547.

[4]Arnold Toynbee, *Civilization on Trial* (Oxford Univ. Press, 1948), p. 239.

world history goes in an exactly opposite direction from what he had labored to achieve in the earlier part of his work. He now sees Christianity, and Judaism, its parent, and Communism which he considers an illegitimate child of Christianity, as possessed of a dogmatic certainty about the truth which seems to him one of the chief obstacles to the union of humanity. (Notice that his criterion has now become a sociological one, the unification of mankind, rather than a spiritual or religious one. Consequently, religions must be quite subordinated to the hoped-for achievement of this sociological goal.)

Toynbee Versus Toynbee on Religious Syncretism

Let us examine more closely the implications of the religious syncretism which Arnold Toynbee proposed in volumes 7 to 10 of *A Study of History* and see how it is related to the judgment which Toynbee himself pronounced in volumes 5 and 6 of the same work. These volumes were published some fifteen years earlier, that is, in 1939. A good starting point is Toynbee's attitude toward the Jewish religion in its Old Testament form.

Where Arnold Toynbee in his earlier volumes had commended the Jews for their resistance to the process of syncretism which was going forward in the ancient world, both during the time of the Hebrew Prophets and during the Hellenistic age, he now finds the Jewish religious attitude to be the source of many of the troubles that afflict the modern world. For, in his view, Judaism has communicated to Christianity its belief in a chosen people and the idea of a unique divine revelation which all men are obliged to accept. As against this view, Toynbee prefers the attitude of an Oriental religion like Mahayana Buddhism, which is so open and flexible that it can embrace all kinds of religious belief and experience in its conception of spiritual reality—except, of course, the specific beliefs and ideas of the Judaeo-Christian tradition.

Christopher Dawson has written two critiques of this move toward religious syncretism on the part of Arnold Toynbee. One of these was reprinted in the Summer 1983 issue of *The Dawson Newsletter* (II, no.2), entitled "Dr. Toynbee's Turning Away." The other appeared in the article on "Arnold Toynbee and the Study of History" in the Dawson anthology, *Dynamics of World History*.   From the latter I quote this passage:

> On the one hand the religions of the Far East—Hinduism and Mahayana Buddhism—adapt themselves well enough to Dr. Toynbee's ideal of religious syncretism, but they do so by denying the significance of history and creating a dream world of cosmological and mythological fantasy in which aeons and universes succeed one another in dazzling confusion and where the unity of God and the historical personality of Buddha are lost in a cloud of mythological figures: Buddhas and Bodhisattvas, gods and saktis, demigods and spirits.[5]

One wonders whether Toynbee, who had devoted his life to the study of history, and has produced over five thousand pages giving the results of this study, is aware of how lacking in significance all his work appears when viewed from the standpoint of Mahayana Buddhism. Surely that is a high price to pay in order to seek refuge in an Oriental syncretist religion.

So far as Toynbee's condemnation of Judaism is concerned—that is, in his 1954 publication of the later volumes of the *Study of History*—it is instructive to compare this with his positive evaluation of the Jewish religion back in 1939, in the sixth volume of this same work. He wrote:

> The same religious intolerance of any rival was also manifestly one of the qualities which enabled the God of Israel, after he had become the God the Christian Church, to outrun all his competitors once again in the later "Battle of the Gods" fought out within the Roman Empire. His rivals—a Syriac Mithras, an Egyptian Isis, a Hittite Cybele—were ready to enter into any compromise with each other and with any other cult that they severally encountered. This easy-going, compromising spirit was fatal to the rivals of the God of Tertullian, when they had to face an adversary who would be content with nothing less than "total" victory, because anything less would be, for Him, a denial of His very essence.[6]

Yet it is precisely this easy-going, compromising spirit which Toynbee now urges Christianity to adopt in the religious situation of our present age, which is also one of the mingling and mixing of religions, as

---

[5]*Dynamics of World History*, p. 398.
[6]*A Study of History*, Somervell Abridgement, Vol. I., p. 504.

was the case in the Roman Empire. Why should Christians be prepared to do so, when such compromise is, according to Toynbee himself, a denial of the very essence of the God they believe in?

Moreover, somewhat earlier, Toynbee points out that the Jewish conception of God had an appeal to the human heart which the gods of syncretism do not have:

> For mankind in the mass [Toynbee writes], God's essence is that He is a living God with whom a living human being enters into a relationship that is recognizably akin to the spiritual relationships into which he enters with other living human beings. This fact of being alive is the essence of God's nature for human souls that are seeking to enter into communion with Him; and this quality of being a person, which is the essence of God as Jews and Christians and Muslims worship Him today, is likewise the essence of God as He makes His appearance in the Old Testament. . . . When this living God of Israel encounters in turn the various abstractions of the philosophers, it becomes manifest that, in the words of the Odyssey, "he alone breathes and the rest are shadows".

Toynbee then links this fact of personality with the trait of exclusiveness which is characteristic of the Jewish conception of God; and he concludes:

> . . . We may find that the exclusiveness which is an enduring as well as a primitive trait in Yahweh's character has also some value which is indispensable for the historic role which the God of Israel has played in the revelation of the Divine Nature.[7]

It would appear then that Toynbee's proposal for syncretism in religion would have the effect of denying to mankind an understanding of the true nature of God. What real value does an artificial religious unity in the world possess, under these circumstances?

What makes this attraction toward religious syncretism on the part of Toynbee so incongruous is that it is precisely this attitude which he warned against in the fifth volume of his Study published in 1939. At that time he identified syncretism as a characteristic refuge of philosophers living in an age of social disintegration, and he provided numerous examples from history in support of this statement. He wrote:

---

[7]*Ibid.*, p. 503.

"In the field of religion the syncretism of amalgamation of rites, cults and faiths is the outward manifestation of that inward sense of promiscuity which arises from the schism in the soul in an age of social disintegration."[8]

After a survey of different philosophies attempting religious syncretism, especially in the Hellenic world, and noting their progress downwards, Toynbee passes a negative verdict on their efforts:

> [P]hilosophy, succumbing to less edifying religious influences, descends from devoutness into superstition. Such is the miserable end of the philosophies of the dominant minority. . . . In the last act of the dissolution of a civilization the philosophies die while the higher religions live on and stake out their claims upon the future. . . . In fact, when philosophies and religions meet, the religions must increase while philosophies must decrease.

Notice that this is a paraphrase of the words of St. John the Baptist concerning his relationship of being precursor to Jesus. It thus suggests that the philosophies, such as that of Plato, are in fact merely a preparation for the advent of the higher religions, in this case, Christianity.

Toynbee then asks why it is that the philosophic attempt at syncretism meets with so little success. He writes:

> What, then, are the weaknesses that doom philosophy to discomfiture when it enters into the lists as the rival of religion? The fatal and fundamental weakness, from which all the rest derive, is a lack of spiritual vitality. This lack of *élan* lames philosophy in two ways. It diminishes its attractiveness for the masses and it discourages those who feel its attractions from throwing themselves into missionary work on its behalf.[9]

This is even true today with regard to Christianity itself, where the spirit of indifferentism, of saying that all religions are equally acceptable to God, is so widespread and so destructive of the missionary impulse. Pope Paul VI took notice of this in his message on evangelization and he saw it as one of the chief obstacles to active missionary endeavor. He said that, "It is all the more serious because it comes from within. . . . It is

---

[8]*Ibid.*, p. 472.
[9]*Ibid.*, pp. 480-481.

manifested in fatigue, disenchantment, compromise, lack of interest and above all, lack of joy and hope."[10]

In our age, therefore, not only Arnold Toynbee, but also many Catholic writers of a neo-Modernist viewpoint, are giving support to the ideas of religious syncretism.

To return to Arnold Toynbee, it should be noted that in 1939 he set up in opposition to the false solution of syncretism, the course taken by the Hebrew Prophets in their battle against the gods of the pagan peoples who surrounded the Israelites. These threatened to infiltrate and destroy the unique character of the Hebrew worship of Yahweh. Toynbee stated:

> No doubt the remarkable and momentous feature of the religious history of Israel in that age is the exceptional success of the Prophets in combating the sense of promiscuity and diverting the stream of Israelitish religious development out of the false channel of syncretism into a new and arduous course which was peculiar to Israel itself.[11]

Incidentally, notice that Toynbee's use of the word "promiscuity," which is used most often in connection with sexual promiscuity, that is, fornication or prostitution, implies by its very use a condemnation of syncretism. It implies a whoring after strange gods, which is in fact the way the Hebrew prophets described the temptations to idolatry and syncretism with which the Israelite people were faced.

Yet, after having written so eloquently of the debasing character of religious syncretism, its lack of sensitivity to genuine spiritual values, it is precisely this syncretism which is his proposal for the religious situation of our own time. He puts this rather obliquely:

> In the same context [i.e., the establishment of a universal state due to the unification of the modern world economically] we considered the possibility that, within such a framework, the respective adherents of the four living higher religions might come to recognize that their once rival systems were so many alternate approaches to the One True God along avenues offering diverse partial approaches to the Beatific Vision. We threw out the idea that, in this light, the historic living churches might eventually give

---

[10]Pope Paul VI, *Evangelii Nuntiandi* (1975), sec. 80.
[11]Somervell Abridgement, Vol. I, p. 475.

expression to this unity in diversity by growing together into a single Church Militant.[12]

The four living higher religions, as Toynbee identifies them, are Christianity, Islam, Hinduism, and Mahayana Buddhism. Are these, in fact, simply "alternate approaches to the One True God?" So far as Christianity and Islam are made the basis for the comparison, we can recognize that their conception of God has a great deal in common, being derived from the God of Israel as set forth in the Old Testament. But there immediately arises the basic difference that Christianity believes that Jesus of Nazareth is the only-begotten Son of God, and that it is only through Him that mankind can come to salvation. Islam, on the other hand, while giving to Jesus the status of a prophet, rejects this basic Christian belief. Is God in fact a Trinity of Persons such as the Christian believes, with Jesus as the Word in whom the Father's Image is reflected? Or is God one Person alone, as is held by Islam? Thus, even in these two religions which seem somewhat close together in some respects, there is a fundamental disagreement as to the nature of the One True God. Does Toynbee expect these two religions of Islam and Christianity to overlook or ignore this difference in order to promote some kind of factitious world unity?

When it comes to Hinduism and Mahayna Buddhism, the term One True God is an anomaly. For that term is based on the Jewish conception of the God of Israel as alone being truly God when compared with the polytheistic deities worshipped by the pagan peoples who surrounded the Jews. But in Hinduism and Mahayna Buddhism, polytheism is at the very center of their religion. They do not worship One True God, but many gods. So Toynbee is prostituting the use of this term and rendering it void of any real meaning when he speaks of the four higher religions as "so many alternate approaches to the One True God." It is significant, I believe, of Toynbee's evasiveness in this matter that he did not mention what these four higher religions were in this particular context: if he were to have set down the names of Hinduism and Mahayana Buddhism along with Islam and Christianity as all capable of being easily reconciled with each other, the enormity of his proposal would have been too easily recognized.

When we examine some forms of Hinduism, we find there a belief

---

[12]Somervell Abridgement, Vol. II (Oxford Univ. Press, 1957), pp. 118-119.

in an impersonal Absolute as a Supreme Being. But this is not the personal God in which Jews, Muslims, and Christians believe. It is lacking in all the attributes of personality which Toynbee earlier said were necessary for a belief in God. And this Absolute did not create the universe. In fact, in some forms of Hinduism, it is believed that nothing at all exists except this one impersonal Absolute, and that everything else is merely a part of it; in such a context, it is a contradiction even to speak of everything else, for these things do not really exist at all. G.K. Chesterton has remarked on the fundamental incompatibility of such a belief with the Christian conception of God. Writing in the early 1900s about this kind of belief then being propagated in England, Chesterton said:

> It is just here that Buddhism is on the side of modern pantheism and immanence. And it is just here that Christianity is on the side of humanity and liberty and love. Love desires personality; therefore love desires division. It is the instinct of Christianity to be glad that God has broken the universe into little pieces, because they are living pieces.... This is the intellectual abyss between Buddhism, and Christianity; that for the Buddhist or Theosophist personality is the fall of man; for the Christian it is the purpose of God, the whole point of his cosmic idea.[13]

Yet it is these religions at opposite ends of the spectrum of religious teaching and experience which Arnold Toynbee proposes to class together under the rubric of "alternate approaches to the One True God."

Is not this a striking example of the schism in the soul — and in the mind — which afflicts the philosophic historian in an age of social disintegration? Why, then, did Toynbee plunge recklessly forward into such religious promiscuity when he had much earlier in his work set up clear signposts of warning against it?

---

[13]*Orthodoxy,* pp. 244-45.

12
Atman-Brahman or the Living God?

Today one of the most pressing challenges to Christianity comes under the form of Oriental and especially Indian types of religion. Their advocates claim that mystical experience, whether in the East or the West, shows the superiority of Oriental religion to Christianity. In this view, Oriental mysticism has reached the supreme heights of contemplation, while Christian mysticism is still lingering in the foothills, unable to strike out for the distant mountain peaks which the Oriental mystics have already attained. The reason for this weakness on the part of Christian mysticism, according to advocates of Oriental religion, lies in the fact that it is far too much concerned with the personal aspects of Divinity instead of going beyond these to the worship of an impersonal Absolute. They tell us we must accept the need of the soul to be joined to a reality which is ultimate precisely because it is not personal, and therefore not timebound, not limited to the categories of thought and feeling in which the phenomenal self—the self of everyday life—finds it reassuring to live and worship.

And since the testimony of the mystics is based on experience rather than on creeds, it is said that their beliefs are more reliable than any merely doctrinal explanation of the nature of God. On this interpretation, the truth to which the mystics offer their united witness is that the Ultimate Reality with which the mystic achieves union is an undifferentiated Absolute, not the Living God of Scripture.

Here is one statement of the claims made for Indian philosophy and mysticism, as given by Christopher Isherwood in his introduction to the volume, *Vedanta for Modern Man*. (This book was intended to provide a common platform for Western intellectuals seeking to replace Christianity with Indian Vedanta as the religion of the West.) Referring to the Ultimate Reality behind the phenomenal universe, to which Vedantists give the name Brahman, Isherwood writes:

> Brahman is beyond all attributes. Brahman is not conscious, Brahman is consciousness. Brahman does not exist; Brahman *is* existence. Brahman is the Atman (the Eternal Nature) of every human being, creature, and object. Vedanta teaches us that Life has

no other purpose than this—that we shall learn to know ourselves for what we really are; that we shall reject the superficial ego-personality which claims that "I am Mr. Smith; I am other than Mr. Brown," and know, instead, that "I am the Atman; Mr. Brown is the Atman; the Atman is Brahman; there is nothing anywhere but Brahman; all else is appearance, transience, and unreality."

And then, with reference to Vedanta's conception of mystical experience, and its transcendence of all creeds:

> Vedanta also teaches the practice of mysticism; it claims, that is to say, that man may directly know and be united with his eternal Nature, the Atman, through meditation and spiritual discipline, without the aid of any church or delegated minister. . . . It does exalt the validity of the mystic's direct experience far above the authority of creeds, dogmas, and scriptures.[1]

This is, in fact, a propaganda manifesto and involves a rewriting of the facts of Indian religion in order to make Hinduism more acceptable to the modern taste for religious individualism. One would assume that Mr. Isherwood had never heard of high-caste Brahmins and of the rigid caste system of India, which was based on the spiritual superiority of the priestly class to all others. One would think that he had never heard of the *guru* as a prominent feature of Indian religion, that is, the concept of a spiritual guide whose direction is required so that the neophyte may advance along the road of enlightenment. And, to the degree that the *guru* feels unrestrained by "creeds, dogmas, and scriptures," it is quite likely that the pupil's dependence on him will be far greater than where there is some objective standard to be governed by. That is, a standard embodied in those very dogmas and scriptures which Isherwood holds to be an obstacle to the achievement of any authentic mystical experience.

It may be that it was an awareness of this very real danger which led later Indian thought to its emphasis on revelation, and the limitation this imposed on religious individualism. Christopher Dawson writes concerning this fact:

> [I]n spite of its genuinely philosophical character, and its reliance on direct spiritual intuition, the Vedanta itself claims the

---

[1] Christopher Isherwood, *Vendanta for Modern Man* (Harper Bros. 1951), p. ix.

authority of revelation in the strict sense of the word. "The authority of the Veda," writes Sankara, "with regard to the matter stated by it is independent and direct just as the light of the sun is the direct means of our knowledge of form and color; the authoritativeness of human dicta, on the other hand, is of an altogether different kind, as it depends on an extraneous basis and is mediated by a chain of teachers and tradition." Nay more, the truth of the supreme intuition is itself established by the authority of Scripture and not vice versa. (In a note, Dawson identifies Sankara as follows: "Sankara [c. A.D. 788-850] taught the strict monist [Advaita] interpretation of the Vedanta and is usually regarded as the greatest philosopher of Hinduism.")[2]

Now, if this is the attitude taken by the greatest philosopher of Hinduism toward the intuition of the Vedanta, it would seem that it is a special Western interpretation of the Vedanta, not the classical Indian one, to which Isherwood is inviting us when he tells us that "the mystic's direct experience [is] far above the authority of creeds, dogmas, and scriptures."

Moreover, from the standpoint of spiritual formation and moral character, the Vedantist religion of Aldous Huxley and Isherwood suffers from a striking deficiency. As the worshiper becomes more aware of his "eternal Nature," the identification of his own Atman with the Brahman, he loses a sense of humility before the ultimate mystery of the Transcendent, because he himself is now merged with it. And he tends to look down on all those who have not attained the height which he has achieved through his own unaided efforts.

With regard to Isherwood's proposal for a religion that would constitute a vast improvement on Christianity, because it would recognize that nothing really exists except the Brahman, and that individual persons like Mr. Smith and Mr. Brown are mere illusions, it does not seem that it is very much different from the religion of Theosophy promoted by Mrs. Besant half a century earlier. This drew its inspiration from her contact with Indian religious philosophy. Of that earlier version of a Westernized "non-dualism," Chesterton observed:

> According to Mrs. Besant this universal Church is simply the universal self. It is the doctrine that we are really all one person; that there are no real walls of individuality between man and man.

---

[2] *Orthodoxy*, pp. 244-5.

If I may put it so, she does not tell us to love our neighbors; she tells us to be our neighbors. . . . And I never heard of any suggestion in my life with which I more violently disagree. I want to love my neighbor not because he is I, but precisely because he is not I. . . . If the world is full of real selves, they can be really unselfish selves. But upon Mrs. Besant's principle the whole cosmos is only one enormously selfish person.[3]

Now let us consider the basic argument the Vedantists give for saying that the ultimate reality is a formless absolute. This is related to the fact that mystics generally, Christian as well as non-Christian, seek to rid the mind of forms and images that would interfere with preparing for union with this Reality. The Vedantic monists assume that getting rid of finite forms is a proof that, when one is faced with the Divine, all form is thereby obliterated, and that this Reality itself is beyond form. But this conclusion does not necessarily follow.

It is quite possible that one reason for ridding the mind of finite forms and images is the disproportion existing between finite forms and the Form of the Infinite Being who has given these other forms all the reality they possess. It may be a discipline which is practiced so as not to confuse one type of being with the other.

In the Christian conception of creation, the difference between the way in which creatures possess their being, and the way in which the Creator is the fullness of being ("I Am Who Am," as Scripture puts it in the account of the Burning Bush in *Exodus*) is so great that we can compare them only by way of analogy. But it is *being* which both Creator and creature possess, however different their manner of possessing it. And since form is the principle of the actuation of being, making being pass from the potential to the actual, a being without form is a contradiction in terms.

This is explained by the teaching of St. Thomas Aquinas on the nature of God. St. Thomas describes God as Pure Act, the fullness of actuality. And from this actuality is derived the possibility of Creation, the communication of God's actuality to other beings in the degree to which their natures allow them to receive it. And before Creation, God the Father communicates to His Son the fullness of the being which is His own; for the Son, being of an infinite nature with the Father, is able to receive that being in the completeness in which it exists in the Father.

---

[3]*Orthodoxy*, pp. 242-3.

Moreover, the generosity of the giving of being by the Father to the Son forms a prototype to what takes place when created things receive their being from God under the limitations imposed by their own finite natures. And they are meant to imitate the Son in giving back to the Father in love and generosity the gift they have received.

As against this background for the relation of the mystic to God, the Vedantist mistakes the means for the goal. That is, the purification of the mind of images and forms for what is to be attained at the end of the journey. C.S. Lewis has an account of how the description of the Ultimate Reality by mystics, in their attempt to mark off the otherness of that Being from all created things, can lead to this misconception:

> Let us dare to say that God is a particular Thing. Once he was the only Thing: but He is creative, He made other things to be. He is not those other things. He is not "universal being": if He were there would be no creatures, for a generality can make nothing. He is "absolute being" —or rather *the* Absolute Being—in the sense that He alone exists in His own right. But there are things which God is not. In that sense He has a determinate character. Thus He is righteous, not a-moral; creative, not inert . . .
>
> Why, then, do mystics talk of Him as they do, and why are many people prepared in advance to maintain that, whatever else God may be, He is not the concrete, living, willing and acting God of Christian theology?[4]

Lewis then uses a parable about limpets, a few of whom have caught a glimpse of Man. These try to explain to their fellows the nature of Man. This results in a description of Man based on negatives. Man does not have any of the usual features with which limpets are familiar. It is these negative aspects which dominate limpet thinking about Man. Lewis then asserts:

> Our own situation is much like that of the erudite limpets. . . . When we have removed from our idea of God some puny human characteristic, we (as merely erudite or intelligent enquirers) have no resources from which to supply that blindingly real and concrete attribute of Deity which ought to replace it. Thus at each step in the process of refinement our idea of God contains less, and the fatal pictures come in (an endless, silent sea, an empty sky beyond all

---

[4]C.S. Lewis, *Miracles* (Macmillan Co., 1947), p. 106.

stars, a dome of white radiance) and we reach at last mere zero and worship a nonentity.[5]

There is a second point on which Christianity differs from the Vedanta on the nature of God and the universe. The world of transcendent Being to which the soul is to be admitted, either partially in the mystical experience, or fully in the Beatific Vision for those who have attained Heaven after death, is not a world where nothing exists except God. Rather it is a realm in which God's glory is reflected in a multitude of different levels of angels and saints, related to one another in a hierarchical structure, each being possessed of his own particular individuality, and his own particular participation in the life of God. Here we have the analogy in Heaven of the different degrees of actuality, that is, of realized being, which are to be found in the forms of the different creatures in the visible universe.

Moreover, the Christian conception of Ultimate Reality is so far from being merely an all-embracing monist Absolute, that it comprises the existence and interrelationship of Three Divine Persons within God Himself. Contrasting this with the opposite conception of Brahman as the Universal Self wherein all individualities are merged and lose their specific identity, Chesterton speaks of "the image of a council at which mercy pleads as well as justice, the conception of a sort of liberty and variety existing even in the inmost chamber of the world.... For to us Trinitarians (if I may say it with reverence)—to us God Himself is a society."[6]

---

[5]*Ibid.*, pp. 108-109.
[6]*Orthodoxy*, p. 249.

13
The Limitations of Eric Voegelin

The death of Eric Voegelin at age 84 affords us the opportunity to examine the significance of his work. This is all the more necessary because Voegelin's ideas have been promoted as giving great assistance to political conservatives and to orthodox Christians in their struggle against the secular ideologies. It is the purpose of this article to suggest that the nature of that assistance must be sharply qualified so far as Christians are concerned.

Let us first consider some of the major facts about Voegelin's career. He was born in Cologne, Germany in 1901, but shortly thereafter his family moved to Austria, and it was there he received his education and his doctor's degree. In 1924 he came to America on a two-year fellowship, attending lectures of John Dewey at Columbia and Alfred North Whitehead at Harvard. While in America, he also became acquainted with the ideas of George Santayana and William James. All of these thinkers exercised a great influence on his intellectual development. Their ideas were added to what he had already received from German idealist philosophy, with its emphasis on the importance of the subjective element in one's approach to reality.

Voegelin returned to Austria in 1926 and stayed there until 1938, the year of Hitler's takeover of that country, when he managed to escape from Austria and reach the United States. He remained in America from 1938 to 1958. The last sixteen years of this period he taught political science at Louisiana State University in Baton Rouge.

It was while he was in the United States that the volumes for which he is best known were written and published. These include *The New Science of Politics* in 1952, and the first three volumes of his philosophy of history, called *Order and History,* which appeared in 1956 and 1957. These volumes were entitled: *Israel and Revelation, The World of the Polis,* and *Plato* and *Aristotle.* He planned three other volumes to complete the work to be entitled *Empire and Christianity, The Protestant Centuries,* and *The Crisis of Western Civilization*; but these were never written because of a drastic change in the original plan. In their stead, a fourth volume, *The Ecumenic Age,* dealing with the period of the world empires of the ancient world, was published in 1974. And a fifth volume, summarizing his conclusions, the proofs of which he was working upon at the time of his death, is now awaiting publication.

It will be seen, therefore, that his philosophy of history gives its primary attention to certain periods in the history of the ancient world, and especially to those developments which greatly influenced Western civilization. But there is no general treatment of the Christian centuries nor any study of the interaction between Christianity and Western culture. This constitutes a grave limitation for any philosophy of history. For it is from the West, under the dynamic influence of Christianity, that the world transformation of modern culture has proceeded.

Voeglin left the United States in 1958 to assume a chair of political science in Munich, from which position he retired in 1969. Many of the remaining years of his life were spent in the United States, including some years of residence at the Hoover Institute at Stanford University.

In conservative political circles, Voegelin has continued to be an important influence on thought about politics and philosophy; and it is held that his *New Science of Politics* provides a most effective critique of the modern secular ideologies. But it is the erudition and wide-ranging perspectives offered by his *Order and History* volumes which are most responsible for the high regard in which his work is held.

Let us now consider some of his limitations. First, as a political scientist, he has popularized the idea that there is a striking parallel between ancient Gnosticism and modern secular ideologies, since they both feel a strong sense of alienation from the present or the contemporary world. In addition, both of them also rely upon a secret knowledge possessed by an elite which can win salvation for mankind from the corrupt world in which it is now involved. However, as Voegelin himself admitted at a Vanderbilt University symposium held in 1978, ancient Gnosticism was not interested in politics but instead was seeking escape through gaining access to a transcendent reality; whereas modern ideologies are intensely political and are completely concentrated on this world and on how they plan to make it over by applying their revolutionary principles.

Also, as a political scientist, Voegelin has been almost entirely theoretical, with no definite guidance concerning the political choices which one should make. Since politics is meant to be more practical than philosophy of history, this failure diminishes Voegelin's importance as a political thinker. On this point Professor Eugene Webb, a great admirer of Voegelin's thought, nevertheless observes: "There is little in his writings to indicate even sketchily what practical political paths might best be followed in the confusions of our time."[1]

The second limitation of Voegelin has to do with the scope of his philosophy of history. We have already noted that in the four published volumes of his *Order and History,* there is no specific treatment of the history of Christianity, whether Eastern Orthodox, Catholic, or Protestant. Eugene Webb points out:

> There are areas of rich philosophical and religious experience that Voegelin has scarcely touched in his writings — particularly patristic theology and the entire field of Eastern Orthodox thought and spirituality.... His treatment of Christianity has been sketchy and, except for a few references to later thinkers, has been confined almost entirely to parts of the New Testament.[2]

But, in addition to this striking omission of Christian cultural history, there is also his neglect of the world religions of the Orient, and of Islam and later Judaism. An examination of these is certainly important for any contemporary philosophy of history. Of Voegelin's deficiency in this regard Professor Webb writes:

> He has discussed Asian thought only briefly and has not gone into it in any great depth.... There is need for a similar study of the non-Christian religions in general. Voegelin discusses some of these in various places, but for the most part does not make them the focus of his study....
>
> Another notable omission is Jewish thought since the destruction of the Second Temple.[3]

In a note earlier in his book, Webb lists the specific pages where some attention is given to some of the non-Christian religions:

> Voegelin discusses Muslim thought briefly in *OH* (i.e. *Order and History*), 4:142-45, and *Science, Politics, and Gnosticism,* pp. 113-

---

[1]Eugene Webb, *Eric Voegelin: Philosopher of History* v. of Washington Press, 1981), pp. 199-200).

[2]*Ibid.,* p. 274.

[3]*Ibid.,* pp. 273-274.

114; and Hinduism in *OH*, 4:319-322. He does not discuss Rabbinic Judaism at all, but limits his treatment of Judaism to what he considers the Deuteronomic defection into legalism.[4]

We must remember that the four volumes of *Order and History* run between 1,500 and 2,000 pages, so the scantiness of Voegelin's concern with Islam and Hinduism is quite apparent, as is also his lack of interest in Rabbinic Judaism.

The third limitation of Voegelin has to do with his attitude toward orthodox Christian belief. Although he has written a certain amount about the Christianity of the New Testament, his emphasis on subjectivism and on personal experience of the transcendent by a few gifted individuals puts him at a considerable distance from traditional Christian teaching. In fact, he regards doctrinal teaching with great mistrust, for it seems to him that it seeks to communicate in language an experience which is essentially incommunicable. Consequently, it is only in myth and poetry and allegory that something of the religious experience which moved the great thinkers can be made known to the masses of the people. Doctrine, which is conceptual in character, makes the experience something other than it is.

This seems to ignore the close relation which exists between image and concept, between symbol and language. A myth is communicated by means of language, a symbol requires the help of a concept to make known what is its meaning. The image of Christ Crucified, for example, does not of itself communicate the reality of what is taking place. It requires the language of the Gospels to make clear the nature of that image, which is not simply that of a man done to death by crucifixion, but the Son of God made man offering His life freely as a ransom for the many. Consequently, language is needed to communicate what the symbol signifies.

Writing in *Modern Age* in the Spring of 1978, at the time of the Voegelin conference at Vanderbilt University, Harold Weatherby, professor of English at that university, identified the basic relativism of Voegelin's approach to religious experience, which makes it essentially incompatible with Christianity:

> Voegelin's own rationale is clear enough. He rejects the literal

---

[4]*Ibid.*, p. 221.

and dogmatic in matters of religion because he is convinced that God's revelations to the soul — the theophanies which he calls "leaps in being" and which give order to history — are at once preconscious in origin and penultimate in nature. That is to say that God reveals Himself in the depths of the soul, beyond the reach of conscious articulation, and that that revelation takes place in time and history and cannot, therefore, be regarded as final or conclusive. Consequently the expression of the revelation must be symbolic rather than literal and its interpretation must be historical rather than dogmatic.[5]

Even more striking was the criticism of Professor Gerhart Niemeyer, longtime friend and admirer of Voegelin. He seems to have recognized only with the publication of *The Ecumenic Age,* dealing for the first time specifically with the New Testament, that Voegelin preferred to concentrate on St. Paul rather than on Jesus, and to set aside the historical actuality of Jesus as less relevant or less important than the vision experience of St. Paul. Niemeyer writes:

What is more, Voegelin's exegesis of St. Paul would not have to be changed if one removed Jesus Christ from it altogether. . . . If Voegelin's chapter on the Pauline vision of the resurrected had been adopted as the early Christian theology, the Apostolic Creed might have read: "I believe in God the Father Almighty, Maker of Heaven and Earth: and in St. Paul, his prophet, mighty in vision, and in the Spirit of Freedom which he proclaimed". . . . Noting that he defines "the Resurrection" as "St. Paul's vision of the resurrected," we may infer that that standpoint is the same characterized by St. Paul when he saw that the Gospel of Jesus Christ must be "a foolishness to the Greeks"[6]

It was the rationalism of the Greeks which led them to regard the cross and the Resurrection as mere foolishness; and, despite Voegelin's exaltation of myth and mystery, it is in fact the rationalism of his approach to religion which leads him to reject or ignore the factual character of the life of Jesus. Speculations and images within the mind, however arrived at, are easier to control than the hard facts of external reality. The latter are felt to be a vulgar intrusion, as is also the

---

[5]Harold Weatherby, *Myth, Fact, and History: Voegelin on Christianity* in *Modern Age,* Spring, 1978, vol. 22, No. 1., p. 144.

[6]Gerbart Niemeyer, *Eric Voegelin's Philosophy and the Drama of Mankind* in *Modern Age,* Winter, 1976, Vol. 20, no. 4, p. 35.

intellectual demand of doctrine. Rationalism rejects both of them and both for the same reason — they break in from the outside and shatter the beautiful images which the rational mind has been able to construct.

One of Voegelin's most important themes, in fact that which constitutes his "leaps in being," is man's experience of the transcendent, as against the immanence of modern ideologies. Now one would assume that the emphasis on man as a being capable of this transcendent experience would naturally lead one to a belief in immortality, to the existence for mankind of a realm beyond the devouring grave. Yet it would appear that Voegelin's attitude toward immortality is at least ambiguous, if it does not amount to outright denial of it. The existence of a life beyond death intrudes upon the speculations of which the philosopher himself is the master and controlling agent. In the following passage Eugene Webb speaks of Voegelin's attitude toward immortality:

> But on the other hand, he is wary about allowing this experience [i.e. of the divine] to be turned into a doctrine of immortality, and his frequent references to Anaximander's dictum that all things must perish once again into the *Apeiron* (the Boundless) from which they came, must make the reader wonder whether Voegelin's own idea of what awaits the soul after death is a complete dissolution of the individual existent back into absolute being. To attempt to believe with certainty that the human person will continue in individual existence after death would be to speculate beyond experience, and it is obvious why Voegelin would wish to avoid this; but the Christian faith in the risen life to come is not, at its most lucid and authentic, an intellectual speculation, but rather an act of trust in the divine generosity. This act of trust is itself rooted in concrete experiences of the soul.[7]

Thus one finds that after all his pursuit through human history of man's experience of the transcendent, Voegelin thinks it doubtful that this experience is anything more than some fleeting glimpses of it which the present life affords to a few favored individuals. In this perspective, his philosophy of history seems to cancel itself out, and to come down on the side of immanence, rather than transcendence. Indeed, without immortality, it makes of human life no more than what Shakespeare has

---

[7]Eugene Webb, *Eric Voegelin's Theory of Revelation* in *Eric Voegelin's Thought: A Critical Appraisal* edited by Ellis Sandoz (Duke Univ. Press, 1982), pp. 172-173.

Macbeth give voice to in his utter disillusion with life: "It is a tale told by an idiot, full of sound and fury, signifying nothing."

As against that kind of conclusion, we prefer to set the challenge of Maritain to Henri Bergson, another philosopher of history concerned with the meaning of human existence:

> Truly, philosophers play a strange game. They know very well that one thing alone counts, and that all their medley of subtle discussions relates to one single question: why are we born on this earth? Do they not see that people come to them from all points of the compass, not with a desire to partake of their subtlety but because they hope to receive from them one word of life? If they have such words, why do they not cry them from the housetops, asking their disciples to give, if necessary, their very blood for them? If they have no such words, why do they allow people to believe they will receive from them something which they cannot give? For mercy's sake, if ever God has spoken, if in some place in the world, were it on the gibbet of One Crucified, He has sealed His truth, tell us; that is what you must teach. Or are you indeed masters in Israel only to be ignorant of these things?[8]

---

[8]Jacques Maritain, *Ransoming the Time* (Charles Scribner's Sons, 1946), pp. 112-113.